Learning Puppet Security

Secure your IT environments with the powerful security tools of Puppet

Jason Slagle

BIRMINGHAM - MUMBAI

Learning Puppet Security

Copyright © 2015 Packt Publishing

All rights reserved. No part of this book may be reproduced, stored in a retrieval system, or transmitted in any form or by any means, without the prior written permission of the publisher, except in the case of brief quotations embedded in critical articles or reviews.

Every effort has been made in the preparation of this book to ensure the accuracy of the information presented. However, the information contained in this book is sold without warranty, either express or implied. Neither the author, nor Packt Publishing, and its dealers and distributors will be held liable for any damages caused or alleged to be caused directly or indirectly by this book.

Packt Publishing has endeavored to provide trademark information about all of the companies and products mentioned in this book by the appropriate use of capitals. However, Packt Publishing cannot guarantee the accuracy of this information.

First published: March 2015

Production reference: 1240315

Published by Packt Publishing Ltd.
Livery Place
35 Livery Street
Birmingham B3 2PB, UK.

ISBN 978-1-78439-775-3

www.packtpub.com

Credits

Author
Jason Slagle

Reviewers
Vlastimil Holer
Jeroen Hooyberghs
Michael J. Ladd
Stephen McNally
Marcus Young

Commissioning Editor
Dipika Gaonkar

Acquisition Editor
Meeta Rajani

Content Development Editor
Akshay Nair

Technical Editors
Tanmayee Patil
Sebastian Rodrigues

Copy Editors
Sonia Michelle Cheema
Rashmi Sawant
Wishva Shah

Project Coordinator
Mary Alex

Proofreaders
Simran Bhogal
Maria Gould
Paul Hindle
Linda Morris

Indexer
Tejal Soni

Production Coordinator
Shantanu N. Zagade

Cover Work
Shantanu N. Zagade

About the Author

Jason Slagle is a veteran of systems and network administration of 18 years. Having worked on everything from Linux systems to Cisco networks and SAN storage, he is always looking for ways to make his work repeatable and automated. When he is not hacking a computer for work or pleasure, he enjoys running, cycling, and occasionally, geocaching.

Jason is a graduate of the University of Toledo from the computer science and engineering technology program with a bachelor's degree in science. He is currently employed by CNWR, an IT and infrastructure consulting company in his hometown of Toledo, Ohio. There, he supports several prominent customers in their quest to automate and improve their infrastructure and development operations. He occasionally serves as a part-time instructor at the University of Toledo.

Jason has previously worked as a technical reviewer on *Puppet 3: Beginner's Guide* and *Puppet Monitoring and Reporting*.

> I would like to thank my wife, Heather, and my son, Jacob. They've been greatly supportive during this process.
>
> Additionally I'd like to thank my mentor, Allen Rioux. Without you, none of this would have been possible.

About the Reviewers

Vlastimil Holer is a systems engineer, with focus on automation. He has worked with Unix-like systems for more than a decade, and first used Puppet in 2008 while preparing and managing the growing deployment of the GoodData cloud BI on Amazon EC2. Currently, he works on the CERIT Scientific Cloud project at Masaryk University, where he manages and automates their computing, cloud, and storage infrastructure.

Jeroen Hooyberghs is an open source and Linux consultant, working for Open Future in Belgium. In this position as well as in his earlier roles in Linux system administration, he obtained technical expertise through a lot of open source solutions, such as Puppet. In 2014, he became a Puppet Certified Professional and Official Puppet Trainer. As a reviewer, he contributed to *Mastering Puppet* and *Puppet Cookbook, Third Edition*.

Michael J. Ladd is a senior manager of systems engineering at Leapfrog Online LLC of Evanston, Illinois. He has been working with Linux systems for more than 15 years, and has been using Puppet for over 5 years. In addition to wrangling computers, Michael enjoys writing music and working through an ever-growing list of books to read. He writes very occasionally at `www.mjladd.com`, and can be reached at `mjladd@gmail.com`.

> I would like to thank my admirable wife, Jen, for her support and encouragement, and my spirited daughter, Piper.

Stephen McNally received his MBA from Tennessee Technological University in 2013 with focus on management information systems. Stephen has experience in procuring, deploying, maintaining, administering, and decommissioning some of the world's fastest supercomputers. Most notably, his team deployed the first academic petascale supercomputer, Kraken. Stephen has IT experience in multiple industries, including automotive manufacturing, healthcare, and research computing. He oversees all aspects of HPC operations as the group leader for some of the world's brightest and most talented administrators and programmers.

> I would like to thank my wife, Christina, and my son, Sutton, for providing their love and support during this process.

Marcus Young recently graduated with a degree in computer science and mathematics, before getting involved in system administration and DevOps. He currently works in software automation using open source tools and technologies. His hobbies include playing ice hockey and brewing beer. He also enjoys hardware projects based on microcontrollers and single-board computers. He is currently working on *Implementing Cloud Design Patterns for AWS*.

www.PacktPub.com

Support files, eBooks, discount offers, and more

For support files and downloads related to your book, please visit www.PacktPub.com.

Did you know that Packt offers eBook versions of every book published, with PDF and ePub files available? You can upgrade to the eBook version at www.PacktPub.com and as a print book customer, you are entitled to a discount on the eBook copy. Get in touch with us at service@packtpub.com for more details.

At www.PacktPub.com, you can also read a collection of free technical articles, sign up for a range of free newsletters and receive exclusive discounts and offers on Packt books and eBooks.

https://www2.packtpub.com/books/subscription/packtlib

Do you need instant solutions to your IT questions? PacktLib is Packt's online digital book library. Here, you can search, access, and read Packt's entire library of books.

Why subscribe?

- Fully searchable across every book published by Packt
- Copy and paste, print, and bookmark content
- On demand and accessible via a web browser

Free access for Packt account holders

If you have an account with Packt at www.PacktPub.com, you can use this to access PacktLib today and view 9 entirely free books. Simply use your login credentials for immediate access.

Table of Contents

Preface	**v**
Chapter 1: Puppet as a Security Tool	**1**
What is Puppet?	**2**
Declarative versus imperative approaches	3
The Puppet client-server model	5
Other Puppet components	6
PuppetDB	6
Hiera	7
Installing and configuring Puppet	**8**
Installing the Puppet Labs Yum repository	8
Installing the Puppet Master	9
Installing the Puppet agent	10
Configuring Puppet	10
Puppet services	11
Preparing the environment for examples	**12**
Installing Vagrant and VirtualBox	12
Creating our first Vagrantfile	13
Puppet for security and compliance	**17**
Example – using Puppet to secure openssh	**18**
Starting the Vagrant virtual machine	19
Connecting to our virtual machine	20
Creating the module	20
Building the module	20
The openssh configuration file	22
The site.pp file	23
Running our new code	23
Summary	**25**

Chapter 2: Tracking Changes to Objects — 27
Change tracking with Puppet — 28
The audit meta-parameter — 28
How it works — 29
What can be audited — 29
Using audit on files — 30
Available attributes — 30
Auditing the password file — 31
Preparation — 31
Creating the manifest — 31
First run of the manifest — 32
Changing the password file and rerunning Puppet — 33
Audit on other resource types — 34
Auditing a package — 35
Modifying the module to audit — 36
Things to know about audit — 39
Alternatives to auditing — 40
The noop meta-parameter — 41
Purging resources — 42
Using noop — 42
Summary — 45

Chapter 3: Puppet for Compliance — 47
Using manifests to document the system state — 48
Tracking history with version control — 50
Using git to track Puppet configuration — 50
Tracking modules separately — 53
Facts for compliance — 55
The Puppet role's pattern — 55
Using custom facts — 56
The PCI DSS and how Puppet can help — 58
Network-based PCI requirements — 58
Vendor-supplied defaults and the PCI — 59
Protecting the system against malware — 67
Maintaining secure systems — 71
Authenticating access to systems — 71
Summary — 71

Chapter 4: Security Reporting with Puppet — 73
Basic Puppet reporting — 73
The store processors — 75
Example – showing the last node runtime — 77

PuppetDB and reporting	**79**
Example – getting recent reports	83
Example – getting event counts	85
Example – a simple PuppetDB dashboard	86
Reporting for compliance	**88**
Example – finding heartbleed-vulnerable systems	88
Summary	**91**
Chapter 5: Securing Puppet	**93**
Puppet security related configuration	**93**
The auth.conf file	94
Example – Puppet authentication	95
Adding our second Vagrant host	95
The fileserver.conf file	98
Example – adding a restricted file mount	99
SSL and Puppet	**102**
Signing certificates	103
Revoking certificates	104
Alternative SSL configurations	106
Autosigning certificates	**107**
Naïve autosign	108
Basic autosign	108
Policy-based autosign	110
Summary	**114**
Chapter 6: Community Modules for Security	**115**
The Puppet Forge	**116**
The herculesteam/augeasproviders series of modules	**120**
Managing SSH with augeasproviders	122
The arildjensen/cis module	**125**
The saz/sudo module	**129**
The hiera-eyaml gem	**132**
Summary	**137**
Chapter 7: Network Security and Puppet	**139**
Introducing the firewall module	**139**
The firewall type	**141**
The firewallchain type	**146**
Creating pre and post rules	**147**
Adding firewall rules to other modules	**151**
Is allowing all to NTP dangerous?	153
Summary	**155**

Chapter 8: Centralized Logging — 157
- Welcome to logging happiness — 158
  - Installing the ELK stack — 159
- Logstash and Puppet — 164
- Installing Elasticsearch — 164
  - Installing Logstash — 167
- Reporting on log data — 171
  - Installing Kibana — 172
- Configuring hosts to report log data — 176
- Summary — 180

Chapter 9: Puppet and OS Security Tools — 181
- Introducing SELinux and auditd — 182
  - The SELinux framework — 182
  - The auditd framework for audit logging — 186
- SELinux and Puppet — 187
  - The selboolean type — 187
  - The selmodule type — 190
  - File parameters for SELinux — 191
- Configuring SELinux with community modules — 192
- Configuring auditd with community modules — 197
- Summary — 200

Appendix: Going Forward — 201
- What we've learned — 201
- Where to go next — 202
  - Writing and testing Puppet modules — 202
  - Puppet device management — 203
  - Additional reporting resources — 204
  - Other Puppet resources — 205
  - The Puppet community — 206
- Final thoughts — 207

Index — 209

Preface

Using Puppet is currently one of the hottest trends right now in the IT industry. As the industry moves away from manual provisioning towards automation, the usage of Puppet and its associated tools will only continue to grow.

With the rise of automation, and the repetitive tasks that security often entails, it makes perfect sense for Puppet to be a strong security tool. With proper configuration, Puppet can assist in securing your servers, showing compliance with various standards, and generally easing the workload of security-related personnel.

This book is a practical introduction to Puppet for security professionals. It will guide you into the world of automation, showing you how to make repetitive tasks a breeze. With the knowledge learned here, you can begin the process of bringing your system configurations into code, where they can be audited and treated much like you would treat a code base.

Starting with the beginning, and assuming that you only have the knowledge of Linux operating systems, we will explore the basics of Puppet. From there on, we will cover examples and concepts of increasing complexity and skill until you are ready to start on your own. In doing this, we will cover using the Puppet code for auditing, as well as using reports and other data to show compliance. We'll explore centralized logging, and learn how you can use Puppet to make your SELinux tasks easier.

What this book covers

Chapter 1, Puppet as a Security Tool, provides an introduction to Puppet. We'll build a development environment that we'll use in all the chapters, and explore some simple examples with Puppet.

Chapter 2, Tracking Changes to Objects, explores various ways to audit changes to resources, such as files. Puppet provides a number of ways to handle this, and we'll review their pros and cons.

Chapter 3, Puppet for Compliance, looks at the use of Puppet for compliance purposes. Version control for our manifests will be introduced, and it will explain how the manifests can be used for auditing and compliance purposes. We'll also review some specific examples of how Puppet can help with the PCI DSS.

Chapter 4, Security Reporting with Puppet, looks at how to report on some of the things we covered in the previous chapters. We'll build reporting on various system facts, as well as some simple reporting covering when Puppet last ran on our hosts.

Chapter 5, Securing Puppet, covers what it takes to secure Puppet itself. Since Puppet is in charge of all of your systems, ensuring that it is secure is important. We'll cover the various security configuration files Puppet uses, as well as how it uses SSL to ensure security.

Chapter 6, Community Modules for Security, takes a look at various modules that are available at the Puppet Forge. We'll explore modules to make managing various configuration files easier, as well as modules that provide some security hardening of hosts.

Chapter 7, Network Security and Puppet, will explore using Puppet to manage the firewall of the local host. We'll primarily be concentrating on the Puppet module, which manages iptables and its associated set of tools that are used to manage firewall rules. We'll also cover how to extend your modules to handle firewall resources.

Chapter 8, Centralized Logging, introduces the use of Puppet to manage centralized logging using Logstash. We'll cover the installation of Logstash as well as its dashboard component, Kibana. We'll then build a simple module to ship logs to a central server.

Chapter 9, Puppet and OS Security Tools, covers using Puppet to manage SELinux and auditd. We'll cover the options available for Puppet for SELinux, as well as community modules for both SELinux and auditd.

Appendix, *Going Further*, covers information on developing good modules, an analysis of Puppet device management, useful reporting tools, and a brief discussion on the Puppet community.

What you need for this book

The examples in this book are all written using CentOS 6. The source present in this book uses Vagrant to run the examples. Vagrant is a wonderful tool to use for development, as it allows you to specify how full virtual machines should be configured.

To use Vagrant, you'll need the following software:

- **VirtualBox**: This is the virtualization container we'll use. You can find it at http://www.virtualbox.org.
- **Vagrant**: This tool is what we'll use to manage our virtual machines. You can get it at http://www.vagrantup.com.

Who this book is for

This book is targeted at experienced system administrators who focus on security, and it also targets security professionals. It assumes an intermediate to advanced level of system administration ability, but does not require any previous experience with Puppet.

Convention

In this book, you will find a number of styles of text that distinguish between different kinds of information. Here are some examples of these styles, and an explanation of their meaning.

Code words in text, database table names, folder names, filenames, file extensions, pathnames, dummy URLs, user input, and Twitter handles are shown as follows: "If not specified, this defaults to `$vardir/reports`, so `/var/lib/puppet/reports` on CentOS."

A block of code is set as follows:

```
node default {
        include openssh
        include users
        include clamav
        include puppetdb
        include puppetdb::master::config
}
```

When we wish to draw your attention to a particular part of a code block, the relevant lines or items are set in bold:

```
node default {
        include openssh
        include users
        include clamav
        include puppetdb
        include puppetdb::master::config
}
```

Any command-line input or output is written as follows:

```
# sudo service puppetmaster restart
```

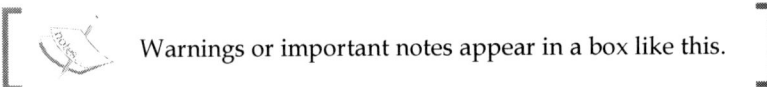

Warnings or important notes appear in a box like this.

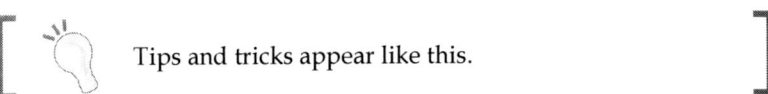

Tips and tricks appear like this.

Reader feedback

Feedback from our readers is always welcome. Let us know what you think about this book—what you liked or may have disliked. Reader feedback is important for us to develop titles that you really get the most out of.

To send us general feedback, simply send an e-mail to feedback@packtpub.com, and mention the book title via the subject of your message.

If there is a topic that you have expertise in and you are interested in either writing or contributing to a book, see our author guide on www.packtpub.com/authors.

Customer support

Now that you are the proud owner of a Packt book, we have a number of things to help you to get the most from your purchase.

Downloading the example code

You can download the example code files for all Packt books you have purchased from your account at http://www.packtpub.com. If you purchased this book elsewhere, you can visit http://www.packtpub.com/support and register to have the files e-mailed directly to you.

Errata

Although we have taken every care to ensure the accuracy of our content, mistakes do happen. If you find a mistake in one of our books—maybe a mistake in the text or the code—we would be grateful if you would report this to us. By doing so, you can save other readers from frustration and help us improve subsequent versions of this book. If you find any errata, please report them by visiting http://www.packtpub.com/submit-errata, selecting your book, clicking on the **errata submission form** link, and entering the details of your errata. Once your errata are verified, your submission will be accepted and the errata will be uploaded on our website, or added to any list of existing errata, under the Errata section of that title. Any existing errata can be viewed by selecting your title from http://www.packtpub.com/support.

Piracy

Piracy of copyright material on the Internet is an ongoing problem across all media. At Packt, we take the protection of our copyright and licenses very seriously. If you come across any illegal copies of our works, in any form, on the Internet, please provide us with the location address or website name immediately so that we can pursue a remedy.

Please contact us at copyright@packtpub.com with a link to the suspected pirated material.

We appreciate your help in protecting our authors, and our ability to bring you valuable content.

Questions

You can contact us at questions@packtpub.com if you are having a problem with any aspect of the book, and we will do our best to address it.

Puppet as a Security Tool

Imagine you're sitting at home one day after a long day of work. Suddenly, you get a phone call that a new security vulnerability was found and all 300 of your servers will need to be patched. How would you handle it?

With **Puppet**, finding which one of your servers was vulnerable would be an easier task than doing so by hand. Furthermore, with a little additional work, you could ensure that every one of your servers is running a newer nonvulnerable version of the Puppet package.

In this chapter, we will touch on the following concepts:

- What is Puppet?
- Declarative versus imperative systems
- The Puppet client-server model
- Other components of the Puppet ecosystem used for security
- Installing Puppet
- How Puppet fits into a security role

Once this is complete, we will build the environment we'll use to run examples in this book and then run our first example.

Much of the information in this chapter is presented as a guide to what we will accomplish later on in this book.

What is Puppet?

The Puppet Labs website describes open source Puppet as follows:

> *Open source Puppet is a configuration management system that allows you to define the state of your IT infrastructure, then automatically enforces the correct state.*

What does this mean, though?

Puppet is a configuration management tool. A configuration management tool is a tool that helps the user specify how to put a computer system in a desired state. Other popular tools that are considered as configuration management tools are Chef and CFEngine. There are also a variety of other options that are gaining a user base, such as Bcfg2 and Salt.

Chef is another configuration management tool. It uses pure Ruby **Domain-specific Language (DSL)** similar to Puppet. We'll cover what a domain-specific language is shortly. This difference allows you to write the desired state of your systems in Ruby. Doing so allows one to use the features of the Ruby language, such as iteration, to solve some problems that can be more difficult to solve in the stricter domain-specific language of Puppet. However, it also requires you to be familiar with Ruby programming. More information on Chef can be found at `http://www.getchef.com`.

CFEngine is the oldest of the three main tools mentioned here. It has grown into a very mature platform as it has expanded. Puppet was created out of some frustrations with CFEngine. One example of this is that the CFEngine community was formally quite closed, that is, they didn't accept user input on design decisions. Additionally, there was a focus in CFEngine on the methods used to configure systems. Puppet aimed to be a more open system that was community-focused. It also aimed to make the resource the primary actor, and relied on the engine to make necessary changes instead of relying on scripts in most cases.

> Many of these issues were addressed in CFEngine 3, and it retains a very large user base. More information on CFEngine can be found at `http://www.cfengine.com`.

Bcfg2 and Salt are both tools that are gaining a user base. Both written in Python, they provide another option for a user who may be more familiar with Python than other languages. Information on these tools, as well as a list of others that are available, can be found at `https://en.wikipedia.org/wiki/Comparison_of_open-source_configuration_management_software`.

Configuration management tools were brought about by a desire to make system administration work repeatable, as well as automate it.

In the early days of system administration, it was very common for an administrator to install the operating system needed as well as install any necessary software packages. When systems were simple and few in number, this was a low effort way of managing them.

As systems grew more complex and greater numbers of them were installed, this became much more difficult. Troubleshooting an application as it began to run on multiple systems also became difficult. The difference in software versions on installed nodes and other configuration differences created inconsistencies in the behavior of multiple systems that were running the same application. Installation manuals, run books, and other forms of documentation were often deployed to try to remedy this, but it was clear that we needed a better way.

As time moved on, system administrators realized that they needed a better way to manage their systems. A variety of methods were born, but many of them were home built. They often used SSH to manage remote hosts. I also built several such systems at various places before coming across Puppet.

Puppet sought to ease the pain and shortcomings of the early days. It was a big change from anything that was present at the time. A large part of this was because of its declarative nature.

Declarative versus imperative approaches

At the core of Puppet is software that allows you to specify the state of the system and let Puppet get the system there. It differs from many of the other products in the configuration management space due to its declarative nature.

In a declarative system, we model the desired state of the resources (things being managed).

Declarative systems have the following properties:

- Desired state is expressed, not steps used to get there
- Usually no flow control, such as loops; it may contain conditional statements
- Actions are normally idempotent
- Dependency is usually explicitly declared

>  The concept of actions being idempotent is a very important one in Puppet. It means that actions can be repeated without causing unnecessary side effects. For example, removing a user is idempotent, because removing it when it doesn't exist causes no side effects. Running a script that increments to the next user ID and creates a user may not be idempotent, because the user ID might change.

Imperative systems, on the other hand, use algorithms and steps to express their desired state. Most traditional programming languages, such as C and Java, are considered imperative. Imperative systems have the following properties:

- They use algorithms to describe the steps to the solution
- They use flow control to add conditionals and loops
- Actions may not be idempotent
- Dependency is normally executed by ordering

In Puppet, which is declarative, the users can describe how they want the system to look in the end, and leave the implementation details of how to get there up to the types and providers within Puppet. Puppet uses types, which represent resources, such as files or packages. Each type can optionally be implemented by one or more provider.

Types provide the core functionality available in Puppet. The type system is extensible, and additional types can be added using pure Ruby code. Later on in this chapter, we'll use the file and package types in our example.

Providers include the code for the type that actually does the low level implementation of a resource. Many types have several providers that implement their functionality in different ways. An example of this is the package type. It has providers for RPM, Yum, dpkg, Windows using MSI, and several others. While it is not a requirement that all types have multiple providers, it is not uncommon to see them, especially for resources that have different implementation details across operating systems.

This system of types and providers isolates the user from having to have specific knowledge of how a given task is done. This allows them to focus on how the system should be configured, and leave specific implementation details, such as how to put it in that state, to Puppet.

A few tools, such as Chef, actually use more of a hybrid approach. They can be used in a declarative state, but also allow the use of loops and other flow control structures that are imperative. Puppet is slowly starting to gain some support for this in their new future parser, however these are experimental and advanced features at this point.

While the declarative approach may have a larger learning curve, especially around dependency management, many sysadmins find it a much better fit with their way of thinking once they learn how it works.

The Puppet client-server model

Puppet uses a client-server model in the most common configurations. In this mode, one or more systems, called Puppet Masters, contain files called manifests. Manifests are code written in the Puppet DSL. A DSL is a language designed to be used for a specific application. In this case, the language is used to describe the desired state of a system. This differs from more general purpose languages, such as C and Ruby, in that it contains specialized constructs for the problem being solved. In this case, the resources in the language are specific to the configuration management domain.

Manifests contain the classes and resources which Puppet uses to describe the state of the system. They also contain declarations of the dependencies between these resources.

Classes are often bundled up into modules which package up classes into reusable chunks that can be managed separately. As your system becomes more complicated, using modules helps you manage each subsystem independently of the others.

The client systems contain the Puppet agent, which is the component that communicates with the master. At specified run intervals (30 minutes by default), the agent will run and the following actions will take place:

1. Custom plugins, such as facts, types, and providers, are sent to the client, if configured.
2. The client collects facts and sends them to the master.
3. The master compiles a catalog and sends it to the client.
4. The client processes the catalog sent by the master.
5. The client sends the reporting data to the master, if configured.

The catalog, sent to the client by the master, contains a compiled state of the system resources of the client. The client then applies this information using types and providers to bring the system into the desired state. The following illustration shows how data flows between the components:

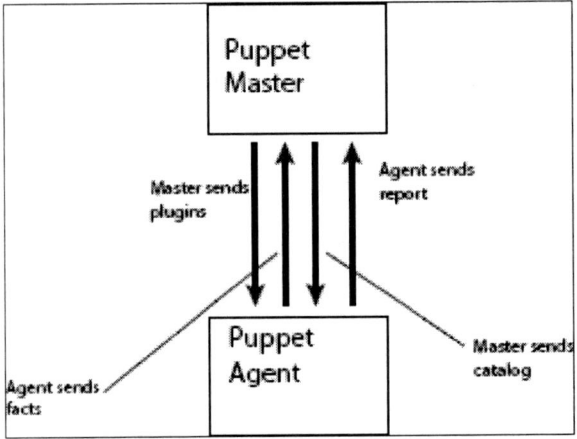

It is also possible to run Puppet in a masterless mode. In this mode, the Puppet manifests and other needed components, such as custom facts, types, and providers, are distributed to each system using an out of band method, such as scp or rsync. Puppet is then applied on the local node using cron or some other tool.

cron has the advantage of not requiring the server setup with open ports that the master-based setup has. In some organizations, this makes it easier to get past information security teams. However, many of the reporting and other benefits we will explore in this book are less effective when run in this fashion. The book *Puppet 3: Beginners Guide*, *John Arundel*, *Packt Publishing*, has a good amount of information about such a masterless setup.

Other Puppet components

Puppet has a number of other components that form part of the Puppet ecosystem, which are worth exploring due to their use as security tools. The specific components we are going to explore here include PuppetDB and Hiera.

PuppetDB

PuppetDB is an application used to store information on the Puppet infrastructure. Released in 2012, PuppetDB solved performance issues present in the older storeconfigs method that stored information about Puppet runs.

PuppetDB allows you to store facts, catalogs, reports, and resource information (via exported resources). Mining this data, using one of the reporting APIs, is an easy and powerful way to get a view of your infrastructure. More information on PuppetDB will be presented in *Chapter 3*, *Puppet for Compliance*, as well as *Chapter 4*, *Security Reporting with Puppet*.

Hiera

Hiera was a new feature introduced in Puppet 3. It is a hierarchal data store, which helps to keep information about your environment. This allows you to separate data about the environment from code that acts on the environment. By doing so, you can apply separate security policies to the code that drives the environment and data about the systems.

Before Hiera, it was not uncommon to see large sections of Puppet code dedicated to maintaining sites or installation of specific information on the systems under management. This area was often difficult to maintain if the ability to override parameters using many different factors was needed.

By adding a hierarchy that can depend on any facts, it becomes much easier to store the data needed for the systems under management. A model of most specific to least specific can then be applied, which makes it much easier to override the default data at a site, environment, or system level.

For example, let's say you had a set of development environments where a certain group of development accounts needed to get created, and SSH access to those accounts was granted. However, these accounts and the access granted should only exist in the development machines, and not in production. Without Hiera, there would likely be site-specific information in the modules to manage the SSH configuration, and perhaps in the user creation module to manage the users. Using Hiera, we can add a fact for the type of system (production or development) and store which users get created there, or have access. This moves the list of users with access to the system out of the code itself, and into a data file.

As our examples get more complicated later in this book, we will explore using Hiera to store some system data.

> **Downloading the example code**
> You can download the example code files for all Packt books you have purchased from your account at http://www.packtpub.com. If you purchased this book elsewhere, you can visit http://www.packtpub.com/support and register to have the files e-mailed directly to you.

Installing and configuring Puppet

Puppet can be installed in a variety of ways. Since this book is focused on the security-related aspects of Puppet and is not a beginner's guide, we will cover the most common way it is installed on our target system. There are many good reference books available for more in-depth information on installing Puppet, including *Puppet 3: Beginner's Guide*, *John Arundel*, *Packt Publishing*.

In our examples, we'll be using CentOS 6 as our operating system. If you are using a different operating system and following along on your own, please see the installation instructions for your operating system at http://www.puppetlabs.com, or follow along using Vagrant as outlined later.

Since we will be using Vagrant for our examples, the base box we are using already has the Puppet repository installed on it as well as the Puppet agent. We'll provide instructions for the installation of these elements for those who wish to use CentOS without using Vagrant.

Installing the Puppet Labs Yum repository

The currently recommended way to install Puppet on CentOS machines is to use the Puppet Labs Yum repository. This repository, which can be found at https://yum.puppetlabs.com, contains all the Puppet Labs software as well as the dependencies required to install them, such as several Ruby gems not present in the main CentOS repository. On installation, Ruby and these dependencies will also be installed.

Adding this repository is relatively simple. Execute the following command as a root (or using `sudo`, as shown here):

```
sudo rpm -ivh https://yum.puppetlabs.com/puppetlabs-release-el-6.noarch.rpm
```

After running this command, you will see an output similar to this:

```
Retrieving https://yum.puppetlabs.com/puppetlabs-release-el-6.noarch.rpm
Preparing...
########################################### [100%]
   1:puppetlabs-release
########################################### [100%]
```

Once this is complete, you're done! The Puppet Labs repository is added and we can use it to install the current version of any of the Puppet Labs products.

Chapter 1

Installing the Puppet Master

The next step is to install the Puppet Master. As mentioned earlier, this system acts as the controller that all of your client agents will then use to communicate with to receive catalog information. This package is normally installed on only a few systems that act as servers for configuration management information.

Installing the master with the repository is as easy as executing the following command:

```
sudo yum -y install puppet-server
```

This will instruct yum to install the Puppet server without confirmation. The output will be as follows:

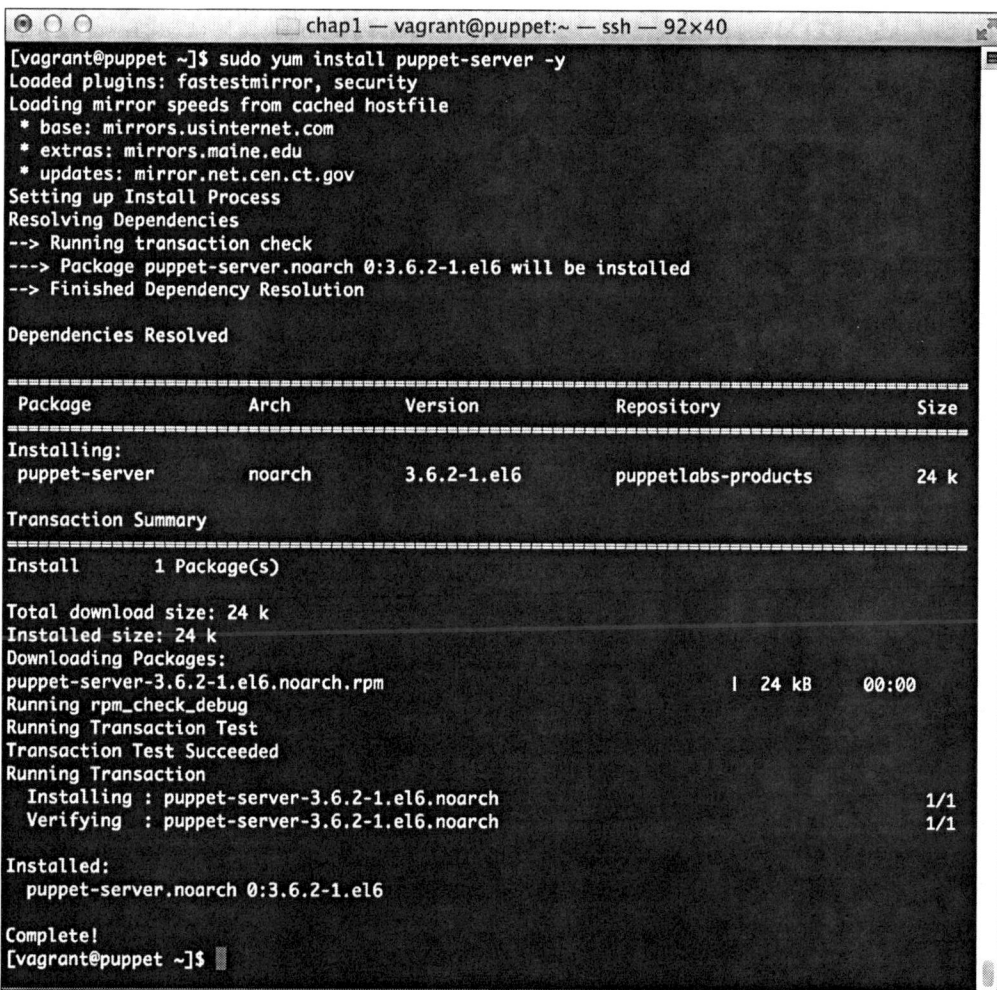

Installing the Puppet agent

On all the systems that we wish to manage by using Puppet, we'll need to install the Puppet agent. This agent is a piece of software that is responsible for communicating with the master and applying changes.

Installing the Puppet agent is very easy and similar to installing the master in the preceding section. You simply run the following:

```
sudo yum -y install puppet
```

After this is complete, you'll see that the the Puppet agent is installed on the local machine and is ready to talk to the master.

Configuring Puppet

Now that we have a perfectly working Puppet Master, we need to configure it. Installation of the packages will include a base level configuration. There are some changes we will want to make to the base Puppet configuration to enable some features that we'll use in the future. As we go through this book, we'll make changes to these files several times.

The main configuration files in use by Puppet are present in the /etc/puppet directory.

In this directory, there are a number of configuration files that control how Puppet behaves. Information on these files can be found at https://docs.puppetlabs.com/puppet/3.7/reference/config_about_settings.html. For now, we only need to concern ourselves with the Puppet configuration file.

Open the /etc/puppet/puppet.conf file with your favorite editor (make sure that you use sudo) and edit it to look similar to the following:

```
[main]
    # The Puppet log directory.
    # The default value is '$vardir/log'.
    logdir = /var/log/puppet

    # Where Puppet PID files are kept.
    # The default value is '$vardir/run'.
    rundir = /var/run/puppet

    # Where SSL certificates are kept.
    # The default value is '$confdir/ssl'.
    ssldir = $vardir/ssl

[agent]
```

```
    # The file in which puppetd stores a list of the classes
    # associated with the retrieved configuratiion.  Can be loaded
 in
    # the separate ``puppet`` executable using the ``--
loadclasses``
    # option.
    # The default value is '$confdir/classes.txt'.
    classfile = $vardir/classes.txt

    # Where puppetd caches the local configuration.  An
    # extension indicating the cache format is added
automatically.
    # The default value is '$confdir/localconfig'.
    localconfig = $vardir/localconfig
    report = true
    pluginsync = true
[master]
    reports = store
```

We've made a handful of changes to the file from the default version and will cover them here.

The first change is adding the `report = true` section to the agent configuration section. This will cause clients to send reports containing information about the Puppet run. We'll use these reports for later analysis in *Chapter 4, Security Reporting with Puppet*.

The second change is to add `pluginsync = true` to the agent section. While this has become the default in the more recent versions of Puppet, it does not hurt to add it in. This causes the clients to sync custom facts, providers, and other Puppet libraries from the master. We will see how this is used in later chapters.

The final change we have made is to add the master section and add `reports = store`. This causes the master to save reports to the local filesystem on the Puppet Master. We'll use this later to do analysis of our Puppet runs for security-related purposes.

Puppet services

Both the Puppet Master and the agent are usually run as services. This allows the agent to check its run frequency and apply any changes. We've not explicitly started the services here, although we'll need to start the master in order to use it from our agent. To do this, we run the following command:

```
sudo service puppetmaster start
```

In order for the Puppet Master to start at boot, we'll also issue the following command to enable it to autostart:

```
sudo chkconfig puppetmaster on
```

It's pretty common to use Puppet to manage Puppet, and in a later chapter, we'll do this to show how we can use Puppet to secure the Puppet Master.

> It's worth noting that Puppet running with a default web server configuration will not scale beyond a few dozen hosts. Scaling Puppet is outside the scope of this book. More information on scaling Puppet can be found at http://docs.puppetlabs.com/guides/scaling.html.

Preparing the environment for examples

As mentioned in the preface, we're going to use Vagrant to run our examples. In case you missed it, Vagrant is a tool that helps you automate the creation of virtual machines for testing. In this case, it's a great tool for us to use to quickly build-out our build and example environments.

We'll be using CentOS 6 in these examples, but most of them should run without much modification on other platforms. You will need to adjust the package names and perhaps configure the filenames for other operating systems. Many community modules, which we will explore in later chapters, support multiple flavors of Linux as well as other Unix-like systems. The powerful descriptive language of Puppet makes this easy to do.

While the use of Vagrant is not required, it will help us to maintain a clean environment for each of the examples we run, and will also ease the creation of virtual machines. If you choose not to use Vagrant for this, you can still run the examples using the manifests and modules provided with the source accompanying this book.

Installing Vagrant and VirtualBox

In order for us to use Vagrant, we must first install it. To do this, we need to install the required dependencies followed by Vagrant itself. We'll be using VirtualBox to host the virtual machines in these examples, since it is the most supported virtual machine provider.

VirtualBox can be downloaded from http://www.virtualbox.org. On this site, you will find packages for installing a variety of operating systems. You simply need to pick the package for your chosen operating system and install it using the instructions found on the site.

Once we have VirtualBox installed, we can approach installing Vagrant. Vagrant has several methods of installation. These methods include OS packages for Linux, as well as installers for OS X and Windows. Older versions of Vagrant supported installation via the Ruby gem utility, but this has been removed in later versions.

Vagrant can be found at http://www.vagrantup.com. Once you're there, you can download the package or installer for your OS. Once downloaded, you can install the package using your operating system's package manager, or by executing the downloaded package. In Windows and OS X, this is sufficient to have a working installation of Vagrant.

More in-depth installation instructions can be found on the **Documentation** tab on the Vagrant website; however, the package or installer will do most of the work.

It is worth noting that if you are using Windows, you will perform most of the work we're doing in a command shell on the DOS command box. However, if you use a local editor, you should be able to follow along with no issues.

Creating our first Vagrantfile

Now that we have Vagrant installed, we'll create our first Vagrant configuration. Vagrant uses a file called Vagrantfile to control its operation.

First, we start by creating a directory for our project. In this case, we'll call it puppetbook. We'll end up building on this setup in later chapters to automate configuration of our examples. This will allow us to focus on the Puppet tasks, and not so much on getting our test systems into the desired state.

Inside this directory, we'll create a directory called master_manifests. The purpose of this directory is to hold the Puppet manifests that we'll use to provision the base VM.

We'll be using the Puppet provisioner to do our work. This is one of a handful of methods you can use to provision a Vagrant virtual machine. Using this provisioner, we'll write a Puppet manifest that will describe the desired state of our machine. Vagrant will then use this manifest to run Puppet locally and configure the system.

Next, we'll create a `Vagrantfile`. In your favorite editor, go ahead and open `Vagrantfile`. Add the following contents. We'll cover what each one does in a moment:

```
Vagrant.configure(2) do |config|
  config.vm.define :puppetmaster do |master|

    master.vm.box = "centos65-x64-puppet"
    master.vm.box_url = "http://puppet-vagrant-boxes.puppetlabs.com/centos-65-x64-virtualbox-puppet.box"
    master.vm.hostname = "puppet.book.local"
    master.vm.network "private_network", ip: "10.78.78.30", netmask: "255.255.255.0"

    master.vm.provision "shell", inline: "yum -y update puppet"

    master.vm.provision "puppet" do |puppet|
      puppet.manifests_path = "master_manifests"
      puppet.manifest_file = "init.pp"
    end

  end
end
```

> It's possible that by the time you read this, the Vagrant box referenced in the preceding code will be deprecated. This book was written using the Puppet Labs CentOS 6 machine images. You can go to `http://puppet-vagrant-boxes.puppetlabs.com/` and find a replacement. You want a CentOS 6 x86_64 box with Puppet (called plain there) and VirtualBox addons.

Go ahead and save the file. We'll cover what each file does here:

```
Vagrant.configure(2) do |config|
```

This line sets up Vagrant using configuration version 2. It uses Ruby blocks to create a Vagrant configuration with the `config` variable:

```
config.vm.define :puppetmaster do |master|
```

This line defines a virtual machine called `puppetmaster`. Vagrant supports multimachine setups, which is a feature we'll use later on in the book. For now, we'll define a single machine. Much like the preceding code, we use a block called `master`:

```
master.vm.box = "centos65-x64-puppet"
```

This defines the box we'll use for our Puppet Master. It is a symbolic name, but it makes sense to name it according to what it is. If you refer to the same box later, it'll use the same base and not download the box files an additional time:

```
master.vm.box_url = "http://puppet-vagrant-
boxes.puppetlabs.com/centos-65-x64-virtualbox-puppet.box"
```

This defines the URL we'll download our box file from. In this case, we're grabbing it from the hosted Puppet Vagrant boxes on Puppet Labs. We could get a box from any number of other places, but the Puppet Labs boxes come with the Puppet agent preinstalled and the Puppet repository is already available and ready for use. If you wish to explore other box options, there is a directory of them available at http://www.vagrantcloud.com:

```
master.vm.hostname = "puppet.book.local"
```

This command simply sets the host name of our machine. It is important for the master as it influences the certificate name that gets created at installation:

```
master.vm.network "private_network", ip: "10.78.78.30", netmask:
"255.255.255.0"
```

This line creates a private network for our virtual machines to use. We assign it the IP address 10.78.78.30/24 (78 is PU on a phone dial pad):

```
master.vm.provision "shell", inline: "yum -y update puppet
```

"Wait," you say, "I thought we were using the Puppet provisioner?"

As it turns out, the Puppet Labs base box comes with Puppet 3.4 installed. The current version we wish to use in this book is 3.7.3. We use the yum statement to upgrade Puppet before the provisioner starts. Otherwise, we get issues when the Puppet run updates the agent:

```
master.vm.provision "puppet" do |puppet|
```

Here, we tell Vagrant we're going to use the Puppet provisioner, and open a block called puppet to do so:

```
puppet.manifests_path = "master_manifests"
```

Here, we give the path to the manifest directory. This is relative to the path that the Vagrantfile is in. As you can recall, we created this directory earlier:

```
puppet.manifest_file = "init.pp"
```

We define the Puppet manifest to be called `init.pp`. This is the default name of a Puppet manifest. Vagrant defaults to `default.pp` if it's not specified:

```
    end
  end
end
```

These lines undo each of the preceding blocks and close out the file.

If we run Vagrant now, it will throw an error because it cannot find the `init.pp` file, so let's go ahead and create it inside the `master_manifests` directory. To save space, we'll call out each block and describe its function rather than giving the entire file and explaining it:

```
package { 'puppet-server':
  ensure => 'present',
}
```

The preceding resource declaration will install the Puppet Master. By specifying the `ensure` value of `present`, we make sure it's installed; however, we tell Puppet that we do not care about the version and do not wish to upgrade it:

```
file { '/etc/puppet/puppet.conf':
  ensure  => 'present',
  owner   => 'root',
  group   => 'root',
  mode    => '0644',
  source  => '/vagrant/master_manifests/files/puppet.conf',
  require => Package['puppet-server'],
}
```

The preceding resource declaration has a good amount more going on. Here, we're going to manage a file called `/etc/puppet/puppet.conf`. We ensure that it is present, then set the owner, group, and mode to set the values. Using the `source` parameter, we source the file from the local filesystem. Vagrant, by default, will mount the directory containing the `Vagrantfile` as `/vagrant`, so we can take advantage of that mount to get the file without otherwise copying it.

The last line here shows off the explicit dependency management of Puppet. We require that the `puppet-server` package is installed before we install the configuration file. This will ensure that the directory is created, and the package installation does not overwrite the configuration file:

```
service { 'puppetmaster':
  ensure  => 'running',
  require => File['/etc/puppet/puppet.conf'],
}
```

This last resource declaration ensures that the Puppet Master service is running. It depends on the configuration file being there.

In a real-world example, we're likely to use `subscribe` instead of `require` here. This would restart the service if the configuration file changed. However, since we're using the local Puppet provisioner and not running this code under a Puppet Master, this code will only be run once, so it is unnecessary to use `subscribe`.

We need one last file to make the system work. The file resource depends on a file called `master_manifests/files/puppet.conf`. We've covered the contents of this file in the Puppet installation section, so we will not repeat them here. You simply need to copy the file to the directory for the provisioner to use.

When we're done, the complete directory structure of this setup will look as follows:

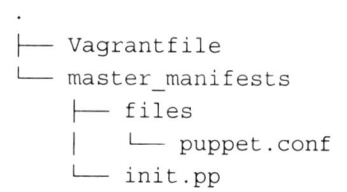

```
.
├── Vagrantfile
└── master_manifests
    ├── files
    │   └── puppet.conf
    └── init.pp
```

Once we're set up, we're in a good position to run the examples that we'll present in this book. As these examples get more complex, we'll add the necessary data to this structure to add things such as client machines.

Puppet for security and compliance

Puppet is a perfect tool for security and compliance. So much security work involves ensuring that a given version of a service is on every server, or whether a user account exists or not.

Much of this work is also very tedious and repetitive. When work such as this is done across many servers, the likelihood that some of them will be different grows. These snowflakes, or systems that are unique and unlike other systems, can cause security issues or can be hard to troubleshoot.

On top of being able to maintain a system in a fixed state, we can use some Puppet resources, such as PuppetDB, to do some fairly in-depth reporting. Using custom facts, you can collect any information you wish to send to a central place. This can include things such as software versions, hardware configuration, and much more. By using this information, we can start to work toward creating a full configuration management and security platform.

Through Puppet, you will be able to centrally manage the major configuration aspects of all of your systems. Keeping this configuration in version control and treating it as code gives you all the benefits that developers have been able to enjoy for years. You'll quickly be able to see how the state of a system has evolved over time, as well as look where bugs might have been introduced and have caused security issues.

Additionally, there is an increasing movement to use Puppet for compliance and auditing. By demonstrating that Puppet is indeed running on a system and showing the manifests running on it, you can ensure that a system is in a given state. This information can be shown to auditors as documentation on how systems are configured.

Getting to the point of 100-percent coverage in system configuration using Puppet requires commitment and time. Using community modules, as we'll explore later, can lessen that work. However, the results of doing this are very high. Disaster recovery can be made simpler because systems can quickly be rebuilt. Installing the latest tripwire on all systems becomes as simple as updating the manifests and letting the systems check in. These benefits can make the job of a security professional much easier.

As we progress through this book, we will explore many of these abilities in-depth, but for now, let's look at a simple example we can use to learn some of the Puppet concepts and language.

Example – using Puppet to secure openssh

Now that we've got the system set up for our use, we can finally approach the main example for this chapter. In this example, we're going to use what has traditionally been one of the first things used to show off Puppet and install SSH. However, in this case, we're going to use a hardened configuration utilizing some options recommended by the security community.

The example of securing SSH is one that we will return to several times in this book as we expand upon our configuration management toolkit and branch out into things such as firewall management.

Starting the Vagrant virtual machine

Since this is our first time using Vagrant, we'll cover how to start a virtual machine. In the directory with the `Vagrantfile`, run the following command:

```
vagrant up
```

Once this is done, you'll see the output from Vagrant indicating the actions it's taking, as well as output from the commands it runs—this includes the Shell provisioner and the Puppet provisioner. When it's done, you'll end up with something that is similar to the following:

```
  Cleanup     : puppet-3.4.2-1.el6.noarch                              2/2
  Verifying   : puppet-3.6.2-1.el6.noarch                              1/2
  Verifying   : puppet-3.4.2-1.el6.noarch                              2/2

Updated:
  puppet.noarch 0:3.6.2-1.el6

Complete!
==> puppetmaster: Running provisioner: puppet...
Running Puppet with init.pp...
Warning: Setting manifestdir is deprecated. See http://links.puppetlabs.com/env-settings-dep
recations
   (at /usr/lib/ruby/site_ruby/1.8/puppet/settings.rb:1095:in `issue_deprecations')
Notice: Compiled catalog for puppet.book.local in environment production in 0.33 seconds
Warning: The package type's allow_virtual parameter will be changing its default value from
 false to true in a future release. If you do not want to allow virtual packages, please expl
icitly set allow_virtual to false.
   (at /usr/lib/ruby/site_ruby/1.8/puppet/type.rb:816:in `set_default')
Notice: /Stage[main]/Main/Package[puppet-server]/ensure: created
Notice: /Stage[main]/Main/File[/etc/puppet/puppet.conf]/content: content changed '{md5}58e2f
9765e2994db8e8ab19a3513356e' to '{md5}050756d308081f08193ea71a10a92740'
Notice: /Stage[main]/Main/Service[puppetmaster]/ensure: ensure changed 'stopped' to 'running
'
Notice: Finished catalog run in 10.03 seconds
jslagle@Jasons-MacBook-Pro:~/pupbook/src/chap1 $
```

You'll notice some warnings on the screen here. These are options that are changing with the newer version of Puppet. Our manifest could add an `allow_virtual` setting to get rid of the second warning. The first warning, however, is a result of how Vagrant is calling Puppet.

Connecting to our virtual machine

Once your machine has booted, simply issue the following command to connect:

`vagrant ssh`

This will connect you to the machine using `ssh`. Once this is complete, we can start working on our module.

Creating the module

We'll be using a Puppet module to secure SSH. As such, we should go ahead and create the directory to hold our module. You can issue the following commands to create the module skeleton on the guest virtual machine:

```
sudo mkdir -p /etc/puppet/modules/openssh/manifests
sudo mkdir -p /etc/puppet/modules/openssh/files
```

These directories will hold the manifests for Puppet to compile as well as our configuration file. For our first simplistic example, we will use a static SSH configuration file. In later chapters, we will build upon it and make it dynamic with the various options that are available.

> It's also possible to make the `/etc/puppet/modules/openssh` directory a symlink to a directory in `/vagrant`. If you create the directory in `/vagrant`, you can use any editor on your host system to edit the files and have it immediately available in the guest. This saves you the trouble of having to configure a good editing environment on the guest machine.

Building the module

Now that we have the framework, we'll build our first module. Much like the preceding code, we'll go through it section by section covering what each resource does. The manifest we're building will be very similar to the one we used to provision the Puppet Master for the use of.

First, we'll edit the `/etc/puppet/modules/openssh/manifests/init.pp` file to create the module's main manifest. This manifest is the main unit of the Puppet code, which is invoked when we include the module. As we go through each of the sections, we'll go through what they do. A complete manifest file can be found on this book's website, but you should really build it along with us. This will help you with understanding and memorization:

```
class openssh {
```

The preceding line defines the class. The class in the `init.pp` file is always named after the module. It's a new construct we've not seen before that is unique to creating modules:

```
package { 'openssh-server':
  ensure => 'latest',
}
```

The preceding section is similar to the `puppetmaster` section. The only difference is that we're using `latest` instead of `present`. Being a security-related package, it may make sense to make sure that you keep `openssh` up to date.

Alternatively, if your environment requires it, you could specify a fixed version to install. This might be useful if you require pretested versions or have validated versions. You must weigh the benefits, ensuring that you run the most recent version of the software, including the risk of almost immediately installing it when it is available, and that you're using the latest tag:

```
file { '/etc/ssh/sshd_config':
  ensure => 'present',
  owner  => 'root',
  group  => 'root',
  mode   => '0600',
  source => 'puppet:///modules/openssh/sshd_config',
}
```

> As your Puppet code becomes more complex, care must be taken on how you name your files inside your module. It can sometimes be useful to create the full path to the file under the modules directory, so there is no confusion as to the destination of the time. We omit these here only because our modules are simple, and it makes the examples easier to follow.

This is similar to the Puppet Master configuration file, but we introduced a new construct here. We're sourcing the file from `puppet master` by using the special `puppet://` uniform resource identifier (URL). When Puppet runs, it will fetch the file from the master for use on the agent. The source file should be present in the `/etc/puppet/modules/openssh/files` directory on the master:

```
service { 'sshd':
  ensure => 'running',
}
```

Here, as before, we ensure that ssh is running when we run Puppet:

```
    Package['openssh-server']
    -> File['/etc/ssh/sshd_config']
    ~> Service['sshd']
}
```

This is also a new construct called resource chaining. It is an alternative way to specify that we do things in the order listed: first, the package, followed by the file, and then the service. Note the tilde on the service dependency. This shows that we're notifying the service. It means that if the configuration file changes, the service will be restarted.

> In a declarative system, there needs to be a way to ensure that things are run in the correct order. One of the more difficult things for new Puppet users is to grasp the concept that their manifests don't necessarily run in a top-down order. This concept is so hard that in recent versions of Puppet, the default has been changed to a process in the manifest order by default. More information on resource ordering and this change can be found at http://puppetlabs.com/blog/introducing-manifest-ordered-resources.

The openssh configuration file

To build the configuration file we're going to use, we'll start with the openssh configuration file shipped with CentOS and make a few changes. First, we'll copy the existing configuration file with the following command:

```
sudo cp /etc/ssh/sshd_config /etc/puppet/modules/openssh/files/
```

Next, we'll edit the file with your favorite editor. Make sure you run it in sudo as you won't have permission to edit the file. We'll uncomment and change the following lines in the file:

```
    PermitRootLogin no
    MaxAuthTries 3
```

We'll start with these changes to demonstrate how the process works. Then, save the file.

Next, we need to make sure the Puppet agent can read it. We'll set the permissions in such a manner that the Puppet user can read it. Execute the following:

`sudo chgrp puppet /etc/puppet/modules/openssh/files/sshd_config`

`sudo chmod 640 /etc/puppet/modules/openssh/files/sshd_config`

The site.pp file

Now, we need to bring it all together to tell Puppet to use our module. By default, Puppet runs a file called `site.pp` on the master to determine what actions to take when a node checks in. We need to add the new module to the file for Puppet to run it.

The file lives in `/etc/puppet/manifests` on our Vagrant guest. Go ahead and open it in your favorite editor and add the following section:

```
node default {
  include openssh
}
```

This adds a default node declaration and includes our `openssh` module on that node. It will ensure that our new module gets used.

Running our new code

Now that we've got it all built, let's go ahead and see the fruits of our labor. Execute the following command:

`sudo puppet agent --test`

Puppet as a Security Tool

You should see the output as follows:

```
[vagrant@puppet ~]$ sudo puppet agent --test
Info: Retrieving plugin
Info: Caching catalog for puppet.book.local
Warning: The package type's allow_virtual parameter will be changing its default value from
false to true in a future release. If you do not want to allow virtual packages, please expl
icitly set allow_virtual to false.
   (at /usr/lib/ruby/site_ruby/1.8/puppet/type.rb:816:in `set_default')
Info: Applying configuration version '1407420269'
Notice: /Stage[main]/Openssh/File[/etc/ssh/sshd_config]/content:
--- /etc/ssh/sshd_config        2014-01-16 04:36:24.975584986 -0800
+++ /tmp/puppet-file20140807-3398-f6n71q-0      2014-08-07 07:04:30.455879230 -0700
@@ -39,9 +39,9 @@
 # Authentication:

 #LoginGraceTime 2m
-#PermitRootLogin yes
+PermitRootLogin no
 #StrictModes yes
-#MaxAuthTries 6
+MaxAuthTries 3
 #MaxSessions 10

 #RSAAuthentication yes

Info: /Stage[main]/Openssh/File[/etc/ssh/sshd_config]: Filebucketed /etc/ssh/sshd_config to
puppet with sum 95f289e1ad7e3e8df4600beb48355a01
Notice: /Stage[main]/Openssh/File[/etc/ssh/sshd_config]/content: content changed '{md5}95f28
9e1ad7e3e8df4600beb48355a01' to '{md5}fee58d906943947e41151738c2cbab68'
Info: /Stage[main]/Openssh/File[/etc/ssh/sshd_config]: Scheduling refresh of Service[sshd]
Notice: /Stage[main]/Openssh/Service[sshd]: Triggered 'refresh' from 1 events
Notice: Finished catalog run in 0.76 seconds
[vagrant@puppet ~]$
```

> If you're running these examples outside Vagrant, you will have a bit more work to do. We're using Vagrant to set our hostname to Puppet, and the master by default has its own certificate signed. If you are running without Vagrant, you will need to add a host file entry or DNS pointing to your master, and you may need to sign the certificate. We'll cover certificate singing in *Chapter 5*, *Securing Puppet*.

Victory! You can see that Puppet changed the file to disallow root logins and change the maximum authentication attempts to 3.

As with any new technology, the learning curve can seem somewhat overwhelming at first. We've now gone through a rather lengthy example to effectively make a two-line edit to a configuration file on a single machine. This was a short and simple example to explore some base concepts of Puppet. Using this concept, we could apply this same edit to hundreds or even thousands of machines in our infrastructure with very little additional effort. We'll also be exploring more in-depth examples as we gain a skillset. With some practice, you will find that applying changes across one of many machines becomes second nature with Puppet.

Summary

In this chapter, we built a foundation for things we will do in chapters to come. First, we covered what Puppet is, and how it differs from other tools in its space. We gave a brief introduction to some of the other Puppet components we'll be using in this book as well.

Moving on from this, we covered how to install Puppet on CentOS. We went through a full installation example and covered the basics of configuration files.

Then, we covered the configuration and installation of Vagrant and used it to run our first example. In this example, we configured SSH with a secure configuration file.

Finally, we introduced how Puppet fits into a security ecosystem. While keeping with the basics, we've begun exploring how Puppet can be used to process simple configuration tasks to secure your systems.

This chapter focused on several high-level concepts. As we get further into the book, we'll go more in-depth in examples and they will get much more powerful. As an introductory chapter, the hope was to get you up and running with a working manifest. In future chapters, we will assume a base level of knowledge and link to references you can use if needed.

Additionally, if you wish to get some more information on the base Puppet language before we proceed, there are several books available. Some of them were mentioned earlier in this chapter, and we'll cover more as we proceed through the book. The documentation at `http://docs.puppetlabs.com` is also very informative, if a little dry at times.

In the next chapter, we'll begin to use our knowledge gained here to explore how Puppet can be used to track changes to resources on our filesystems.

2
Tracking Changes to Objects

Have you ever wanted to know whether the content of the files on your server has changed or whether the packages installed on the server have changed? Perhaps you have developers who have access to edit files. Maybe you need to gather information on what has changed for production use.

If you have changed the tracking requirements that require you to report on specific items changing on our system, then the Puppet auditing and change tracking system can be a great solution.

Change tracking is the act of monitoring systems for changes and reporting on them. It is a component of more comprehensive auditing, which includes the reporting and other activities surrounding it, ensuring that a system is in compliance. There are numerous software packages available that do this. Many of them are special-purpose tools, such as Tripwire, OSSEC, and AIDE. Puppet can be used to configure many of these tools, which often require fairly extensive setups. Additionally, some of these tools require commercial licenses to obtain the full feature set.

With proper configuration, you can use Puppet to do change tracking. Beyond this, Puppet can be used to make sure that changed resources return to their expected states, including correcting the content, owner, or mode of the file.

In this chapter, we will cover the following topics:

- How change tracking works in Puppet
- An overview of the audit meta-parameter
- Examples of using the audit meta-parameter
- Caveats of the audit meta-parameter
- Using noop to get a similar workflow to the audit meta-parameter

Change tracking with Puppet

Puppet has a variety of ways to track changes. In its normal mode of operation, Puppet will track (and correct) changes to any resources in its catalog. This is by its nature what it's designed for. This can let you know that items have changed, but at the same time let you know that you can correct them to be the way you want them to be specified.

If you don't have a set state for your resources and you just want to know whether they have changed, you can use the audit meta-parameter. There is some evidence that this will be deprecated in Puppet 4; however, it is currently still available as this book is being written.

Finally, one can use noop to monitor changes. In this mode, Puppet will report on any changes to a resource from its baseline; however, it will not make an effort to change them back.

Noop can be used in a variety of fashions and will be covered at the end of the chapter.

The following table summarizes the available change tracking options:

	Declared resources	Audit	Noop
Requires definition of the baseline of a resource	Yes	No	Yes
Corrects the resource if it becomes out of compliance	Yes	No	No (although you can run without noop to do so)
Allows you to specify what parameters are monitored	No, only what's in the baseline is monitored	Yes	No, see declared resources
Supported in later Puppet versions	Yes	No	Yes

We'll cover the audit and noop methodologies later in the section. We've already covered what can be done with declared resources in the previous chapter, and we will continue to build on it in the later chapters.

The audit meta-parameter

The audit meta-parameter is the primary change tracking method currently in Puppet. It was introduced in Puppet 2.6, and it provides a way to monitor a resource without enforcing a state on it.

With the introduction of Puppet Enterprise 1.2, Puppet Enterprise gained a compliance dashboard that allowed you to configure and track file changes. This dashboard has since been removed, but it relied heavily on the audit meta-parameter and allowed you to quickly set up auditing.

The audit meta-parameter is a bit of a divergence in the Puppet world. The declarative nature of Puppet is to model the desired state of a resource and allow Puppet to get it there. The audit meta-parameter can allow you to say that you may not care about the state of an item, but you want to know if it changes.

How it works

The audit system works by keeping track of the state of the attributes you monitor. At the end of every run, it persists the state of those objects.

If at the start of a run Puppet notices that the current state of an object changes, it raises an alert. Additionally, information on these changes is reported back to the master as part of any reports. This report data can be used to generate logs of changes to attributes.

Internally, Puppet implements auditing by persisting the state of the audited objects to a YAML file. This data is stored on each of the agent nodes, and not on the master server. On each Puppet run, YAML is read and the state in the file is compared to the existing state.

> **What is YAML?**
>
> YAML is a markup language. Originally, it was called "Yet another markup language". It is now known as "YAML Ain't Markup Language". YAML is a way to store data in a file similar to formats such as JSON. Puppet stores much of its internal data in the YAML format, and as we approach reporting and other processing of Puppet data, we will need to parse and create YAML files.

What can be audited

Being a meta-parameter, audit can be applied to any resource. The code to handle the audit meta-parameter is present in the Puppet core. In theory, any attribute on any resource should be permitted to be audited, but there are likely cases that are untested and do not work well.

Using audit on files

The most common use case for audit is auditing whether a given file has changed. The audit system was designed for a particular customer's needs by Puppet. Indications are that this need was largely around auditing files. For this reason, support around auditing files as well as documentation is the strongest for auditing the file type.

To use audit on a file, we add the audit meta-parameter to its declaration. For example:

```
file { '/etc/shells':
  audit => 'all',
}
```

This tells Puppet that it should audit every attribute on the file /etc/shells. If anything on this file changes, it will log messages in the local log file as well as generate report events indicating the changes.

Available attributes

On paper, any attribute is available to be audited. However, some attributes do not make sense. The Puppet language reference as of version 3.6 lists many available attributes for the file type. A current available list can be found at https://docs.puppetlabs.com/references/latest/type.html#file. The attributes that directly change the files and represent their state on the system are listed in the following table, along with a brief description of what they do:

Attribute	Purpose
content	This is the md5sum checksum of the content. This changes whenever the file content changes.
ctime	This denotes the creation time of the file per the Unix operating system's stat system call.
ensure	This contains the type of file, directory, or link if managed by Puppet.
group	This denotes the Unix group of the file.
mode	This is the file's Unix mode.
mtime	This denotes the last modification of the file per the Unix operating system's stat system call.
owner	This denotes the Unix user who owns the file.

Attribute	Purpose
selrange	This denotes the SELinux range component of the file on systems supporting SELinux.
selrole	This denotes the SELinux role of the file on systems supporting SELinux.
seltype	This denotes the SELinux type of the file for systems supporting SELinux.
seluser	This denotes the SELinux user of the file for systems supporting SELinux.
type	This contains the type of the file—typically, the same as ensure if managed.

Some of these attributes will not be present on all systems. For instance, on a non-Linux system, the SELinux attributes will not be present. Additionally, on a Windows system, there is an underlying mapping in place to turn the Windows concepts of file security into a fake Unix mode.

Auditing the password file

Now that we've seen how the audit resource works on files, it's time to perform an example. Building on our last exercise, we will audit the password file and see the results.

Preparation

The following steps need to be performed to audit the password file:

1. If you're following along from the last example, go ahead and start the virtual machine with the following command:

   vagrant up

2. Once the system is up, go ahead and SSH into it using the following command:

   vagrant ssh

You should now be logged in to the system.

Creating the manifest

Unlike the last chapter, we are going to build this manifest straight into the /etc/puppet/manifests/site.pp file. Since the example is short and for demonstration purposes, it does not make sense to create an entire module to hold it.

> As previously mentioned, it is considered bad form to add Puppet resources directly to the main manifest in most cases. We do so here to keep the length of the examples to a minimum since we'll have plenty of opportunities to create modules. For this and other best practice information on writing Puppet code, see `https://docs.puppetlabs.com/guides/style_guide.html`.

Inside the `/etc/puppet/manifests` directory, we'll edit the `site.pp` file. Once we are in the file, edit the default node to have an additional file resource as follows:

```
node default {
  include openssh
  file { '/etc/passwd':
    audit => 'all',
  }
}
```

First run of the manifest

Once this is done, execute Puppet. To do so, run the following command:

`sudo puppet agent -test`

The output should be as follows:

```
[vagrant@puppet ~]$ sudo puppet agent --test
Info: Retrieving plugin
Info: Caching catalog for puppet.book.local
Info: Applying configuration version '1421010717'
Notice: /Stage[main]/Openssh/Package[openssh-server]/ensure: audit change: previously recorded value 5.3p1-94.el6 has been changed to 5.3p1-104.el6_6.1
Notice: /Stage[main]/Main/Node[default]/File[/etc/passwd]/ensure: audit change: newly-recorded value file
Notice: /Stage[main]/Main/Node[default]/File[/etc/passwd]/content: audit change: newly-recorded value {md5}f613d4b669f05a354674be315902c47a
Notice: /Stage[main]/Main/Node[default]/File[/etc/passwd]/target: audit change: newly-recorded value notlink
Notice: /Stage[main]/Main/Node[default]/File[/etc/passwd]/owner: audit change: newly-recorded value 0
Notice: /Stage[main]/Main/Node[default]/File[/etc/passwd]/group: audit change: newly-recorded value 0
Notice: /Stage[main]/Main/Node[default]/File[/etc/passwd]/mode: audit change: newly-recorded value 644
Notice: /Stage[main]/Main/Node[default]/File[/etc/passwd]/type: audit change: newly-recorded value file
Notice: /Stage[main]/Main/Node[default]/File[/etc/passwd]/seluser: audit change: newly-recorded value
Notice: /Stage[main]/Main/Node[default]/File[/etc/passwd]/selrole: audit change: newly-recorded value
Notice: /Stage[main]/Main/Node[default]/File[/etc/passwd]/seltype: audit change: newly-recorded value
Notice: /Stage[main]/Main/Node[default]/File[/etc/passwd]/selrange: audit change: newly-recorded value
Notice: /Stage[main]/Main/Node[default]/File[/etc/passwd]/ctime: audit change: newly-recorded value Thu Jan 16 09:37:14 -0800 2014
Notice: /Stage[main]/Main/Node[default]/File[/etc/passwd]/mtime: audit change: newly-recorded value Thu Jan 16 09:37:14 -0800 2014
Notice: Finished catalog run in 0.57 seconds
[vagrant@puppet ~]$
```

In the preceding screenshot, Puppet records the initial value of all of the elements of the file. It will use this data later to determine whether any of it changes.

Changing the password file and rerunning Puppet

After we confirm that things look good, we'll go ahead and add a user. This will have the effect of changing the password file. We can also change a user password or perform any number of other operations on user accounts.

We're going to add a `puppettest` user. To do so, execute the following command:

```
sudo useradd puppettest
```

Once this is complete, we will need to run Puppet again to see the outcome. Run the following command:

```
sudo puppet agent -test
```

Again, observe the output, as shown in the following screenshot:

```
[vagrant@puppet ~]$ sudo useradd puppettest
[vagrant@puppet ~]$ sudo puppet agent --test
Info: Retrieving plugin
Info: Caching catalog for puppet.book.local
Info: Applying configuration version '1421010717'
Notice: /Stage[main]/Main/Node[default]/File[/etc/passwd]/content: audit change: previously recorded value {md5}f613d4b669f05a354674be315902c47a has been changed to {md5}154ac6b71d6752cd3d2e80eabf602694
Notice: /Stage[main]/Main/Node[default]/File[/etc/passwd]/ctime: audit change: previously recorded value Thu Jan 16 09:37:14 -0800 2014 has been changed to Sun Jan 11 13:14:21 -0800 2015
Notice: /Stage[main]/Main/Node[default]/File[/etc/passwd]/mtime: audit change: previously recorded value Thu Jan 16 09:37:14 -0800 2014 has been changed to Sun Jan 11 13:14:20 -0800 2015
Notice: Finished catalog run in 0.59 seconds
[vagrant@puppet ~]$
```

In the preceding screenshot, we can see that three different attributes have changed. The first attribute is the `content` attribute. This makes perfect sense since we changed the file.

The second attribute that has changed is the `ctime` attribute. This tells us that something rewrote the entire file.

The final attribute that has changed is `mtime`. We would expect this also since the file was changed.

The Puppet agent logs these changes in its local log file, but this data is also present in the report output. We'll cover how we can use this data in *Chapter 4, Security Reporting with Puppet*.

Audit on other resource types

While a file is the most common resource that can be audited, any resource can be audited. This even includes custom types. Additionally, even classes and defines can be audited; however, the mechanism is a bit different. In the case of defines and classes, the meta-parameter is inherited by all of the resources contained in that class or define, but not in any that are included inside it.

The basic mechanism of the audit parameter works in the same way as it does in the file case. You need to specify a list of attributes to monitor and Puppet will persist their state. If the state changes between runs, then it will trigger an audit alert. An example of auditing just the `owner` and `mtime` (modified time) attributes of the `sshd` daemon in `/usr/sbin` is as follows:

```
file { '/usr/sbin/ssh':
  audit => [ 'owner', 'mtime' ],
}
```

However, as one would expect, the attributes to be audited differ for each type. The package type, for example, only supports auditing the `ensure` value. This makes sense since it's the only value that has a concrete state on the system. In this case, it represents the currently installed version of the package.

Determining the attributes that can be audited for a given resource requires some trial and error. The following table shows some of the more prevalent resource types and the auditable resources:

Resource	Auditable attributes
cron	`ensure`, `command`, `environment`, `hour`, `minute`, `month`, `monthday`, `special`, `target`, `user`, and `weekday`
group	`ensure`, `attributes`, `gid`, and `members`
mount	`ensure`, `atboot`, `blockdevice`, `device`, `dump`, `fstype`, `options`, `pass`, and `target`
package	`ensure`, `package_settings`
service	`ensure`, `enable`, and `flags`
user	`ensure`, `attributes`, `auths`, `comment`, `expiry`, `gid`, `groups`, `home`, `iterations`, `keys`, `password`, `password_max_age`, `password_min_age`, `profiles`, `project`, `roles`, `salt`, `shell`, and `uid`

Not all of these resources can be audited in all cases. For instance, many of the user resources are only appropriate on Solaris systems.

Determining what resources can be audited on other resources can be done by reviewing `https://docs.puppetlabs.com/references/latest/type.html`. Look for the entries that say they represent the concrete state on the system. These attributes are usually able to be audited. One can also use the output of the Puppet resource command on a resource to get an idea. For more information on the Puppet `resource` command, see `https://docs.puppetlabs.com/references/3.7.latest/man/resource.html`.

Auditing a package

In this example, we'll extend our `openssh` module to audit the version installed. We'll then downgrade the package so that the version changes. Afterwards, we can verify whether the audit worked as expected.

> In a production environment, it would make sense to audit at least the `sshd` binary along with the package. It's quite possible for the attacker to change the binary without even touching the package. Auditing the package is more useful to find system administrators upgrading packages to unauthorized versions by accident.

Tracking Changes to Objects

Modifying the module to audit

First, make sure the Vagrant machine is running. If you need to restart your Vagrant machine, see the first exercise to get it running.

Once it is running, go ahead and SSH it into the machine. Again, if you need a reference, refer to the earlier chapter.

Now we'll edit the `openssh` manifest and add the `audit` parameter. Edit the `/etc/puppet/modules/openssh/manifests/init.pp` file with your favorite editor. Make sure to use `sudo` if you are working on the live file.

Locate the package declaration and change it to look like the following:

```
package { 'openssh-server':
  ensure => 'latest',
  audit  => 'all',
}
```

Go ahead and save the file. Once complete, run Puppet using the following command:

```
sudo puppet agent --test
```

The output of the command should be as follows:

```
Last login: Wed Aug  6 10:59:02 2014 from 10.0.2.2
Welcome to your Packer-built virtual machine.
[vagrant@puppet ~]$
[vagrant@puppet ~]$ ls
[vagrant@puppet ~]$ sudo vi /etc/puppet/
auth.conf       fileserver.conf  modules/
environments/   manifests/       puppet.conf
[vagrant@puppet ~]$ sudo vi /etc/puppet/modules/openssh/
files/    manifests/
[vagrant@puppet ~]$ sudo vi /etc/puppet/modules/openssh/manifests/init.pp
[vagrant@puppet ~]$ sudo puppet agent --test
Info: Retrieving plugin
Info: Caching catalog for puppet.book.local
Warning: The package type's allow_virtual parameter will be changing its default value from
false to true in a future release. If you do not want to allow virtual packages, please expl
icitly set allow_virtual to false.
   (at /usr/lib/ruby/site_ruby/1.8/puppet/type.rb:816:in `set_default')
Info: Applying configuration version '1407460757'
Notice: /Stage[main]/Openssh/Package[openssh-server]/ensure: audit change: newly-recorded va
lue 5.3p1-94.el6
Notice: Finished catalog run in 41.04 seconds
[vagrant@puppet ~]$
```

As you can see, it recorded the `ensure` value, setting it to the currently installed package version.

Now that we have done this, let's downgrade the package and see what the outcome is like.

To downgrade `openssh-server`, run the following command:

```
sudo rpm -Uvh --oldpackage \
http://vault.centos.org/6.4/os/x86_64/Packages/openssh-server-5.3p1-84.1.el6.x86_64.rpm \
http://vault.centos.org/6.4/os/x86_64/Packages/openssh-5.3p1-84.1.el6.x86_64.rpm \
http://vault.centos.org/6.4/os/x86_64/Packages/openssh-clients-5.3p1-84.1.el6.x86_64.rpm
```

> The preceding command is all on one line.

The output of the preceding command is shown in the following screenshot:

```
[vagrant@puppet ~]$ sudo rpm -Uvh --oldpackage http://vault.centos.org/6.4/os/x86_64/Packages/openssh-server-5.3p1-84.1.el6.x86_64.rpm http://vault.centos.org/6.4/os/x86_64/Packages/openssh-5.3p1-84.1.el6.x86_64.rpm http://vault.centos.org/6.4/os/x86_64/Packages/openssh-clients-5.3p1-84.1.el6.x86_64.rpm
Retrieving http://vault.centos.org/6.4/os/x86_64/Packages/openssh-server-5.3p1-84.1.el6.x86_64.rpm
Retrieving http://vault.centos.org/6.4/os/x86_64/Packages/openssh-5.3p1-84.1.el6.x86_64.rpm
Retrieving http://vault.centos.org/6.4/os/x86_64/Packages/openssh-clients-5.3p1-84.1.el6.x86_64.rpm
Preparing...                ########################################### [100%]
   1:openssh                ########################################### [ 33%]
   2:openssh-server         warning: /etc/ssh/sshd_config created as /etc/ssh/sshd_config.rpmnew
########################################### [ 67%]
   3:openssh-clients        ########################################### [100%]
[vagrant@puppet ~]$
```

Tracking Changes to Objects

> The preceding command is a handful. Due to the nature of openssh, it doesn't seem to get many updates. Because of dependencies, we need to downgrade multiple packages, resulting in the large command.
>
> When we run Puppet next, it will re-upgrade openssh since we have set it to the latest version. This will ensure that we're not running an old version of important software such as openssh.

Now we want to run Puppet again and observe the output. We'll once again run a command that should be familiar to you by now:

```
sudo puppet agent -test
```

Once it's complete, go ahead and run it again to demonstrate that Puppet did indeed update the package for us based on the latest attribute in the openssh module.

After both the runs are complete, the output should look something like the following:

```
[vagrant@puppet ~]$ sudo puppet agent --test
Info: Retrieving plugin
Info: Caching catalog for puppet.book.local
Warning: The package type's allow_virtual parameter will be changing its default value from false to true in a future release. If you do not want to allow virtual packages, please explicitly set allow_virtual to false.
   (at /usr/lib/ruby/site_ruby/1.8/puppet/type.rb:816:in `set_default')
Info: Applying configuration version '1407460757'
Notice: /Stage[main]/Openssh/Package[openssh-server]/ensure: ensure changed '5.3p1-84.1.el6' to '0:5.3p1-94.el6' (previously recorded value was 5.3p1-94.el6)
Notice: Finished catalog run in 13.81 seconds
[vagrant@puppet ~]$ sudo puppet agent --test
Info: Retrieving plugin
Info: Caching catalog for puppet.book.local
Warning: The package type's allow_virtual parameter will be changing its default value from false to true in a future release. If you do not want to allow virtual packages, please explicitly set allow_virtual to false.
   (at /usr/lib/ruby/site_ruby/1.8/puppet/type.rb:816:in `set_default')
Info: Applying configuration version '1407460757'
Notice: /Stage[main]/Openssh/Package[openssh-server]/ensure: audit change: previously recorded value 5.3p1-84.1.el6 has been changed to 5.3p1-94.el6
Notice: Finished catalog run in 1.78 seconds
[vagrant@puppet ~]$
```

> Notice that we have two different audit-like outputs here. The first one shows that the package has been changed, and the second one shows that it has been changed again from the original value.
>
> This is one of the caveats of audit. If we audit managed resources and they are changed, we end up generating two audit records. This happens because the audit checks are performed at the beginning of the run before Puppet runs. This means that the next time Puppet runs, the audit still has the original value stored and reports that it changed again. We'll cover some of the other caveats of audits in the next section.

Things to know about audit

The audit meta-parameter is a weird fit in the Puppet world. Puppet is about defining the state of your machines, and the audit parameter doesn't do that. Over its lifespan of several years, it has been fairly controversial. Based on the discussion happening on the mailing list as well as comments on the blog post announcing the feature, some users felt that the idea was good, but having it in the manifest was a bad idea.

Audit was a key part of the Puppet Compliance dashboard, which existed in Puppet Enterprise. This dashboard provided a GUI around running audit and also allowed you to convert the rules to baseline Puppet manifests. This made compliance a breeze under light workloads.

In Puppet Enterprise 3.0, the Compliance dashboard, which relied on this technology, was deprecated and removed from Puppet Enterprise. A page at `https://docs.puppetlabs.com/pe/latest/compliance_alt.html` suggests that a noop approach be used instead, which we'll cover in a later section.

Additionally, the Puppet Labs ticket seems to indicate that the audit functionality is going to be deprecated in Puppet 4 (`https://tickets.puppetlabs.com/browse/PUP-893`).

This does not necessarily indicate that you should not use the audit meta-parameter. If you have small compliance needs, it's a good way to get started as you work to build a baseline for use in alternative workflows.

We'll explore some of these possible workflows in the next section.

Alternatives to auditing

The Puppet audit feature essentially works by creating a baseline of a resource. It then monitors that the resource does not change from that baseline.

Using the tools Puppet provides us, we can manually build a baseline and have Puppet run against it. This will allow us to accomplish the same goal as auditing.

We can then apply the baseline we create to either ensure that the resource stays in the baseline state or to monitor that it has left it without changing it back.

We do this using the Puppet `resource` face to give us information on the resource in question. A face is what Puppet calls the mechanism to extend its command-line objects.

We call the Puppet face with the Puppet `resource` command. Go ahead and request for help using the following command:

`puppet help resource`

You'll get an output that will list all of the possible arguments—almost like a man page.

The Puppet `resource` face allows us to export the current state of any object as a baseline. For example, consider the `openssh` package from the earlier section. Try running the following command:

`puppet resource package openssh-server`

The output of the preceding command should look something like the following:

```
package { 'openssh-server':
  ensure => '5.3p1-94.el6',
}
```

This is the full representation needed to put the package in the state it is currently in. In the case of a package, this is only the version that is necessary.

Using this Puppet `resource` command, you can very quickly build a baseline of all of the objects you care about. However, once it's done, how do we use it?

The noop meta-parameter

Puppet has a built-in mechanism to indicate that a resource should be checked but not acted on. This is called the noop mode. Noop is supported in two modes. In the first mode, the entire run can be considered a noop run. This is accomplished by adding the `--noop` flag on the run. In the second method, we use the noop meta-parameter.

The noop meta-parameter is very similar to the audit one. You can add the parameter to any resource. It supports a true and a false value to indicate whether noop is on or off.

It's worth noting that the noop meta-parameter overrides the command-line setting. In other words, even if you have noop set to false in the manifest and execute Puppet with the noop setting as true, the resource will still be applied.

One last tool in the noop tool chain is the resource default. Suppose you have a class for your baseline data and you want to ensure that all of the resources in that class are set with noop as true. We can use the concept of a resource default to do this.

To add a resource default, you can use the type of resource with a capital letter. You can then set the parameter defaults for resources in that scope. In Puppet, a scope defines the search order and set of area in the manifest searched while attempting to resolve a default or variable. In past versions, scoping was much more complicated due to the widespread use of variable inheritance, but that has largely been replaced due to the difficulties in understanding how it worked.

> Defining how Puppet scopes work is outside the scope of this book (isn't that funny?); however, if you're interested in learning more you can find the details at `https://docs.puppetlabs.com/puppet/latest/reference/lang_scope.html#scope-lookup-rules`.

For our purposes here, we'll consider the class to be in the scope since that is the most likely area for you to declare the parameter defaults. In the next example, we'll show the use of parameter defaults in our auditing class.

Purging resources

In our giant bag of tricks around monitoring change, we have one final trick. We call this resource purging.

If you consider the earlier example in this chapter, where we monitor the password file, you might see an issue. While we can monitor the password file, or enforce the state of particular users, we do not have a good way to stop a user from getting added.

Puppet contains a special type called `resources` to manage this. The `resources` type supports relatively few parameters, which are as follows:

Parameter	Description
name	The resource type to manage
purge	A true/false value indicating whether to purge unmanaged resources
unless_system_user	A user-specific flag indicating to skip the system users
unless_uid	A user-specific flag indicating to skip the given `uid` values

The `resources` type also accepts meta-parameters. This means we can manage users, for instance, with purge and noop as true. This has the effect of logging any users that which we are not explicitly managing. In effect, it lets us audit the password file in a much more granular way.

We can do a similar thing with packages that will give us the ability to log or remove any packages that we have not explicitly targeted for installation.

In the next section, we'll go through an example of using noop to emulate the audit meta-parameter.

Using noop

So, what do all of the previous examples look like in action? In this section, we'll set up auditing on the password file using the preceding noop parameters and the resources.

First, start your Vagrant machine and SSH into it.

We'll create a module to hold this called `useraudit`. To do this, let's first create the skeleton of our module much like in *Chapter 1, Puppet as a Security Tool*. On your virtual machine, run the following command:

```
sudo mkdir -p /etc/puppet/modules/useraudit/manifests
```

This module is only going to have manifests, so it's the only directory we'll make.

> For brevity in this book, we're creating bare bones skeleton example modules. The module format is very powerful and contains metadata such as versioning and dependency data. See https://docs.puppetlabs.com/puppet/latest/reference/modules_fundamentals.html or check out the book *Extending Puppet* by *Alessandro Franceschi* for more information.

Now that we have a module structure, let's make the manifest. Create the /etc/puppet/modules/useraudit/manifests/init.pp file and set the content to be as follows:

```
class useraudit {
  User {
    noop => true,
  }
  user { 'bob':
    ensure      => present,
    noop        => false,
    managehome  => true,
  }
  resources { 'user':
    purge              => true,
    unless_system_user => true,
    unless_uid         => 500,
    noop               => true,
  }
}
```

We're doing a number of things here. First, we're setting the user default to enable noop. Then, we create a bob user. This is to demonstrate that we can override noop with the meta-parameter. Finally, we're using the resources type to purge any users in the noop mode. This essentially reports on any users that are not system users or users who were manually exempted from this check with the unless_uid parameter.

Now, we need to add our new class to the sitewide manifest so that it gets included in our test system. To do this, we edit the /etc/puppet/manifests/site.pp file. Make it look as follows:

```
node default {
        include openssh
        include useraudit
}
```

Tracking Changes to Objects

Once this is done, go ahead and run Puppet with the following command:

`sudo puppet agent -test`

Observe the output, which should be similar to the following screenshot:

```
[vagrant@puppet ~]$ sudo puppet agent --test
Info: Retrieving plugin
Info: Caching catalog for puppet.book.local
Warning: The package type's allow_virtual parameter will be changing its default value from false to
 true in a future release. If you do not want to allow virtual packages, please explicitly set allow
_virtual to false.
   (at /usr/lib/ruby/site_ruby/1.8/puppet/type.rb:816:in `set_default')
Info: Applying configuration version '1407539845'
Notice: /Stage[main]/Useraudit/User[nfsnobody]/ensure: current_value present, should be absent (noop
)
Notice: /Stage[main]/Useraudit/User[nfsnobody]/uid: audit change: newly-recorded value 65534
Notice: /Stage[main]/Useraudit/User[bob]/ensure: created
Notice: Finished catalog run in 0.89 seconds
[vagrant@puppet ~]$
```

As you can see, a number of things happened. The first is that Puppet noticed that the `nfsnobody` user existed but wasn't managed. When we created the manifest, we essentially told it to skip all the users below user 500 as well as user 500. The `nfsnobody` user is the `uid` value `65534`, so it was not skipped. We would also want to exempt it from checks by modifying the `unless_uid` line in the preceding code as follows:

`    unless_uid => [500, 65534],`

We can specify a user ID there as well as an array of user IDs or a range of user IDs in the format low-high. This gives us a good amount of flexibility in exempting users from the audit.

The second thing this did is create the `bob` user, which was called out in our manifest.

Now, much like we did earlier, let's create ourselves another user without Puppet and see what happens.

Run the following command to make a dummy user:

`sudo useradd dummy`

Now let's run Puppet again. Go ahead and run the following command:

`sudo puppet agent -test`

You should see an output like the following screenshot:

```
[vagrant@puppet ~]$ sudo puppet agent --test
Info: Retrieving plugin
Info: Caching catalog for puppet.book.local
Warning: The package type's allow_virtual parameter will be changing its default value from false to
 true in a future release. If you do not want to allow virtual packages, please explicitly set allow
_virtual to false.
   (at /usr/lib/ruby/site_ruby/1.8/puppet/type.rb:816:in `set_default')
Info: Applying configuration version '1407539845'
Notice: /Stage[main]/Useraudit/User[nfsnobody]/ensure: current_value present, should be absent (noop
)
Notice: /Stage[main]/Useraudit/User[dummy]/ensure: current_value present, should be absent (noop)
Notice: /Stage[main]/Useraudit/User[dummy]/uid: audit change: newly-recorded value 502
Notice: Finished catalog run in 0.82 seconds
[vagrant@puppet ~]$
```

And success! The output looks very similar to the audit output.

Summary

In this chapter, we looked at the available change tracking methodologies in Puppet. We started by exploring the audit meta-parameter. We looked at how it can be used to manage file and package change tracking.

After this, we looked at some of the limitations of the audit subsystem. It serves a purpose, but has some issues and doesn't quite fit into the Puppet paradigm since it doesn't model state.

Finally, we looked at how we can replicate the workflow using other tools Puppet provides us. By creating our own baseline and using noop, we can duplicate the functionality audit provides, and even pull the system back to the baseline as desired.

In the next chapter, we'll explore how to use these change tracking tools and more to make the compliance department happy. After that, we'll see how we can report on all of this data we've been collecting.

3
Puppet for Compliance

Whether you run one, five, or 10,000 machines; if you're in the business world, you have some level of necessary compliance. Compliance issues can be complicated. There is nothing most system administrators hate more than dealing with an auditor for several days. What if there was a way in which your systems would be self-documenting? These documents would show the system state and can be given to the auditor. With Puppet, this is possible.

In this chapter, we will explore how to do the previously mentioned points. We'll cover the following topics before we wrap it up:

- Using manifests to document the system state
- How version control helps show history
- PCI DSS and Puppet
- How we can use facts to show system information

What is the PCI DSS? The **Payment Card Industry Data Security Standard (PCI DSS)** is a set of standards created for the credit card industry, to address the cardholder security information. The author of this book has personal experience with the PCI DSS in his work with companies that process credit card information. Much of the information that we'll cover that is specific to PCI applies to other compliance frameworks, such as Sarbanes-Oxley, as well.

As the master of the current state of a system, Puppet is in an ideal position to help you with compliance issues. With some education and demonstration, many auditors will accept Puppet manifests, as showing the state a system is in, if accompanied by reporting, showing that Puppet has run.

Using manifests to document the system state

One of the strongest tools in the Puppet compliance tool chest is the concept of the manifest. Since the manifest represents the system's desired state, we can use the data found in it to show what the system looks like.

Consider the following example: you have an audit requirement that says key security-related services and software must be kept up to date. Working with your security team, you've identified a list of packages that fall under this. For the purposes of our example, we'll say they're openssh, kerberos, and openssl.

We can write a manifest that looks like the following, to ensure that this is the case:

```
class compliance(
  $ensure   = latest,
  $packages = ['openssh', 'kerberos', 'openssl']
) {
  package { $packages:
    ensure => $ensure,
  }
}
```

> As we noted earlier, normal practice would dictate that to use the preceding pattern, you would be sourcing these packages from your own local repository and would promote them after testing. Puppet can even help manage your local yum repository configuration with the yumrepo resource.

The preceding class should seem familiar, but we've introduced a few new concepts. First, we will pass an array of resources. Arrays of resources are a quick way to create similar resources, while only sacrificing a bit of readability. Second, we will list the packages as class parameters. Class parameters are a way of passing data to a class. In this case, we can define the class with no parameters and it'd handle the default packages. For example, consider the following declaration of the class:

```
include compliance
```

Using this command, we'd get the openssh, kerberos, and openssl packages set to the latest version. However, we have a system where we need to also do the openldap package. In this case, you can do the following:

```
class { 'compliance':
  packages => ['openssh', 'kerberos', 'openssl', 'openldap'].
}
```

Using this syntax, we make the class more flexible. With Hiera, which we will cover in a future chapter, this becomes even more powerful.

We can then apply the `compliance` class to any system that we want to ensure compliance on. This will have the effect of upgrading any of these packages, as the updates become available whenever Puppet runs.

If we combine this with a report showing when Puppet last ran on each of the machines in the environment, we essentially produce a documentation showing that our environment must be in the state the manifest describes it to be in.

We've seen a lot of examples using packages, but we can also use these methods with any other resource, such as services or files. Often times, in compliance situations, we need to ensure that insecure services are not installed or running.

Keeping insecure packages uninstalled is just an extension of the preceding package example, so we won't show it here. However, we can see how to prevent the service from running. We'll use `xinetd` (which handles telnet and more) and `tftpd` in our examples.

The manifest to do this would be similar to the following:

```
class compliance (
  $services = ['xinetd', 'tftpd']
) {
  service { $services:
    ensure => stopped,
    enable => false,
  }
}
```

This is somewhat similar to our preceding example. However, in this case, we make sure the services are stopped. We also use the `enable` attribute to ensure that the service is set to not start on boot.

> **What about other non-managed services?**
>
> These examples deal with services the OS knows about. It is certainly possible to start the service outside the control of Puppet and it may not be detected with this methodology. There are ways to handle this, but they can quickly become complex and very case-specific. In most cases, you would use an exec resource to ensure that running processes are acceptable.

Tracking history with version control

If we're using Puppet manifests and data for compliance purposes, we will want to track the history of the manifests and data. There are many version control systems out there, and a comparison of them is beyond the scope of this book. However, most of the Puppet communities have standardized on using git.

While we do not aim to be a comprehensive resource on git, or the use of git with Puppet, for the sake of compliance, it makes sense to explore the common workflow that will aid a security professional in their everyday work.

> If you want more details than this book provides on git and Puppet, I recommend that you read *Mastering Puppet*, *Thomas Uphill*, *Packt Publishing* for a Puppet-specific view, or http://git-scm.com/book for a more general overview of git.

Using git to track Puppet configuration

We'll start with the simplest use case. In this case, we'll just track the entire contents of the Puppet configuration directory under git. This is how many users begin their deployments, and it can work while they are small.

We'll start by making sure git is installed. Run the following command in your Vagrant virtual machine:

```
sudo yum -y install git
```

Now that's done, let's go ahead and set git up to track our installation.

We're going to assume that you're leaving off where we left off in *Chapter 2, Tracking Changes to Objects*. If you're dealing with a system in a different state, the output of the various commands may be different, but the concept is identical. We need to perform the following steps:

1. Move into the `puppet` directory with the following command:

    ```
    cd /etc/puppet
    ```

2. Then, let's go ahead and create our git repository:

    ```
    sudo git init
    ```

    You'll be greeted with the output, as follows:

    ```
    Initialized empty Git repository in /etc/puppet/.git/
    ```

3. Now, we have a git repository created. However, it's not very interesting. Let's see what git currently thinks with the `git status` command:

```
[vagrant@puppet puppet]$ git status
# On branch master
#
# Initial commit
#
# Untracked files:
#   (use "git add <file>..." to include in what will be committed)
#
#	auth.conf
#	environments/
#	fileserver.conf
#	manifests/
#	modules/
#	puppet.conf
nothing added to commit but untracked files present (use "git add" to track)
```

4. As you can see, everything is untracked. We can go ahead and solve this. In our very simplistic case, we'll just add the entire Puppet directory with the following command:

```
sudo git add .
```

5. Now, we'll commit it to the git repository, as follows:

```
sudo git commit -m "Initial Commit"
```

We'll see an interesting output showing the files and directories that were added, along with some administrative information:

```
[vagrant@puppet puppet]$ sudo git commit -m "Initial Commit"
[master (root-commit) 7c38a9b] Initial Commit
 Committer: root <root@puppet.book.local>
Your name and email address were configured automatically based
on your username and hostname. Please check that they are accurate.
You can suppress this message by setting them explicitly:

    git config --global user.name "Your Name"
    git config --global user.email you@example.com
```

```
        If the identity used for this commit is wrong, you can fix it
        with:

            git commit --amend --author='Your Name <you@example.com>'

        10 files changed, 390 insertions(+), 0 deletions(-)
        create mode 100644 auth.conf
        create mode 100644
        environments/example_env/README.environment
        create mode 100644 fileserver.conf
        create mode 100644 manifests/example1/site.pp
        create mode 100644 manifests/example3/site.pp
        create mode 100644 manifests/site.pp
        create mode 100644 modules/openssh/files/sshd_config
        create mode 100644 modules/openssh/manifests/init.pp
        create mode 100644 modules/useraudit.full/manifests/init.pp
        create mode 100644 puppet.conf
```

We'd probably want to follow the instructions to set a username and e-mail and amend the commit. This will make it easier to track who made the changes. Note that the -m command-line argument sets the commit message on the command line. If you omit this, it will open your default editor (which is usually vi) to prompt you for a commit message.

In a real production environment, we'd likely want to use a git server solution. This can be as simple as a directory, where we store the common git information, or as complex as an an online service designed to handle git. When doing this, each user would make changes as their own user, and we would use a method (manual, hook, script, and so on) to check out a read-only copy on the Puppet Master. This will allow us to audit and track who made what changes to the Puppet environment. This helps you with auditing by showing the users who made the changes, which can then be compared to an authorized users list.

Our workflow from this point on is the same. We make changes to files, use `git add` to add the files to the git repository, then use `git commit` to commit them with a message.

We can then use a variety of commands in git to review the history of the repository at any given point. The simplest just being `git log`. The output of this would be as follows:

```
[vagrant@puppet puppet]$ git log
commit 7c38a9b721e40b1f7ce556e3876f1b087cd1c42d
Author: root <root@puppet.book.local>
Date:   Tue Aug 19 17:36:33 2014 -0700

    Initial Commit
```

If there were more commits, you would see multiple entries. However, as you can see, it tracks the author, when the change was made, and the comment.

> For more information on git and the various commands, please check out the git website at http://git-scm.org.

Tracking modules separately

As the complexity of your git environment increases, there comes a desire to track the state of modules separately from the main repository. This lets you use different life cycles for the various modules. It also lets individual groups work on various modules.

There are several solutions available to solve this problem. The first one that many users attempted to use was git submodules. The git submodules provide a methodology to store a link from one git repository inside another. The inside version can be pinned to a specific revision, allowing you to independently set the version of the module.

However, while this seems like a workable solution, it presents a number of challenges. As the number of modules you track grows, a lot of spurious commits get made to the main repository, simply to update the submodules to the new versions. Additionally, the steps to do this usually entail no less than three or four git commands. This is cumbersome and hard to manage with many frequently changing submodules.

Several custom solutions to this problem have been developed. The most popular currently are librarian-puppet and r10k.

Both librarian-puppet and r10k handle installation of modules from both the Puppet Forge and version control. The Puppet Forge is an online resource of community modules used for installation. We'll see how to use it, and highlight some security-related modules, in *Chapter 6, Community Modules for Security*.

Librarian-puppet and r10k both use a file called `puppetfile` to handle the installation of modules. In this file, we list modules to be installed and the source we want to get them from. This is normally either version control or the Puppet Forge.

R10k differs from librarian-puppet in having built-in support for dynamic environments. Dynamic environments let you create a separate full set of Puppet code for different life cycles of code. This allows you to quickly and easily develop Puppet code without impacting on production. More information on this feature can be found on the link at the end of this section.

Once we have our `puppetfile` configured, we execute the program of our choice, and it downloads the modules and links them into the `modules` directory. In this way, we do not have to track the modules in our main version control repository.

We'll go over a quick example showing how to install the `stdlib` module using r10k. We don't use it in the later examples in the book, but in cases, where we use the `puppet module` command in later examples, you can just substitute the appropriate r10k configuration. We won't be doing dynamic environments, or any of the other advanced features of r10k, but we will cover the basic use case of installing modules. We need to perform the following steps to install modules:

1. We'll start by installing r10k. This is packaged as a Ruby gem. We need to have the `gem` command installed. We can install it with the following command:

   ```
   sudo gem install r10k
   ```

2. Now, we need to make a `puppetfile`. In our case, the file is very simple, since we're simply installing one module. Create the `/etc/puppet/puppetfile` file and add the following line:

   ```
   mod 'puppetlabs/stdlib', '4.5.1'
   ```

3. Once that's done, we just need to run r10k in the proper mode with the following command:

   ```
   sudo r10k puppetfile install
   ```

The command won't give any output. However, when it completes running, you will find that the `modules/stdlib` directory exists.

These programs will become invaluable as you grow your Puppet environment, and start to treat your infrastructure as code.

> For more information on librarian-puppet, check out its website at `http://librarian-puppet.com/`. Likewise, for more information on r10k, check out its website at `https://github.com/adrienthebo/r10k`.

Facts for compliance

In addition to using Puppet, to show the system state and reporting on that, we can use the powerful fact system to report information on the system. Using this information and reporting mechanisms, we can quickly build the documentation on our systems for use in our compliance audits.

Additionally, the power of creating custom facts really shines here. As we'll see in *Chapter 6*, *Community Modules for Security*, Puppet makes it very easy to grab information on your systems and store it in a common place. With PuppetDB and some reporting glue, you can turn this data into fairly comprehensive compliance documents. We'll explore some simple cases here and see how we can use this data in future chapters.

The Puppet role's pattern

Before we continue discussing facts, we're going to take a short detour to discuss a best practice.

One of the common patterns used in the Puppet world is the concept of a role.

In this pattern, a role defines what we expect a system to do from a business perspective. It becomes a larger part of what's known as the roles and profiles pattern. We use roles to group together specific configurations for a service that is required to deliver a business function.

In some cases, the role is determined from the hostname. In others, it's determined from the data passed into the instance of a virtual machine. However, the role is obtained, it is very often used to determine what set of modules and manifests gets applied to a system.

Let's consider an example. Say, we have a three-tier web application. In this system, we have frontend web servers, application servers, and database servers.

Configuration of these servers is going to differ, as per their compliance needs. Perhaps, the database server stores credit card data, so it needs to ensure that disk encryption is used. Using the role fact, we can get a quick inventory of what each system type is, along with the other data on the system. This is all with just the addition of one custom fact.

We can extend the roles pattern to cover other logical systems. In this case, we'll explore the role of the Puppet Master.

Using custom facts

Puppet uses `facter` as its method for providing state information about the system. In addition to the large number of built-in facts about the system, it's also possible to create your own. There are a couple of ways to do this. One way, is to create Ruby plugins, which provide fact information. The second way, is to use the `facter` external fact methodology. We'll cover this in the following steps:

1. Let's go ahead and implement the simplest form of custom fact, using the built-in `facter` external fact mechanism. First, let's create the external fact directory:

   ```
   sudo mkdir -p /etc/facter/facts.d
   ```

2. Then, edit the `/etc/facter/facts.d/role.yaml` file with your favorite editor and make it look exactly as follows (YAML can be picky about formatting):

   ```
   ---
   role: puppetmaster
   ```

3. Once we're done, run the following command:

   ```
   sudo facter -p role
   ```

   The `-p` flag tells `facter` to behave in a similar manner to a Puppet run. This emits some Puppet-specific facts, as well as loading any custom plugins that have been synced over by Puppet. If all goes well, you should see the output similar to the following:

   ```
   [vagrant@puppet ~]$ sudo facter -p role
   puppetmaster
   ```

This data would then be available in any Puppet manifests as `::role`, as well as for use in Hiera. Furthermore, it will be stored in PuppetDB and any other report processor for later use. As mentioned earlier, we'll explore the reporting aspect of this in the next chapter.

This is a very simple case of extending `facter`. However, as mentioned earlier, the `facter` library will allow a user to implement custom facts in Ruby, as shell scripts or as structured data files (YAML, JSON, and specially formatted text files). With the recent version of Puppet (Puppet 3.4 and later and Facter 2.0.1 and later), one can even sync external facts straight to the client via the plugin sync mechanism. Before this, we'd have to write the facts in Ruby to have plugin sync distribute them. This makes it much easier for system administrators who may not know Ruby to create and use custom facts.

Let's consider a somewhat more in-depth example using a shell script.

A common compliance (and general security) practice, is to ensure that no accounts exist without passwords. We can use an external fact to expose a count of accounts without passwords.

Edit /etc/facter/facts.d/passwordlesscount.sh with your favorite editor. Add the following contents:

```sh
#!/bin/sh

echo -n "passwordlesscount="
getent shadow | cut -d: -f2 | grep -x '' | wc -l
```

Go ahead and save the file and make it executable by executing the command:

`sudo chmod a+x /etc/facter/facts.d/passwordlesscount.sh`

Finally, let's execute the `facter` command again:

`sudo facter -p passwordlesscount`

The output should be 0. If you add a passwordless account, the count increases to 1.

While this is more complicated than our first example, it is still pretty simplistic. However, it shows the power of using facts. With some thought, you can report quite a lot of information using the fact system, such as the number of accounts, whether things have passwords. You can also report the SELinux state, out-of-date package count, and many more. With this information, you can build reports that make showing compliance much easier than collecting the information by hand.

In the next section, we'll show specific examples for using Puppet to deal with compliance challenges that the PCI DSS brings about.

The PCI DSS and how Puppet can help

The PCI DSS is a set of standards for security, created by the Payment Card Industry. It provides a framework on how computer systems handling credit card transactions should be configured. With recent high profile intrusions, including the Target intrusion of late 2013 resulting in the theft of over 40 million cards, as well as the more recent Home Depot attack; it has become even more important that any company, processing credit card information, ensures that they are secure. In this section, we'll approach some specific controls of the PCI DSS standard, and see how you can configure Puppet to remain in compliance. In some cases, we'll provide concrete examples, and in others, we'll provide references to other sections of the book, where these specific problems are solved.

While we will be approaching several key areas of the PCI DSS, this section is not intended to be a comprehensive list of tutorials on how to do all PCI DSS-related hardening. There are many other areas that Puppet can assist with, if configured correctly. Additionally, one should engage a qualified assessor if there are any questions about any of the sections of the PCI DSS.

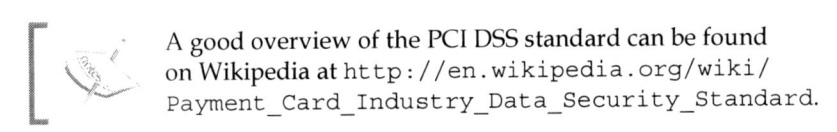

> A good overview of the PCI DSS standard can be found on Wikipedia at `http://en.wikipedia.org/wiki/Payment_Card_Industry_Data_Security_Standard`.

Network-based PCI requirements

The PCI DSS contains a wealth of requirements surrounding secure networks. While many of them (and indeed many of the PCI DSS requirements) are around policy, there are a few concrete ones that Puppet can help you with.

Several of the requirements are surrounding limiting host access to required services. In *Chapter 7, Network Security and Puppet*, we will see how to manage the host firewall with Puppet. Using this methodology, one can configure the firewall to only allow access to individual services. As mentioned earlier, the manifest that allows this shows that the process is in place and alleviated needing to check each individual host.

Additionally, Puppet contains support to manage a variety of network devices directly. There are modules to support Juniper, Cisco, and F5 devices in various stages of their life cycles. Support for these modules continues to build.

As this ecosystem develops, it opens the opportunity to expand management of your devices with a configuration management system. This will bring many of your configuration items into one place, further lowering the burden of providing compliance information to auditors.

We'll briefly touch on the device management aspects in *Appendix, Going Forward*.

Vendor-supplied defaults and the PCI

The second major section of the PCI DSS deals with vendor-supplied security parameters. Again, this is an area that Puppet can help you with. We'll build on some earlier examples and give a more complete example of some of the concepts in this section.

In the simplest sense, we can use use `ensure => 'absent'` to guarantee that the vendor-supplied user resources are not enabled whenever we come across them. However, this is really a default `allow` value. We'll only remove accounts that we explicitly remove. A better course of action is to use a default `deny` value—if we don't manage or know a user, we will remove it. This requires a bit more work to maintain, but it's more secure.

To do this, we'll write a somewhat more complicated user module. Some of the features we'll use here are more in-depth than the features we've discussed. We'll explain some of them and use references for others.

We're going to create a module to handle the user creation. However, this time we'll use the Puppet method of generating a template. This is a better practice for modules you may need to manage with librarian-puppet or r10k.

To begin, let's go ahead and create our module. We can do this in our home directory because we can link it in, or add it to our local librarian-puppet or r10k, and install it later.

Let's run the following command to create the module:

```
puppet module generate pupbook/users
```

You can replace `pupbook` with another username if you'd like.

Once we do this, Puppet will ask us for a series of questions to help write our metadata. It looks as follows—go ahead and answer similarly:

```
[vagrant@puppet ~]$ puppet module generate pupbook/users
We need to create a metadata.json file for this module.  Please answer the
following questions; if the question is not applicable to this module, feel free
to leave it blank.

Puppet uses Semantic Versioning (semver.org) to version modules.
What version is this module?  [0.1.0]
-->

Who wrote this module?  [pupbook]
--> jslagle

What license does this module code fall under?  [Apache 2.0]
-->

How would you describe this module in a single sentence?
--> Module to manage system users

Where is this module's source code repository?
-->

Where can others go to learn more about this module?
-->

Where can others go to file issues about this module?
-->

----------------------------------------
{
  "name": "pupbook/users",
  "version": "0.1.0",
  "author": "jslagle",
  "summary": "Module to manage system users",
  "license": "Apache 2.0",
  "source": "",
  "project_page": null,
  "issues_url": null,
  "dependencies": [
    {
      "version_range": ">= 1.0.0",
      "name": "puppetlabs-stdlib"
    }
  ]
}
----------------------------------------
About to generate this metadata; continue? [n/Y]
-->
```

> Your output can vary a bit depending on the version of Puppet you are running this on.

When you get to this point, go ahead and answer `yes` to generate your module template.

You'll see that several files and directories were created. Some are familiar, such as the manifests directory. I'll briefly explain the others here.

- `Rakefile`: This contains a set of instructions for Ruby to run tasks. In this case, tests.
- `README.md`: This is a general README for the module. In a real module, you would describe it here.
- `metadata.json`: This file contains the metadata generated. The metadata in this file is parsed by tools, such as the puppet module tool, librarian-puppet, and r10k to install dependencies and other actions.
- `tests/init.pp`: This contains a simple class intended to test the module.
- `spec/*`: This contains the directory and its files hold spec tests for the module. It's a good idea to write spec tests on anything more than a simple module.

> An entire book can be written on Puppet testing. We'll not cover the concept of spec tests here other than mentioning them. You can find more information on rspec at http://rspec.info/, and on spec tests for Puppet at http://puppetlabs.com/blog/the-next-generation-of-puppet-module-testing. The source that accompanies this book contains a working, but basic, spec test for this module. It's how the code was tested to ensure that it works.

Now, we'll go ahead and create our define. In puppet, a define is like a macro. It's intended to hold reusable code that can be used to build other things. This is different from how we use, and create, a class that is intended to hold resources that are only declared once.

Let's create the `manifests/users.pp` file. In this file, we'll create a define that both this module and other modules can use to create users. Open the file and make it look like the following:

```
define users::user (
  $userid,
  $password  = '!!',
  $username  = $title,
```

```
        $managehome = true
    ) {

        group { $username:
          ensure => present,
        }

        user { $username:
          ensure   => present,
          password => $password,
          uid      => $userid,
          gid      => $username,
        }

        if ($managehome) {
          file { "/home/${username}":
            ensure => 'directory',
            owner  => $username,
            group  => $username,
            mode   => '0750',
          }
        }

    }
```

We'll use this structure to manage users we create. We do this instead of the user type directly, because we can extend this to manage other resources. Notice that we can handle the creation of the users group (the OS would do this too in most cases, but this way, it's explicit). We can also manage their home directory. We can extend this to manage anything else we want about the user.

There are a handful of community modules that perform the preceding functions, as well as manage things, such as additional groups and SSH keys. The ones that are of particular interest are the camptocamp/accounts and torrancew/accounts modules, which seem to be popular. Also, Puppet Enterprise comes with the pe_accounts module that handles all these things. For more information, see http://forge.puppetlabs.com and search for the account or user.

Next, we'll create a params class. This is a very common pattern in the Puppet module community. It separates the OS-specific data from the core module functionality. This also puts us in a great position to override the functionality on systems, where we need to make it different. A good description of this pattern can be found at https://docs.puppetlabs.com/guides/module_guides/bgtm.html.

Edit the `manifests/params.pp` file and insert the following CentOS 6 specific logic:

```
class users::params {
  case $::osfamily {
    'RedHat': {
      $verarray = split($::operatingsystemrelease,'[.]')
      $majver = $verarray[0]

      case $majver {
        '6': {
          $systemusers =
[0,1,2,3,4,5,6,7,8,10,11,12,13,14,99,81,69,173,68,38,499,89,74,72,
32,29,52,498,65534]
        }
        default: {
          fail("OS Version ${majver} not supported")
        }
      }
    }
    default: {
      fail"OS ${::osfamily} not supported")
    }
  }
}
```

Note that the users array is all on one line. As you can see, we set some defaults based on the family of the OS (it's better to use the family than the version since the Red Hat family, for instance, has a ton of OS releases, such as Scientific and CentOS. Watch out for Fedora though, which is also in that family). Then, we use some Puppet logic to split the `operatingsystemrelease` fact. If you have the `lsb-release` package installed, you get a `lsbmajdistrelease` fact, but it's not hard to just split, and it works with other operating systems, as well as the older version of Puppet. Puppet 3.3+ ships with the `osmajversion` fact that does the same thing. We use this to define a huge array of default system users that we want to allow to exist. We can also choose to represent this array using a custom fact. However, an array support in facts is still somewhat new. The list has a couple of VirtualBox-/Vagrant-specific users, so if you use this in your environment, you should verify and update the preceding list.

Puppet for Compliance

Now, we'll create the structure to use the `resources` type to purge the users while ignoring all the system users. Edit `manifests/init.pp`:

```
#
# Here you should define a list of variables that this module would require.
#
# [*sample_variable*]
#   Explanation of how this variable affects the funtion of this class and if
#   it has a default. e.g. "The parameter enc_ntp_servers must be set by the
#   External Node Classifier as a comma separated list of hostnames." (Note,
#   global variables should be avoided in favor of class parameters as
#   of Puppet 2.6.)
#
# === Examples
#
#  class { users:
#    servers => [ 'pool.ntp.org', 'ntp.local.company.com' ],
#  }
#
# === Authors
#
# Author Name <author@domain.com>
#
# === Copyright
#
# Copyright 2014 Your name here, unless otherwise noted.
#
class users {

}
```

I've cut the screen to make the screenshot look smaller. Notice how the Puppet module generate command includes some documentation to fill out. This can be used by some tools to generate the module documentation for the user. To keep our example short, we'll just remove it. So, go ahead and remove all of the content and replace it with the following:

```
class users (
  $systemusers = $users::params::systemusers
) inherits users::params {
  validate_array($systemusers)

  resources { 'user':
    purge              => true,
    unless_system_user => 1,
    unless_uid         => $systemusers,
  }
```

```
    users::user { 'vagrant':
      userid   => 500,
      password => '$1$WZR2vRP.$tHmVAmIwW1bxpSfZ7y8k3.',
    }
  }
```

Notice how we can use inheritance and the `params` pattern to set the default value of the system users. You can override this with Hiera, or an explicit resource declaration on a per-instance basis.

We can also create the Vagrant user for our VirtualBox here. I used the password hash from the VirtualBox here locally.

To use this module, first, we have to include it in our modules. In a production environment, you'd likely use r10k or librarian-puppet for this, however, in our case, it's sufficient to just copy it. Go ahead and copy the `pupbook-users` directory to `/etc/puppet/modules/users`.

We're using the module to validate that we are, indeed, being passed an array as the argument to the user's command. We need to install it in the `puppetmaster` directory. To do so, run the following command:

sudo puppet module install puppetlabs/stdlib

This command downloads the module from the Puppet Forge and installs it in your module path.

Finally, we need to include the new module we created in your node declaration. In `/etc/puppet/manifests/site.pp`, modify the declaration to look like the following:

```
  node default {
    include openssh
    include users
  }
```

> The `puppetlabs-stdlib` module contains a large number of utility functions, such as the preceding validators. It also contains glue such as run stages that can simplify your environment's dependencies. Nearly every module you write will end up using some function from `stdlib`, so it's useful to study. You can find more information at https://forge.puppetlabs.com/puppetlabs/stdlib.

Now, go ahead and run Puppet with the normal `sudo puppet agent -test` command. You should see the output similar to the following screenshot:

```
[vagrant@puppet ~]$ sudo puppet agent --test
Info: Retrieving plugin
Info: Loading facts in /etc/puppet/modules/stdlib/lib/facter/facter_dot_d.rb
Info: Loading facts in /etc/puppet/modules/stdlib/lib/facter/pe_version.rb
Info: Loading facts in /etc/puppet/modules/stdlib/lib/facter/puppet_vardir.rb
Info: Loading facts in /etc/puppet/modules/stdlib/lib/facter/root_home.rb
Info: Loading facts in /var/lib/puppet/lib/facter/root_home.rb
Info: Loading facts in /var/lib/puppet/lib/facter/puppet_vardir.rb
Info: Loading facts in /var/lib/puppet/lib/facter/facter_dot_d.rb
Info: Loading facts in /var/lib/puppet/lib/facter/pe_version.rb
Info: Caching catalog for puppet.book.local
Warning: The package type's allow_virtual parameter will be changing its default value fr
om false to true in a future release. If you do not want to allow virtual packages, pleas
e explicitly set allow_virtual to false.
   (at /usr/lib/ruby/site_ruby/1.8/puppet/type.rb:816:in `set_default')
Info: Applying configuration version '1408807509'
Notice: /Stage[main]/Users/Users::User[vagrant]/File[/home/vagrant]/mode: mode changed '0
700' to '0750'
Notice: Finished catalog run in 0.77 seconds
[vagrant@puppet ~]$
```

You might also see some other users if you created them in the previous chapters, as well as the custom facts from the `stdlib` module syncing over. However, the final output should look generally, as shown in the preceding screenshot.

As you can see, the only change here was to change the mode on our Vagrant user's home directory.

> At the time of writing, there was a bug present in the Puppet core preventing this example from working properly. It's been filed at https://tickets.puppetlabs.com/browse/PUP-3132, and its progress can be tracked here. The edits necessary to make this work are also present in this ticket. In our case, the output should look, as shown in the preceding screenshot, but in reality, due to the bug, we end up matching many of the users in the system's user list.

For the production use of this module, you must define all of your users in Puppet. This goes for system users, such as Apache if you need Apache installed. However, if this is done correctly, it is a very powerful tool to ensure that no errant users are on the machine, and once again, shows compliance with a number of the PCI DSS requirements.

There are a number of other pieces of this section of the PCI DSS that can be addressed with Puppet. There is a large section of requirements having to do with managing configuration standards for systems. This includes things, such as disabling services, keeping documentation of the system state, and so on. These tasks can all be easily accomplished with Puppet. We'll cover a community module that covers the CIS standard (which is called out specifically as a standard to use) in *Chapter 6, Community Modules for Security*. We can also use an approach, very similar to the earlier one, to manage both the packages and services. The modules to manage packages in particular will be quite large, since it would need to list every permitted package, but it is possible. Use of the `puppet resource` command, covered in the last chapter, will make automating the creation of a baseline package much simpler.

Protecting the system against malware

The next area where Puppet can be a big help is in protecting the system against viruses and malware. By Puppetizing your anti-virus agent, you can ensure that all systems contain an anti-virus. To handle keeping the anti-virus up to date, we can either Puppetize the updates, or expose a fact with the current anti-virus version.

There are a number of well-developed community modules targeting installation and configuration of the ClamAV virus scanner. We will cover these in *Chapter 6, Community Modules for Security*. Instead of covering how to write a module to install and configure ClamAV, we'll focus on exposing a fact for the currently installed ClamAV database.

Before we can do that, we need to get ClamAV installed. We can just use yum to do this, but there's not a task too small to create the Puppet module to handle this for us, as this will improve our skills and be reusable across multiple machines.

In doing this, we will need to use Fedora EPEL—Extra Packages for Enterprise Linux. Luckily, there's a wonderful community module to help us—stahnma/epel, as shown in the following steps:

1. Go ahead and install it with the following command:
   ```
   sudo puppet module install stahnma/epel
   ```

> **What's with the software repositories?**
>
> Software repositories are very important when using Puppet, as the best practice is to install packages using the operating system package manager whenever possible. Ideally, one would run a local mirror of all of the repositories in question that would allow you to precisely control the versions of packages that get installed on systems. This would include repositories, such as EPEL, as mentioned earlier, as well as the base operating system repositories. Using the `yumrepo` resource type, it is possible to use Puppet to manage all of your configured repositories on Red Hat machines.

2. Now that we've got this installed, `cd` back to your home directory, and we'll make a module to hold our ClamAV resources. Run the following command:

   ```
   puppet module generate pupbook/clamav
   ```

3. Answer the questions, as we did in the earlier example on compliance, and we'll get started. First, we'll need to create the resource that installs ClamAV. From the `pupbook-clamav` directory, edit the `manifests/init.pp` file. In this file, we'll include EPEL to ensure that it's installed, as well as add our package declaration. When you're done, it should look as follows:

   ```
   class clamav {
     require epel
     package { 'clamav':
       ensure => present,
     }
     users::user { 'clam':
       managehome => false,
       require    => Package['clamav']=
     }
   }
   ```

4. Save it, and add `include clamav` to the default node definition in the `/etc/puppet/manifests/site.pp` file.

A thing to note here, is that ClamAV creates a user, so we create that user in our manifest, doing it after the package. If we do not, our earlier module will purge the user created by the package. By putting it in the module that installs ClamAV, it keeps it close to the source. This ties into the roles and profiles pattern we briefly introduced earlier, and we will touch on in a later chapter.

Then, we need to copy the `pupbook-clamav` directory to `/etc/puppet/modules/clamav`.

After that, we'll go ahead and run Puppet. This will have the effect of installing ClamAV. So, run Puppet using the following command (you should be getting used to this by now!):

```
sudo puppet agent --test
```

The output will look like the following screenshot:

```
[vagrant@puppet ~]$ sudo puppet agent --test
Info: Retrieving plugin
Notice: /File[/var/lib/puppet/lib/facter/os_maj_version.rb]/ensure: defined content as '{md5}806fb856251b605df379e973c716a41c'
Info: Loading facts in /etc/puppet/modules/epel/lib/facter/os_maj_version.rb
Info: Loading facts in /etc/puppet/modules/stdlib/lib/facter/facter_dot_d.rb
Info: Loading facts in /etc/puppet/modules/stdlib/lib/facter/pe_version.rb
Info: Loading facts in /etc/puppet/modules/stdlib/lib/facter/puppet_vardir.rb
Info: Loading facts in /etc/puppet/modules/stdlib/lib/facter/root_home.rb
Info: Loading facts in /var/lib/puppet/lib/facter/root_home.rb
Info: Loading facts in /var/lib/puppet/lib/facter/puppet_vardir.rb
Info: Loading facts in /var/lib/puppet/lib/facter/os_maj_version.rb
Info: Loading facts in /var/lib/puppet/lib/facter/facter_dot_d.rb
Info: Loading facts in /var/lib/puppet/lib/facter/pe_version.rb
Info: Caching catalog for puppet.book.local
Warning: The package type's allow_virtual parameter will be changing its default value from false to true in a future release. If you do not want to allow virtual packages, please explicitly set allow_virtual to false.
   (at /usr/lib/ruby/site_ruby/1.8/puppet/type.rb:816:in `set_default')
Info: Applying configuration version '1408885758'
Notice: /Stage[main]/Clamav/Package[clamav]/ensure: created
Notice: Finished catalog run in 241.65 seconds
[vagrant@puppet ~]$ less /etc/passwd
[vagrant@puppet ~]$
```

Again, if this is your first run, you may see some more outputs, as some of the EPEL-related items are synchronized over. In general, the output should be similar though.

Now that we have ClamAV installed, we can go ahead and create our fact. We can use the output of the `clamscan -V` command within a `facter` fact to give us the version information. We'll create a fact in our `clamav` module to give us the information.

In our module, we create the `lib/facter` directory inside our module. You can use the `mkdir -p ~/pupbook-clamav/lib/facter` command to do this.

Inside this directory, we're going to create a file called `clamversion.rb`. Go ahead and open this file with your favorite editor. We want it to look like the following:

```
Facter.add(:clamversion) do
  confine :kernel => "Linux"
  setcode do
```

```
        Facter ::Core::Execution.exec ('/usr/bin/clamscan -V
2>/dev/null')
    end
end
```

Save the file, and recopy your module into /etc/puppet/modules. Once complete, we'll rerun Puppet with sudo puppet agent --test. We should see the output like the following:

```
[vagrant@puppet ~]$ sudo puppet agent --test
Info: Retrieving plugin
Notice: /File[/var/lib/puppet/lib/facter/clamversion.rb]/ensure: defined content as '{md5}a2ca0015e6f864e766867d2b2a94b4c2'
Info: Loading facts in /etc/puppet/modules/clamav/lib/facter/clamversion.rb
Info: Loading facts in /etc/puppet/modules/epel/lib/facter/os_maj_version.rb
Info: Loading facts in /etc/puppet/modules/stdlib/lib/facter/facter_dot_d.rb
Info: Loading facts in /etc/puppet/modules/stdlib/lib/facter/pe_version.rb
Info: Loading facts in /etc/puppet/modules/stdlib/lib/facter/puppet_vardir.rb
Info: Loading facts in /etc/puppet/modules/stdlib/lib/facter/root_home.rb
Info: Loading facts in /var/lib/puppet/lib/facter/root_home.rb
Info: Loading facts in /var/lib/puppet/lib/facter/puppet_vardir.rb
Info: Loading facts in /var/lib/puppet/lib/facter/clamversion.rb
Info: Loading facts in /var/lib/puppet/lib/facter/os_maj_version.rb
Info: Loading facts in /var/lib/puppet/lib/facter/facter_dot_d.rb
Info: Loading facts in /var/lib/puppet/lib/facter/pe_version.rb
Info: Caching catalog for puppet.book.local
Warning: The package type's allow_virtual parameter will be changing its default value from false to true in a future release. If you do not want to allow virtual packages, please explicitly set allow_virtual to false.
   (at /usr/lib/ruby/site_ruby/1.8/puppet/type.rb:816:in `set_default')
Info: Applying configuration version '1408886890'
Notice: Finished catalog run in 2.08 seconds
[vagrant@puppet ~]$
```

We can see that it copied our plugin to the master. The md5sum may vary depending on spacing and so on.

Then, we run the following command:

`sudo facter -p clamversion`

We'll get the output similar to the following:

`[vagrant@puppet ~]$ sudo facter -p clamversion`

`ClamAV 0.98.4/19120/Sat Jun 21 04:57:20 2014`

Success! Now, we can report this data with our favorite reporting mechanism.

We also learned how to write custom facts using a Puppet module. These will automatically get synced to all of your agents.

Maintaining secure systems

There is a section of the DSS that handles maintaining secure systems. One of the objectives in this section, is that we keep our system patched and up to date.

By using manifests, such as those we saw in *Chapter 1, Puppet as a Security Tool*, we can identify security-related packages and make sure they are kept at a given version, or that we keep them at the latest. This will ensure that the security patches are installed.

Authenticating access to systems

A later section of the PCI DSS standard covers authentication best practices. Using many of the same methods we used in the vendor defaults section, we can ensure that only permitted and documented users have access to systems.

In this section, there are also controls around authentication lockouts and timeouts. We can use some of the same methods we learned here to secure `openssh` to do some of these things. We'll explore some of these examples in *Chapter 6, Community Modules for Security*, when we take a look at using `augeasproviders` to manage the SSH configuration.

Summary

In this chapter, we looked at how to use Puppet to solve various compliance challenges. We looked at how to use Puppet manifests to document the system state. This can be unbelievably helpful in showing how a system is configured.

Additionally, we then looked at how version control can help you show the history of the system configuration, when various things changed, as well as possibly help us show who made the changes.

Finally, we looked at specific challenges that the PCI DSS creates, and how we can use Puppet to solve them, including several examples of the use of Puppet to automate some of the PCI DSS requirements.

Compliance is a journey, not a destination. As we learn more and get more familiar with the Puppet ecosystem, we will learn many more ways to use Puppet to assist us in our compliance needs. We'll explore some additional resources to review in *Appendix, Going Forward*.

In the meantime, in the next chapter, we'll move on and explore how we can use Puppet to generate security and compliance-related reporting.

4
Security Reporting with Puppet

By now, we've been over a lot of use cases involving using Puppet for security. However, we have a recurring theme. We've gathered data, written manifests, and created facts. However, what do we do to turn this into proven security and compliance information?

We need to take the data and information from our runs and turn it into reports. Puppet has a comprehensive system to store data, and we'll use this to create reports showing the state of our system and to show compliance.

In this chapter, we plan to cover the following topics:

- Basic reporting in Puppet
- Using PuppetDB to create reports
- Reporting on compliance

We'll use several examples to show how these topics will help us on our security journey. By the end of this chapter, you should be comfortable creating reports using the basic Puppet data, as well as reporting via PuppetDB. There are additional resources that we'll then direct you, to expand your skills.

Basic Puppet reporting

Puppet has several methods that can be used for low end reporting needs. Some of these methods, such as parsing the local run output data files or logs, can be performed on the client, but most of them rely on the Puppet Master to properly perform.

Puppet's reporting system is based on a concept of report processors. Many different report processors exist. A summary of some of the most common ones are listed in the following table:

Processor	Description
HTTP	This posts the report information to the URL given as a configuration parameter.
Store	This stores the completed Puppet reports in files on the filesystem. These can then be post-processed to do reporting.
Tagmail	This report processor can be configured to send e-mails based on "tags", which can be applied to classes.
PuppetDB	This stores the reports in the PuppetDB database. This can then be queried to create reports.

Report processors can also be written in Ruby to handle custom requirements, as needed. There are community report processors readily available that use this report customization support to allow reporting to IRC, Nagios (an open source reporting system), Twitter, SNMP, and many others. There are also other products, such as The Foreman that enables reporting, as well as other functions.

In this chapter, we will explore the use of store and the PuppetDB report processors. We'll take a look at what we can do with these processors to create relevant security reports.

Another common report processor that is in wide use is the HTTP processor. This processor allows you to post the report results to an application listening on a given URL. Your application can be configured to receive the Puppet reports and update the information accordingly. Using this method requires software development that is out of the scope for this book. However, an excellent resource on Puppet reporting that covers many of the concepts in this chapter is the book *Puppet Reporting and Monitoring*, Michael Duffy, Packt Publishing, available at https://www.packtpub.com/networking-and-servers/puppet-reporting-and-monitoring.

> A complete list of built-in processors can be found at https://docs.puppetlabs.com/references/latest/report.html. Additionally, much more information on reporting, including links to some of the community processors mentioned earlier can be found at https://docs.puppetlabs.com/guides/reporting.html.

The store processors

The simplest report processor available within Puppet is the store processor. As mentioned earlier, this processor simply stores the report data as a file on the Puppet Master.

This file is in a YAML format. This is a human-readable text format that is also systematically parsable. It contains information on the entire Puppet run, in a format called internally Puppet::Transaction::Report.

> This report format is versioned and has been through five versions at the time of writing (the first version was 0). Since we are concentrating on more recent Puppet versions, we will explore Version 4. Information on each of the individual versions that have existed can be found at https://docs.puppetlabs.com/guides/reporting.html#report-formats.

The report information contains a wealth of useful information for security reporting, such as when Puppet last ran, the status of resources, and so on.

When we initially configured Puppet way back in *Chapter 1*, *Puppet as a Security Tool*, we configured it to enable the store processor. As such, if you've been following along, we should already have some reports that we can examine. Let's go ahead and take a look at some of the elements of one of the stored reports.

We'll take a look at a report for a run that installed the ClamAV virus scanning software. This is one of the last runs we did in the last chapter, and it does a good job of showing what a successful run looks like.

> **What if the Puppet report directory is owned by root?**
>
> There is some chance that the Puppet report directory ended up owned by root due to the Vagrant configuration of your virtual machine. If this is the case, execute the following command:
>
> `sudo chown puppet /var/lib/puppet/reports/puppet.book.local`
>
> Once complete, if you wish to follow along, remove the `clamav` package with `sudo yum -y remove clamav` and rerun Puppet with `sudo puppet agent -test`. This will regenerate the report and allow you to follow along. Managing the ownership of the report directory seems like a good job for Puppet!

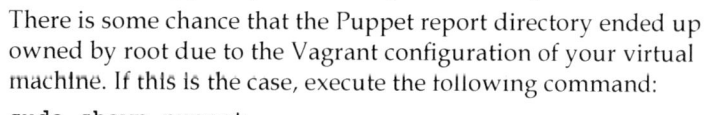

The reports get dropped to the directory specified by the `reportdir` configuration option in the `puppet.conf` configuration file. If not specified, this defaults to `$vardir/reports`, so `/var/lib/puppet/reports` on CentOS.

We'll go ahead and pop into this directory and take a look at the files. There should be one for each run we've done. They add up quickly, and there are community modules to manage this data, such as the one at https://forge.puppetlabs.com/rcoleman/puppet_maint. If you only see one, see the earlier note. The YAML file we're looking at has also been included with the source code for this chapter. The filename is `201409080013.yaml`.

First, let's take a look at the top-level elements. The contents should look as follows:

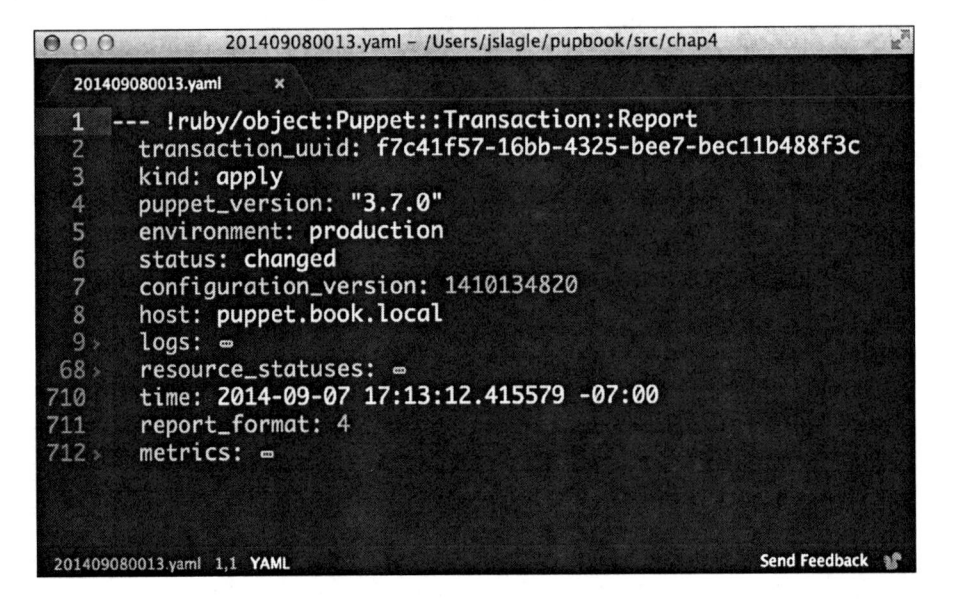

```
--- !ruby/object:Puppet::Transaction::Report
transaction_uuid: f7c41f57-16bb-4325-bee7-bec11b488f3c
kind: apply
puppet_version: "3.7.0"
environment: production
status: changed
configuration_version: 1410134820
host: puppet.book.local
logs:
resource_statuses:
time: 2014-09-07 17:13:12.415579 -07:00
report_format: 4
metrics:
```

> The preceding screenshot was captured in an editor on the host system. However, you can get Vim to do a similar thing with the following Vim commands:
> - `:set shiftwidth=2`
> - `:set foldlevel=1`
> - `:set fdm=indent`
> - `:set number`

Immediately, we can see some useful things. Notice that the `report_format` value is 4, which is consistent with what we expected it to be based on the version of Puppet we're running.

We can also see the hostname of the machine we're running on. In this case, it's `puppet.book.local`. You can use this if you consume reports from many hosts.

Next, we can see the general status of the run. In this case, it is changed. This status can be one of the three options: changed, failed, or unchanged. Changed indicates that work was done during this run. Since we installed ClamAV, we would expect this to be changed.

If, however, we notice that it was failed, we might want to flag the host for further inspection, or parse the logs section of the report to find out why it has failed.

Now, we'll move on to examine the kind parameter. This covers what type of run we did this time. This can be "inspect" if we're running an inspection run for auditing, or an "apply" run if we're running normally. We can use this to differentiate our audit runs and report on just them.

There are two final pieces of information we want to consider. The first is configuration_version and the second is time. These both will assist us in determining when we last ran. The configuration_version value is a string that contains, by default, the epoch time that the configuration was parsed. This will often be cached and is a good indication of when the configuration was last considered. We can also set a custom script to set this data in our configuration file. We can, for instance, set this as a version control commit ID, or any other data.

The time data is quite straightforward. It is the time when the run was started. We can use this data to determine whether we have a recent run. We can also, for instance, set up alerting of a run we do not see for a given host, at least, so often.

Example – showing the last node runtime

In our very simple case, let's whip together a really simple shell script that can parse through a directory of reports and output the last run time and status for each of our hosts in a nice table.

I'll do this in a shell script to demonstrate how flexible the YAML report format is. If you go more in-depth with reporting this way, you would likely want to use a programming language that supports YAML natively. However, for simple cases, we can take advantage of the fact that they're just text files and do the limited amount of parsing we need to do.

Let's edit a file called report.sh in your home directory, and make the content look as follows:

```
#!/bin/bash

if [ $# -eq 1 ]; then
  DIR=$1
else
```

```
    DIR="."
fi

cat << EOF
<!doctype html>

<html lang="en">
<head>
<title>Puppet Run Report</title>
</head>
<body>
<table border=1>
<tr><th>Hostname</th><th>Last Run</th><th>Status</th></tr>
EOF
for i in $(find ${DIR} -mindepth 1 -maxdepth 1 -type d)
do
   FILE=$(ls -t $i/*.yaml|head -n 1)
   if [ -f ${FILE} ]; then
      HOST=$(grep "^  host:" $FILE |cut -c 9-)
      RUN=$(grep "^  time:" $FILE | cut -c 9-)
      STATE=$(grep "^  status:" $FILE | cut -c 11-)
   fi
   echo
"<tr><td>${HOST}</td><td>${RUN}</td><td>${STATE}</td></tr>"
done

cat << EOF
</table>
</body>
</html>
EOF
```

Taking a look at the code, it's pretty simplistic. First, we set a variable for the directory to process. We process the current directory if one is not passed.

Then, we output a header for the HTML. We use a bash syntax that lets us read until a tag to make this easier.

After this, we get on to the meat of the script. We go through each subdirectory in the directory we're processing and look for the most recent YAML file. In each of these files, we grab the three pieces of information that we're outputting. We use a simple combination of `grep` and `cut` to grab that information, since we're dealing with text files.

We then output a line about the host we read from the file and loop. This should give an output of one line for each host.

Finally, we output some trailing footer information to make a complete HTML file.

While I am not an HTML whiz, this is a perfectly serviceable output, albeit a bit plain. The output from our example will look something like the following:

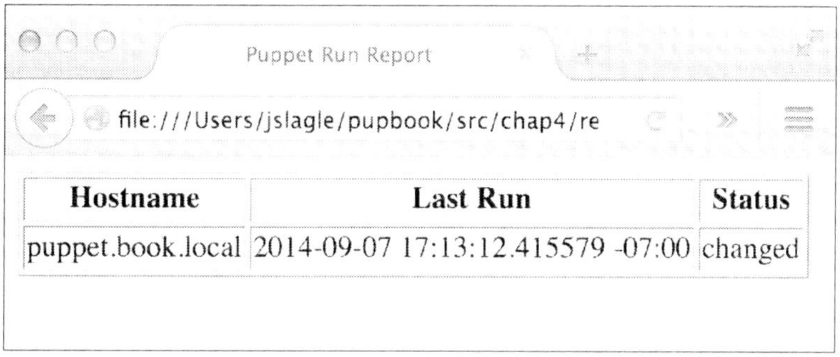
Puppet Run Report
file:///Users/jslagle/pupbook/src/chap4/re
Hostname
Last Run
Status
puppet.book.local
2014-09-07 17:13:12.415579 -07:00
changed

If you had more hosts, we'd expect to see more information there.

There is considerably more information that we can gather from the reports. The reports contain logs from the runs that were performed, as well as information on all of the resources contained within the catalog.

> A wealth of information on the Version 4 report format can be found at `https://docs.puppetlabs.com/puppet/3/reference/format_report.html#report-format-4`.

Now, let's move on and see how we can scale this to more easily gather information about our hosts.

PuppetDB and reporting

We briefly touched on what PuppetDB was in *Chapter 1, Puppet as a Security Tool*. It is a backend database engine that stores information on your Puppet environment.

We can query this information directly to see the current status of a host, get information on its current resources, and more. Additionally, it contains a complete set of reports if configured to do so.

PuppetDB contains a very rich API allowing us to use RESTful API calls via HTTP to retrieve information.

Security Reporting with Puppet

> REST, which is shorthand for Representational State Transfer, is a method of laying out an API using representations of a given resource. In this case, the resources will be information about Puppet. It makes querying and modifying information using HTTP fairly straightforward.

Before we can play with PuppetDB, we need to install it. Luckily, there's a handy Puppet module provided by Puppet Labs that can help us.

Go ahead and spin up your machine (refer to *Chapter 1*, *Puppet as a Security Tool* or *Chapter 2*, *Tracking Changes to Objects* if you need a refresher), and let's get PuppetDB installed so that we can explore it.

First, let's get the PuppetDB module installed. To do so, run the following command:

```
sudo puppet module install puppetlabs-puppetdb
```

This will install the PuppetDB module, as well as several prerequisites we will need to run it. These include modules to manage PostgreSQL, and a number of utility modules. It'll also bring in a module to manage the local firewall. We'll use the same module in *Chapter 7*, *Network Security and Puppet*.

Now, we need to add the module to our manifest, so Puppet will install it (and even configure it) for us.

We'll use all of the defaults for a single host installation. since that is sufficient for our local testing. Let's edit our `site.pp` file in `/etc/puppet/manifests` and add lines so that it looks like the following:

```
node default {
  include openssh
  include users
  include clamav
  include puppetdb
  include puppetdb::master::config
}
```

We added the two `include` lines at the bottom. The first will install PuppetDB and all of its prerequisites, such as Java and PostgreSQL. The second will configure your Puppet Master to use PuppetDB.

Chapter 4

Now, let's run Puppet with our usual `sudo puppet agent --test` command. It will scroll a ton of stuff on your screen as it synchronizes the types and providers—copying the needed libraries to the client system. It'll then get to the meat of installing PuppetDB and configuring the master. In the end, it should give the output like the following:

```
Notice: Unable to connect to puppetdb server (puppet.book.local:8081): Connection refused - connect(2)
Notice: Failed to connect to puppetdb; sleeping 2 seconds before retry
Notice: /Stage[main]/Puppetdb::Master::Storeconfigs/Ini_setting[puppet.conf/master/storeconfigs]/ensure: created
Notice: /Stage[main]/Puppetdb::Master::Storeconfigs/Ini_setting[puppet.conf/master/storeconfigs_backend]/ensure: created
Notice: /Stage[main]/Puppetdb::Master::Routes/File[/etc/puppet/routes.yaml]/ensure: defined content as '{md5}779d47e8d0c320b10f8c31cd9838fca1'
Info: Class[Puppetdb::Master::Routes]: Scheduling refresh of Service[puppetmaster]
Notice: /Stage[main]/Puppetdb::Master::Puppetdb_conf/Ini_setting[puppetdbport]/ensure: created
Notice: /Stage[main]/Puppetdb::Master::Puppetdb_conf/Ini_setting[soft_write_failure]/ensure: created
Notice: /Stage[main]/Puppetdb::Master::Puppetdb_conf/Ini_setting[puppetdbserver]/ensure: created
Info: Class[Puppetdb::Master::Puppetdb_conf]: Scheduling refresh of Service[puppetmaster]
Notice: /Stage[main]/Puppetdb::Master::Config/Service[puppetmaster]: Triggered 'refresh' from 2 events
Notice: Finished catalog run in 239.24 seconds
Error: Could not send report: Broken pipe
[vagrant@puppet ~]$
```

We can notice that we receive a broken pipe error. This is due to the Puppet Master restarting during our run; hence, it is unavailable to receive the report. If you run Puppet again, you'll notice that it runs fine. However, if you're still running the user audit code from the last chapter, the `users` module tries to delete the PuppetDB and Postgres users. For now, we'll just remove this manifest by removing the line from the `site.pp` file. Edit `/etc/puppet/manifests/site.pp` and remove the `include users` line, as well as the `include clamav` line. Removing the `clamav` line is necessary because it uses our `users` module. You can also modify the module to handle the new users by either adding the user definition or adding the new users to the system user's parameter.

We need to make one last change. The PuppetDB module doesn't configure our master to store reports in PuppetDB, and we need this to do our work. We'll fix that now.

Edit the `/etc/puppet/puppet.conf` file. In this file, in the `[master]` section, find the line, as follows

```
reports = store
```

Security Reporting with Puppet

Replace that line with the following:

```
reports = store, puppetdb
```

Then, restart the `puppetmaster` service with the following command:

```
sudo service puppetmaster restart
```

Once this is done and you run Puppet, it should run normally. In fact, you likely won't even notice that PuppetDB is there. However, it is there and it's waiting to assist you.

As was previously mentioned, PuppetDB uses a RESTful API for access. In a nutshell, that means we'll be making HTTP queries to get the report information.

To get that information, we'll need to use a query API. The query API supports a large number of endpoints, or URLs available to serve the information, and covering them all would quickly turn our book into an entire book on reporting, so we'll focus on specific ones to get some quick reports.

> If you want to explore the APIs more in-depth, the earlier mentioned *Puppet Reporting and Monitoring* book is a wonderful resource. You can also find information on the query API at https://docs.puppetlabs.com/puppetdb/2.2/api/query/v3/query.html.

Let's go ahead and duplicate the information in the basic report in the last section via PuppetDB to show a basic report. We'll explore some additional endpoints later in this chapter.

First, we need to get our interesting report into PuppetDB. To do that, we'll simply, manually remove the `clamav` package and let Puppet reinstall it. To do so, run the following commands:

```
sudo yum -y remove clamav
sudo puppet agent --test
```

We should go ahead and create a report showing ClamAV being installed. This is similar to our earlier report.

Now, we'll use the report's endpoint to get information about the reports on a node. However, we'll want to approach this in a slightly different way than we did earlier.

First, we'll use the node's endpoint to get a list of nodes. We can do this on the command line using `curl`, as follows:

```
curl -Gs 'http://localhost:8080/v3/nodes'
```

This will give the output similar to the following:

```
[ {
  "name" : "puppet.book.local",
  "deactivated" : null,
  "catalog_timestamp" : "2014-09-08T02:31:52.988Z",
  "facts_timestamp" : "2014-09-08T02:31:45.760Z",
  "report_timestamp" : "2014-09-08T02:32:17.916Z"
} ]
```

This output is in JSON. It's a bit harder to parse in bash, but we can use a helper library to assist us. This is present in EPEL, so we can install it as follows:

```
sudo yum -y install jq
```

We can then use the `jq` program to process this JSON output in bash.

> **Why all this bash scripting?**
>
> In reality, you wouldn't likely use bash to do this work. While it's possible using tools, such as `jq`, we'd be better served with a more fully featured language. I have used bash here, since it's something most Linux admins will know offhand, and since the previous example is bash. There even exists helper libraries in languages, such as Ruby and Python to assist you with these reporting queries.

If we pipe the previous output to `jq` with a specially formatted query string, we can get the information we're after. The command is as follows:

```
curl -Gs 'http://localhost:8080/v3/nodes' |jq -r '.[].name'
```

The `jq` command will return the name tag of each of the elements of the array. This is the list of hostnames we care about.

Example – getting recent reports

For each hostname, we need to get the most recent report. To do this, we'll use the report's endpoint in PuppetDB and restrict it to the node we care about. This is a bit more complicated as a `curl` command, because we need to filter the data we are querying to just a single node.

We'll start by statically listing our host, and then we'll build the pieces into a script.

The command to do this is a doozy. We'll run the command and then break it into usable chunks:

```
curl -Gs 'http://localhost:8080/v3/reports' --data-urlencode 'order-by=[{"field": "end-time", "order": "desc"}]' --data-urlencode 'query=["=", "certname", "puppet.book.local"]' --data-urlencode 'limit=1'
```

> If your output is a blank set ([ ]), make sure you're reporting to PuppetDB, and that you've completed a run. See the previous section for details.

The preceding command should be on one single line.

We use a handful of PuppetDB arguments here. We pass these to `curl` with `-data-urlencode` and `curl` turns them into the POST or GET arguments, as needed. The first one, `order-by`, lets us order our output. In this case, we order by the end time of the run in a descending order.

The second argument is a query argument. There exists a very powerful set of operators available for use in the PuppetDB query language. A complete document explaining the syntax can be found at https://docs.puppetlabs.com/puppetdb/2.2/api/query/v3/query.html. In this case, what we're after is quite simple. We want the reports of a given host. In this case, our host would be, `puppet.book.local`.

The final argument is a limit. This simply limits the number of results we get back. In this case, we're limiting to 1.

Together, this will return the output like the following:

```
[ {
  "hash" : "0081fb5b58c05c1a24bfc4893f035f6f6ccd9ad3",
  "puppet-version" : "3.7.0",
  "receive-time" : "2014-09-08T02:51:40.951Z",
  "report-format" : 4,
  "start-time" : "2014-09-08T02:51:18.863Z",
  "end-time" : "2014-09-08T02:51:38.248Z",
  "transaction-uuid" : "cb40f17e-dd9a-4246-991e-29390d2cc663",
  "configuration-version" : "1410143505",
  "certname" : "puppet.book.local"
} ]
```

This returns a good amount of information on the run. Already, you can see that we have the start and end time of the run. As a matter of fact, the only data we're missing is the run status.

As it would turn out, PuppetDB doesn't actually store that status like a stored report does. There is currently a feature request in it to add this information to the PuppetDB backend. You can track that request at `https://tickets.puppetlabs.com/browse/PDB-36`.

PuppetDB instead stores the status of each individual event that happened on the node. We can use this information to display an even more useful summary in our example report.

Example – getting event counts

We'll now take a look at how we can use the individual event data to create reporting on aggregate event counts.

To do this, we'll use one final endpoint, the event-counts endpoint. This endpoint, as you might imagine, provides information on event counts from a run. We'll query it based on the hash of the report returned earlier. This will give us information on an individual run.

We need to summarize these events by some value. In this case, we can use the node `certname` since we're querying an individual report.

The command to get the information is as follows:

```
curl -Gs 'http://localhost:8080/v3/event-counts' --data-urlencode 'query=["=", "report", "0081fb5b58c05c1a24bfc4893f035f6f6ccd9ad3"]' --data-urlencode 'summarize-by=certname'
```

Once again, that is all on one line and be sure to use the hash of the report you ran in the previous section, or you will get no data.

It should return the results, as follows:

```
[ {
  "subject" : {
    "title" : "puppet.book.local"
  },
  "subject-type" : "certname",
  "failures" : 0,
  "successes" : 1,
  "noops" : 0,
  "skips" : 0
} ]
```

Security Reporting with Puppet

However, there's our information, even containing information on skipped resources (resources are skipped if a resource it depends on fails) and noop resources. If there was no report, or if there were no changed resources, you would receive an empty hash.

Example – a simple PuppetDB dashboard

We can use the information obtained to this point, in order to build a script such as our earlier one. The script will be somewhat more complicated but can report on more data. In the simplest case here, we'll report on the number of successful and failed resources, or simply return unchanged if no resources changed. If there are no changed resources, the preceding event counts will return null.

The script to do this is as follows:

```
#!/bin/bash

cat << EOF
<!doctype html>

<html lang="en">
<head>
<title>Puppet Run Report</title>
</head>
<body>
<table border=1>
<tr><th>Hostname</th><th>Last Run</th><th>Status</th></tr>
EOF

HOSTS=$(curl -Gs 'http://localhost:8080/v3/nodes' |jq -r \
'.[].name')
for H in ${HOSTS}
do
  REPINFO=$(curl -Gs 'http://localhost:8080/v3/reports' \
--data-urlencode 'order-by=[{"field": "end-time", "order": \
"desc"}]' --data-urlencode "query=[\"=\", \"certname\", \
\"${H}\"]" --data-urlencode 'limit=1')
  REPHASH=$(echo ${REPINFO}|jq -r '.[0].hash')
  START=$(echo ${REPINFO}|jq -r '.[0].["start-time"]')
  ECOUNT=$(curl -Gs 'http://localhost:8080/v3/event-counts' \
--data-urlencode "query=[\"=\", \"report\", \"${REPHASH}\"]" \
--data-urlencode 'summarize-by=certname')
  ELEN=$(echo ${ECOUNT}|jq '.|length')
  if [ $ELEN -eq 0 ]; then
    STATUS="unchanged"
```

```
    else
      SUC=$(echo ${ECOUNT}|jq '.[0].successes')
      FAIL=$(echo ${ECOUNT}|jq '.[0].failures')
      STATUS="${SUC} successes, ${FAIL} failures"
    fi
    echo "<tr><td>${h}</td><td>${START}</td><td>${STATUS}</td></tr>"
  done

  cat << EOF
  </table>
  </body>
  </html>
  EOF
```

I've noted the wrapped lines with \ at the end.

As you can see, the shell of the script is very similar to what we found earlier. However, the main loop has changed. In this case, we build a list of hosts by querying the node's endpoint. We then take this list and gather information about each using first, the report's endpoint and then, the event-count's endpoint. We use some jq magic to format it, and then finally we output the information line.

The output to this command, when run, is very similar to the earlier output, with the addition of the number of successful or failed resources when ran. The output is shown in the following screenshot:

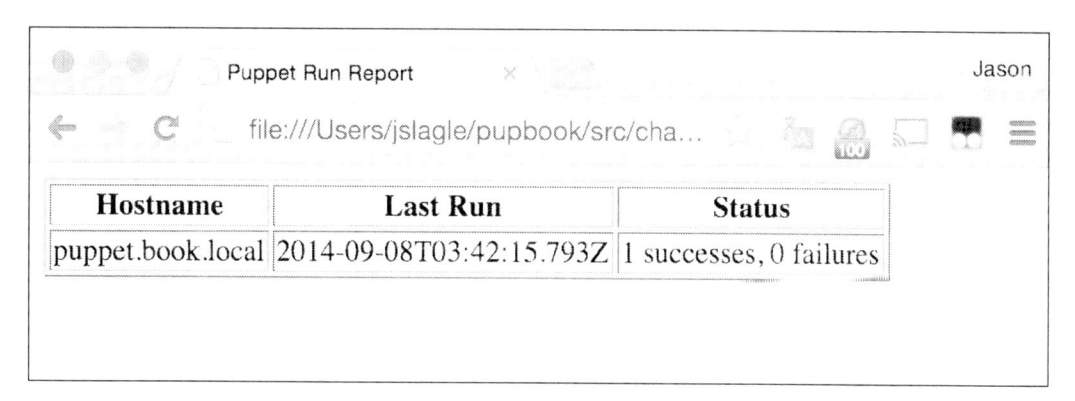

Hostname	Last Run	Status
puppet.book.local	2014-09-08T03:42:15.793Z	1 successes, 0 failures

As you can see, PuppetDB provides a very powerful base to report from. We've not even scratched the surface of what's possible. We'll take a look at some other things we can do next.

Reporting for compliance

When we consider compliance, there are a number of common areas we can report on. To do the actual reporting, we can use whatever method we choose. This could be one of the previously discussed ways, such as processing the stored reports or using PuppetDB.

We already looked at the first big piece in showing compliance. That is, demonstrating when the Puppet run last happened on each of our hosts. We have shown an easy way to accomplish this with both PuppetDB and stored reports, earlier in this chapter. The information on the last run status exists in all of the report formats and can easily be reported on. Setting up alerts on that data is also easily done using concepts, shown earlier wrapped up with some alerting logic.

However, we've not approached reporting on the auditing data. Luckily, reporting on that is not much more difficult.

The report format contains a wealth of information on the run, as well as data on the facts present on a host that can be used to report on the current state of the system. It can also be parsed to show what is changing and when. When put together with the manifest documentation, it can produce a complete history of all the changes that Puppet made to your host over time.

We'll use an example of auditing the openssl package and using it to report on the heartbleed-vulnerable version of openssl, as our compliance example here.

> More information on heartbleed can be found at https://cve.mitre.org/cgi-bin/cvename.cgi?name=CVE-2014-0160.

Example – finding heartbleed-vulnerable systems

Heartbleed became a big issue in mid-2014. It was discovered that certain default versions of openssl were shipped in such a way that they left a remote vulnerability open. Using this vulnerability, one could potentially discover the private SSL key, along with other memory data.

Sysadmins scrambled to patch their systems and ensure that heartbleed was no longer present. For those using Puppet, this became a case of using an ensure value on the resource, as well as some dependency logic to ensure that it was updated, and applications using openssl were restarted. We'll show how to use a noop resource to report on the currently installed version of openssl. One can then extend this to look for the heartbleed vulnerability.

There are a couple of ways in which we can approach this. One way is to expose the `openssl` version as a fact. For certain very critical items, we may go down this route. However, if you are managing many packages in this manner, it quickly becomes overwhelming to try to maintain facts for each package. It is, however, fairly easy to report on this data if these facts are created using the PuppetDB fact's endpoint.

Another methodology is to use the audit meta-parameter. This makes sense since what we are essentially doing is auditing the version of `openssl` installed. This does, however, depend on the deprecated audit meta-parameter, so let's examine one last method.

The first step in doing this, is to create our noop resource. To do that, we will create a noop resource set to pin `openssl` to the latest version. In this case, we're asserting that we always want `openssl` to be the latest, but we want to know if it's going to change, rather than Puppet updating it.

This example will somewhat follow the package auditing example in *Chapter 2, Tracking Changes to Objects*. I'll abbreviate the example here and you can refer to it if you need more in-depth instructions.

First, let's go ahead and set up the `openssl` package for audit, with `ensure => 'latest'`. To do so, we'll edit /etc/puppet/manifests/site.pp and add the following command to our default node definition:

```
package { 'openssl':
  ensure => 'latest',
  noop   => 'true',
}
```

This should run without any issues, auditing the first version installed. The output when running Puppet should be similar to the following screenshot:

```
[vagrant@puppet ~]$ sudo puppet agent --test
Info: Retrieving plugin
Info: Loading facts
Info: Caching catalog for puppet.book.local
Info: Applying configuration version '1421985020'
Notice: /Stage[main]/Main/Node[default]/Package[openssl]/ensure: current_value 1.0.1e-15.el6, should be 0
:1.0.1e-30.el6_6.5 (noop)
Notice: Node[default]: Would have triggered 'refresh' from 1 events
Notice: Class[Main]: Would have triggered 'refresh' from 1 events
Notice: Stage[main]: Would have triggered 'refresh' from 1 events
Notice: Finished catalog run in 8.31 seconds
[vagrant@puppet ~]$
```

Security Reporting with Puppet

As you can see, on our test box, we have an update available but not installed.

To report on this data, we'll use PuppetDB. We'll explore the endpoint required to get the information, as well as the commands needed to do it. However, to save space, we won't show the entire script. The script to report on this data will be found with the book source for reference.

The endpoint we'll use to do this is the `events` endpoint. The `resources` endpoint contains information about the resource, but it does not contain information about its current state. If you did this via stored reports, or your own report processor, you could retrieve the information needed to do it from the `Puppet::Resource::Status` class, and look for, and examine, the child events.

We can query the `events` endpoint for the information required with the following command:

```
curl -sG 'http://localhost:8080/v3/events' --data-urlencode
'query=["and", ["=", "certname", "puppet.book.local"], ["=",
"resource-title", "openssl"]]'
```

We'll get the output similar to the following:

```
[ {
  "containment-path" : [ "Stage[main]", "Main", "Node[default]",
"Package[openssl]" ],
  "new-value" : "latest",
  "containing-class" : "Main",
  "report-receive-time" : "2014-09-08T23:27:32.576Z",
  "report" : "05b824e576a703dc76b34670cead9e3e3d8b8070",
  "resource-title" : "openssl",
  "property" : "ensure",
  "file" : "/etc/puppet/manifests/site.pp",
  "old-value" : "1.0.1e-15.el6",
  "run-start-time" : "2014-09-08T23:27:08.314Z",
  "line" : 9,
  "status" : "noop",
  "run-end-time" : "2014-09-08T23:27:29.863Z",
  "resource-type" : "Package",
  "timestamp" : "2014-09-08T23:27:29.973Z",
  "configuration-version" : "1410218830",
  "certname" : "puppet.book.local",
  "message" : "current_value 1.0.1e-15.el6, should be 0:1.0.1e-
16.el6_5.15 (noop)"
} ]
```

Notice right away that we see the current version, and the message tells us the version we expect. We can use our `jq` command to spit out the current version. The command to do that would be as follows:

```
jq -r '.[0] | .["old-value"]'
```

By piping the first `curl` value to it, we get the output of just the version. This could be used in whatever reporting we're using.

It's worth noting, however, that the preceding command will return all of the events for the `openssl` resource title. In reality, we'd need to include this in a loop like our former script to ensure that we only look at the most recent report for each box. Additionally, if `openssl` is the latest version, the event would be missing. In that case, much like we did with the unchanged resources in the earlier PuppetDB script, we'd just need to return that we have the latest version of OpenSSL installed.

The final step would be to look for vulnerable versions. Looking at the CentOS advisory at `http://lists.centos.org/pipermail/centos-announce/2014-April/020249.html`, we can see that versions before 1.0.1e-16 are vulnerable. As you can see, our system is indeed vulnerable. We can add the vulnerability status to our report if we knew the vulnerable versions on the various operating systems we run.

With some creativity and the PuppetDB API guide, we can produce a rich set of reports on our systems.

Summary

Reporting is something that seems to constantly be a work in progress. We can always make our reports more comprehensive and thorough. In much the same way, the PuppetDB library and the Puppet reporting engine itself has seen a large amount of progress recently.

An entire book could be dedicated to the topic of reporting with Puppet (in fact, as mentioned earlier, one has been!). We've only touched on the beginnings of building a rich reporting environment to get you started with your reporting needs.

Using either stored reports or PuppetDB, we can fairly quickly build in-depth reports on our environment and the resources in them. We can do this in any number of languages.

There exists a good number of available off-the-shelf tools that can also be installed and help us with this. Puppetboard is a great example of one that can provide a lot of quick insights into your Puppet environment from a security standpoint. We'll touch briefly on Puppetboard in *Appendix, Going Forward*.

We've now spent time exploring basic reporting on reports using the store endpoint and some simple shell scripting. We also expanded on that knowledge to handle reporting from PuppetDB, including a good number of examples useful to build a very quick reporting dashboard. Using this information, we're armed to start using the data Puppet provides for reporting purposes.

Now that we've got the basics behind us in setting up Puppet for security and reporting on the data, we'll spend some time in the next chapter talking about how to secure Puppet itself before moving on to more advanced topics.

5
Securing Puppet

As your Puppet Master is a tool that configures your systems, ensuring that it is secure is very important. Puppet can change any facet of the systems under management. Since it can cause great damage to systems as well as create numerous security issues if compromised, it is very important to ensure that your Puppet Master is properly secured. For instance, if your Puppet Master is compromised, it is easy to add a user to every system under management, add that user to `sudoers`, and reconfigure SSH to allow the user to log in.

Luckily, Puppet has a fairly secure, out-of-the-box configuration. However, as your environment grows and you use more advanced features, you'd want to review how to secure your Puppet environment.

In this chapter, we'll explore the following aspects of securing your Puppet installation:

- Puppet security related configuration files
- Puppet SSL configuration
- Autosigning Puppet client certificates

At the end of this chapter, you should have a good understanding of the various Puppet configuration settings that you will require to secure Puppet. Additionally, you should have a good grasp of how Puppet uses SSL and autosigning.

Puppet security related configuration

Present in the Puppet core are several configuration files that control the security and access control of the base Puppet Master. Over time, these configuration files have evolved to add more functionality and more fine-grained access controls. In addition to the main Puppet configuration file, `puppet.conf`, the primary configuration files we'll examine are the files related to the authentication, file server, and autosigning configurations.

The auth.conf file

The `auth.conf` configuration file is the main file controlling access to the Puppet API resources. Internally, it is called the `rest_authconfig` file because it controls access to the RESTful API that the various Puppet commands utilize to perform their functions.

Using this configuration file, you can lock down access to various endpoints. The default configuration settings used by Puppet are sufficient in most cases. These defaults can be found at https://docs.puppetlabs.com/guides/rest_auth_conf.html#default-acls if you wish to review them. If you have special security needs, such as the need to allow off-host systems to use a subsystem, you may consider modifying the settings in this file to handle them. We'll cover an example of one such situation at the end of this section.

The auth configuration file is made up of a series of stanzas that describe paths. Here is a brief example of one of these stanzas:

```
path ~ ^/catalog/([^/]+)$
method find
allow $1
```

The paths found in these configuration sections correspond to URLs in the Puppet API. The options available in each stanza are as follows:

Option	Description
path	This is required. It contains the path component of the URL in question. When prefixed with ~, it is assumed to be a regular expression.
Environment	This is an optional list of environments that the path refers to.
method	This is an optional method to which the path applies. It can be any one of find, search, save, or destroy.
Auth	This defines whether authentication is required. It can be set to yes to indicate that authentication is required, no to forbid authenticated requests, or any to allow both authenticated and non-authenticated requests.
allow	This shows a comma-separated list of hosts allowing regular expressions. Capture arguments are allowed for regular expressions allowing very complex directives.
allow_ip	New in version 3.0, this directive permits IP addresses. They can be specified as whole IPs, IPs with asterisks in them, or CIDR ranges.

Puppet maintains a default internal set of authentication parameters that are utilized if there is no entry with the same path. In the case of a specific entry with the same path as a default entry, the default entry is not applied.

> More information on the `auth.conf` file and the default permissions can be found at https://docs.puppetlabs.com/guides/rest_auth_conf.html.

Additionally, the file is consulted in a top-down manner. This means that typically, you would put the most specific entries at the top, while leaving the more general entries lower in the file.

Example – Puppet authentication

Now let's examine an example of limiting access using the `auth.conf` file. However, to do this, we first need to make some changes to our Vagrant environment, and then we'll move on to the example.

Adding our second Vagrant host

Before we can undertake the examples in this chapter, we need to extend our Vagrant setup to add a second host. In doing this, we'll have a host to test some of our configuration items from so that we can see an allowed case and a disallowed case.

One of the challenges of doing that is getting the resolution of the Puppet-related hostnames right. There are a handful of Puppet-specific Vagrant solutions, such as Beaker, that are used for specific tasks. Beaker is worth mentioning because of its value in testing, but we will not be using it in any of our examples.

Beaker is an acceptance test framework that can configure virtual Vagrant machines using specifications. This can include installing specific versions of Ruby or Puppet. It can also be used to generically provision a set of Vagrant machines using somewhat simplified configuration syntax.

> If you get into testing the modules you write (and you should), you should really look at using Beaker. More information on Beaker can be found on its website at https://github.com/puppetlabs/beaker/.

Beaker is a bit heavy for our usage. We're going to stick to a smaller subset of the features we require for our use, and use a Vagrant plugin. The plugin we're going to use is called `hostmanager`. Its website can be found at https://github.com/smdahlen/vagrant-hostmanager.

Working with hostmanager

The `hostmanager` plugin lets us add some logic to the `Vagrantfile` that results in the `/etc/hosts` file being written with the IPs of all the other machines. We'll use this so that our Puppet agents can find the master:

1. To use the plugin, we first need to install it. This can be done with the following command:

   `vagrant plugin install vagrant-hostmanager`

   This will make the `hostmanager` plugin available for our use.

   > **Are plugins safe?**
   >
   > We use the `hostmaster` plugin for Vagrant here for ease of use. For a development environment, this is fine. However, for a production environment, it is best to have a properly functioning DNS that will eliminate the need for a plugin such as `hostmanager`.

2. Next, we need to add some default configuration options to our `Vagrantfile`. If you're following along with us, you'll note that we're starting from the base files again, as opposed to starting from where we left off in *Chapter 4, Security Reporting with Puppet*. You can use the VM covered in *Chapter 4, Security Reporting with Puppet* but that's not required, as this example does not build upon it. If you're using the source included with the book, the `Vagrantfile` already has the required modifications.

3. In the `Vagrantfile`, we'll add some options to tell `hostmanager` to run, and give it some necessary instructions. At the top of the file, right below the `Vagrant.configure` line, add the following:

   ```
   config.hostmanager.enabled = true
   config.hostmanager.ignore_private_ip = false
   config.hostmanager.include_offline = true
   ```

   This enables the `hostmanager` plugin. It also includes the private IPs of our VMs and the IPs of any offline VMs. These are useful options for our testing setup as they allow us to ping offline hosts, and so on.

4. Now, under the master configuration section, add the following:

   ```
   master.hostmanager.aliases = %w(puppet)
   ```

Chapter 5

This will add an alias for Puppet with no domain. This may not be necessary in your environment, but depending on how your local DNS is configured, your hosts may end up utilizing the wrong host as the Puppet Master. We want them to use our local Vagrant master, and it's possible that they hit our production master if we do not make this change.

Now that this is complete, we'll add our second VM. If we need to add a third VM, it will look very similar to this.

5. Below the end line of the master configuration, we need to add a section for our new `agentone` VM. Add the following lines:

```
  config.vm.define :agentone do |ao|
    ao.vm.box = "centos65-x64-puppet"
    ao.vm.box_url = "http://puppet-vagrant-boxes.puppetlabs.com/centos-65-x64-virtualbox-puppet.box"
    ao.vm.hostname = "agentone.book.local"
    ao.vm.network "private_network", ip: "10.78.78.50", netmask: "255.255.255.0"
    ao.vm.provision "shell", inline: "yum -y update puppet"
  end
```

> The included source has an additional line in the file we just saw. That line is meant for a later example. You can safely delete it for now.

The box URL and the network line should be on one line. This is very similar to the existing master configuration. The only difference is we only currently have the shell provisioner, which will use the shell to update Puppet since we're not setting up the master. We may need to add another provisioner later, but for now, this is sufficient for our use. The complete file, including the additions we just made, is shown here for reference:

```
Vagrant.configure(2) do |config|
  config.hostmanager.enabled = true
  config.hostmanager.ignore_private_ip = false
  config.hostmanager.include_offline = true
  config.vm.define :puppetmaster do |master|

    master.vm.box = "centos65-x64-puppet"
    master.vm.box_url = "http://puppet-vagrant-boxes.puppetlabs.com/centos-65-x64-virtualbox-puppet.box"
    master.vm.hostname = "puppet.book.local"
    master.vm.network "private_network", ip: "10.78.78.30", netmask: "255.255.255.0"
```

```
            master.hostmanager.aliases = %w(puppet)
            master.vm.provision "shell", inline: "yum update puppet -y"
            master.vm.provision "puppet" do |puppet|
              puppet.manifests_path = "master_manifests"
              puppet.manifest_file = "init.pp"
            end

          end
          config.vm.define :agentone do |ao|
            ao.vm.box = "centos65-x64-puppet"
            ao.vm.box_url = "http://puppet-vagrant-
        boxes.puppetlabs.com/centos-65-x64-virtualbox-puppet.box"
            ao.vm.hostname = "agentone.book.local"
            ao.vm.network "private_network", ip: "10.78.78.50", netmask:
        "255.255.255.0"
            ao.vm.provision "shell", inline: "yum -y update puppet"
          end
```

As you can see here, the URL and the network lines should not wrap.

Now that this is complete, we can go ahead and begin the example.

The fileserver.conf file

The second configuration file we'll review is `fileserver.conf`. This file contains the configuration for Puppet's built-in file server.

Much like the `auth.conf` file, in most cases, the default configuration is sufficient. In this section, we'll cover what the options currently are, what the file used to do, and the occasions when we might want to move away from the default configuration.

By default, Puppet will serve files under the `/files` API endpoint to clients. This also handles serving files that are contained within the `files` directory of individual modules. These files are accessed with the `puppet:///modules/modulename/filename` URL within Puppet.

The `fileserver.conf` file allows you to create additional file "mount points". These mount points can serve other directories on the filesystem to Puppet clients. Each mount point can have individual policies and authentication parameters associated with it. This allows you to create, for instance, an area for secured files that can only be accessed by a single host. It also lets you create a set of directories that each host can access, but other hosts cannot access the directory.

Much like the `auth.conf` file before it, the `fileserver.conf` file is made up of a series of stanzas. These files are similar in nature to `ini` files on a Windows machine. Here is an example of one of these entries:

```
[ourfiles]
    path /path/to/ourfiles
    allow *
```

The following is a table of the possible values, for reference:

Option	Description
`[mountpoint]`	This is the name of the file mount. This is the way you reference files in this location. Replace `mountpoint` with the actual mount name you want.
`path`	This is the path to the file on the Puppet Master filesystem.
`allow` or `deny`	This denotes allowing or denying access to the hosts. It can include asterisks. In almost all cases, you should use `allow *` and use the `auth.conf` file to manage access. See the notes that follow for more details on this.

Individual mount point entries start with a header like `[secretfiles]`. In this case, `secretfiles` is the name of our mount point, and it can be accessed via our Puppet module by specifying the source as `puppet:///secretfiles/<file>`.

Under each mount point, you must specify a path using the `path` directive. This is the path to the files on the local filesystem. This can allow you to move files out of your primary version control for security-related purposes. For instance, you can move private SSL keys to a file share that only the hosts that need to use the keys can access.

The final directive is an authorization directive. It can be either `allow` or `deny`. At the first glance, this seems like a way to limit what can access the files, and indeed, this used to be the case. However, in recent versions of Puppet, it is recommended that you use the `auth.conf` file to limit access, and therefore, simply use `allow *` in this file. We'll explore how to limit access via the `auth.conf` file in the next example.

Example – adding a restricted file mount

In this example, we'll add a file mount that only allows access from the `agentone` host. This is a common request for things such as keys that you don't want compromised:

1. We'll be working on our Vagrant Puppet Master here, so use `vagrant up` and `vagrant ssh` to connect to it.

2. To begin, let's edit the /etc/puppet/fileserver.conf file on the Puppet Master file to add support for our additional file server mount. We'll store the data in /srv/secret, so let's start by creating a directory structure there. We'll also store some secret data in the directory. To do so, issue the following commands:

   ```
   sudo mkdir -p /srv/secret/agentone.book.local
   ```

   ```
   echo "sup3r s3kr37" |sudo tee
   /srv/secret/agentone.book.local/secret
   ```

   ```
   sudo chown puppet /srv/secret/agentone.book.local/secret
   ```

3. Once that's done, we'll configure our new file server. Go ahead and edit the /etc/puppet/fileserver.conf file. In it, you will find a bunch of documentation and comments. At the end of the file, add this:

   ```
   [agentone]
       path /srv/secret/agentone.book.local
       allow *
   ```

   This will create the file server mount and allow anything. Remember that we're going to use auth.conf to limit access to the host resources.

4. With that, we should configure auth.conf. When you edit /etc/puppet/auth.conf, you will notice that it has all the default authentication permissions.

   In this case, we need to make sure we insert our new data into the correct place in the file. We'll insert it right before the file stanza, which should be near line 88.

   Locate the section that looks like this:

   ```
   # Allow all nodes to access all file services; this is necessary for
   # pluginsync, file serving from modules, and file serving from custom
   # mount points (see fileserver.conf). Note that the `/file` prefix matches
   # requests to both the file_metadata and file_content paths. See "Examples"
   # above if you need more granular access control for custom mount points.
   path /file
   allow *
   ```

   We'll insert our changes above it. The changes are as follows:

   ```
   path ~ ^/file_(metadata|content)s?/agentone/
   allow agentone.book.local
   ```

5. This should allow only `agentone` to access that resource. Next, we need to restart the Puppet service:

   ```
   sudo service puppetmaster restart
   ```

6. Finally comes the fun part. Let's go ahead and create a node definition referencing the file, and see what happens.

   We'll do this in the `site.pp` file since this is simple and it's a test. As a reminder, typically you'd use a module for all of the manifest code. However, for our testing purposes, we'll use `site.pp` to keep the length of this book reasonable.

   Edit `/etc/puppet/manifests/site.pp` and make it look as follows:

   ```
   node default {
     file { '/tmp/secret':
       ensure => file,
       source => 'puppet:///agentone/secret',
     }
   }
   ```

7. Save it and run Puppet on `agentone` and the master. First, we'll go for `agentone`. Run Puppet there with `sudo puppet agent -test`. First, we'll need to sign the certificate. We'll cover signing in more detail in the next section, so I'll just explain it in brief here.

   The first time you run the agent on `agentone`, you'll receive a message that indicates that the certificate was created and `waitforcert` is disabled. This means that the master has a certificate request for the agent.

8. We need to process the certificate request on the master. As I said before, we'll cover this in more detail in the next section. For now, let's just go ahead and sign it with the following command on the master:

   ```
   sudo puppet cert sign agentone.book.local
   ```

   Now that it's done, we should be able to rerun the agent on `agentone`, and you should see the output as shown in the following screenshot:

   ```
   [vagrant@agentone ~]$ sudo puppet agent --test
   Info: Retrieving plugin
   Info: Caching catalog for agentone.book.local
   Info: Applying configuration version '1412002485'
   Notice: /Stage[main]/Main/Node[default]/File[/tmp/secret]/ensure: defined content as '{md5}788bd3d6
   6f079c8e19d97aa59744c8c6'
   Notice: Finished catalog run in 0.11 seconds
   [vagrant@agentone ~]$
   ```

   As you can see, this has successfully created the file in question.

9. We'll also run this on the Puppet Master to see how it behaves there. Once you do so, you should see the following output:

```
s[vagrant@puppet ~]$ sudo puppet agent --test
Info: Retrieving plugin
Info: Caching catalog for puppet.book.local
Info: Applying configuration version '1412002485'
Error: /Stage[main]/Main/Node[default]/File[/tmp/secret]: Could not evaluate: Could not retrieve fi
le metadata for puppet:///agentone/secret: Error 403 on SERVER: Forbidden request: puppet.book.loca
l(127.0.0.1) access to /file_metadata/agentone/secret [find] authenticated  at :83
Wrapped exception:
Error 403 on SERVER: Forbidden request: puppet.book.local(127.0.0.1) access to /file_metadata/agent
one/secret [find] authenticated  at :83
Notice: Finished catalog run in 0.06 seconds
[vagrant@puppet ~]$
```

You can see here that we're not allowed to access the resource.

This example shows some of the power that auth.conf can provide. With some work, you can extend this pattern to allow a host to only access its own resources, for instance. You can also allow access from a management host to some resources for monitoring or reporting.

Let's move on and explore how Puppet uses SSL for encryption and authentication.

SSL and Puppet

SSL is a core component of Puppet. The Puppet Master uses SSL certificates to authenticate client systems. Proper management of SSL is vitally important to ensure that your Puppet system is secure and behaves properly.

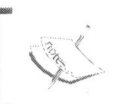

> This section assumes you have some knowledge about the working of SSL. If you require a primer on SSL, a good reference is https://info.ssl.com/ssl-made-easy-for-beginners/.

By default, the Puppet Master will act as an SSL **Certificate Authority (CA)**. As part of the SSL CA, the master will accept certificate requests from new agents. You can then choose whether to sign the certificate on the master. There is also a methodology to enable autosigning. We'll cover this in the next section.

Puppet can also support use of an external certificate authority. You might want to do this if you already have a certificate authority configured to allow you to utilize existing certificates. This avoids the overhead of needing two separate certificate authorities. At the end of this section, we will cover some more information about external CAs and the configurations supported for them.

Signing certificates

Puppet uses the `cert face` command (as a reminder, `face` is a Puppet command) to manage signing and revoking of certificates. By default, when a node starts up for the first time and does not have a certificate, it will create a **Certificate Signing Request** (**CSR**). A CSR is the agent's way of registering itself with the master and requesting access to resources. We'll demonstrate this now.

If you did the last example, issue this command to clean up, and we'll start over:

```
vagrant destroy -f
```

Once the cleanup is complete, restart the Vagrant hosts with the following command:

```
vagrant up
```

Once they boot, use `vagrant ssh agentone` to connect to the agent guest. Once there, we'll run Puppet in our normal way, using `sudo puppet agent -test`.

When a host is new and Puppet is run for the first time, you'll see output like this:

```
Last login: Sun Sep 28 14:17:02 2014 from 10.0.2.2
Welcome to your Packer-built virtual machine.
[vagrant@agentone ~]$ sudo puppet agent --test
Info: Creating a new SSL key for agentone.book.local
Info: Caching certificate for ca
Info: csr_attributes file loading from /etc/puppet/csr_attributes.yaml
Info: Creating a new SSL certificate request for agentone.book.local
Info: Certificate Request fingerprint (SHA256): 3B:2E:2E:C4:17:4D:67:1C:F8:25:F7:8D:5B:33:61:2A:85:21:B9:DA:4F:E9:E7:F2:A1:A9:D3:41:6E:9E:5F:82
Info: Caching certificate for ca
Exiting; no certificate found and waitforcert is disabled
[vagrant@agentone ~]$
```

As you can see, we created an SSL certificate request, and we sent it to the master. We also exited because, by default, we will not wait for the certificate to be signed.

On the master, we should now be able to see the certificate if we check with the Puppet `cert face` command. Open a new terminal, and connect to the master with `vagrant ssh puppetmaster`. Once logged in, we'll issue this command:

`sudo puppet cert list`

We should see an output like what is shown in the following screenshot:

```
jslagle@Jasons-MacBook-Pro:~/pupbook/src/chap5 $ vagrant ssh puppetmaster
Last login: Sun Sep 28 14:41:08 2014 from 10.0.2.2
Welcome to your Packer-built virtual machine.
[vagrant@puppet ~]$ sudo puppet cert list
  "agentone.book.local" (SHA256) 3B:2E:2E:C4:17:4D:67:1C:F8:25:F7:8D:5B:33:61:2A:85:21:B9:DA:4F:E9:
E7:F2:A1:A9:D3:41:6E:9E:5F:82
[vagrant@puppet ~]$
```

As you can see, the certificate request is now present on the master. The next step is to sign it. The command to do so is as follows:

`sudo puppet cert sign agentone.book.local`

The Puppet Master will return some information indicating that the certificate is signed and the request has been removed.

Once this is done, go ahead and run the agent on the `agentone` machine again. You should now see the normal output. In this case, since our `site.pp` file is empty, we won't have any output other than the run being successful. If you happen to still be using the example from *Chapter 4, Security Reporting with Puppet*, you should see it apply all of the same manifests you have in your default node to the machine.

Revoking certificates

Now that you know how to sign a certificate, we may want to ask for the opposite. What happens if we need to get rid of a host? Perhaps we've decommissioned it, or perhaps the host is doing bad things and we need to lock it out of the Puppet infrastructure. In the SSL world, we do this by revoking the certificate.

In the Puppet world, we have two operations that can be used to do this. The first is the `revoke` operation, and the second is the `clean` operation.

If a host has been compromised or is still around but you do not want it checking into Puppet, the proper thing to do is to revoke its certificate. To do this for our example host, we issue the following command:

`sudo puppet cert revoke agentone.book.local`

We'll do that, and then we'll go ahead and rerun the Puppet agent on `agentone`. The output on the master gives only the serial number of the revoked certificate. Once this is done, we actually have to restart the master. To do that, we run the following on our master node:

`sudo service puppetmaster restart`

When we rerun the agent, the output looks significantly worse, as you can see here:

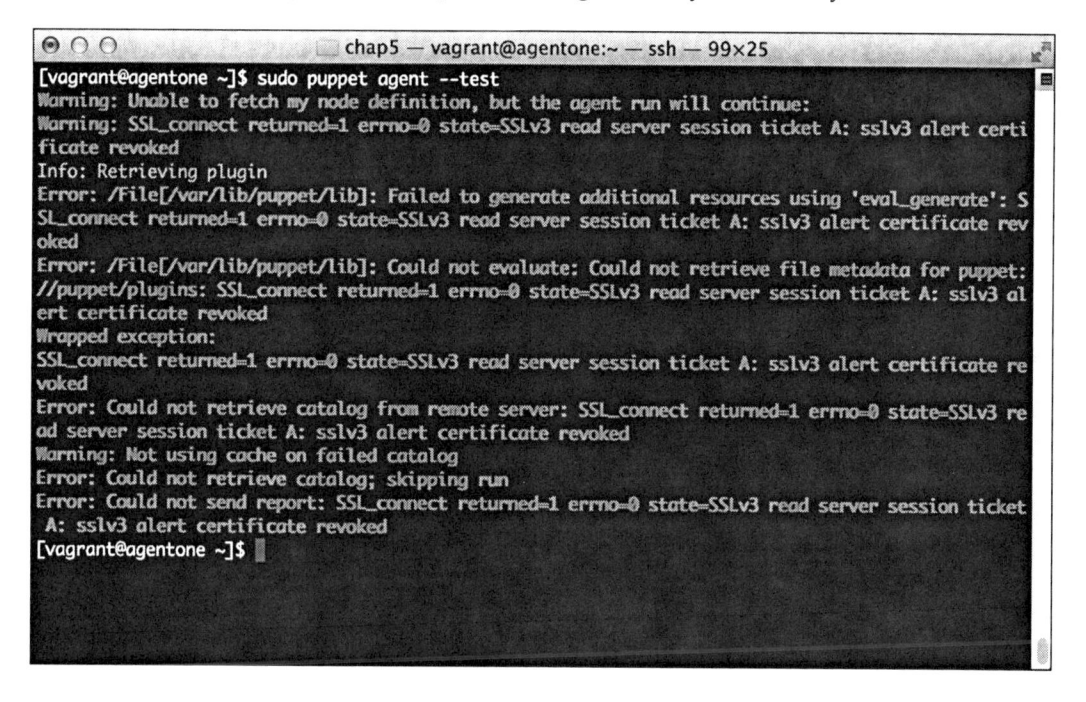

```
[vagrant@agentone ~]$ sudo puppet agent --test
Warning: Unable to fetch my node definition, but the agent run will continue:
Warning: SSL_connect returned=1 errno=0 state=SSLv3 read server session ticket A: sslv3 alert certificate revoked
Info: Retrieving plugin
Error: /File[/var/lib/puppet/lib]: Failed to generate additional resources using 'eval_generate': SSL_connect returned=1 errno=0 state=SSLv3 read server session ticket A: sslv3 alert certificate revoked
Error: /File[/var/lib/puppet/lib]: Could not evaluate: Could not retrieve file metadata for puppet://puppet/plugins: SSL_connect returned=1 errno=0 state=SSLv3 read server session ticket A: sslv3 alert certificate revoked
Wrapped exception:
SSL_connect returned=1 errno=0 state=SSLv3 read server session ticket A: sslv3 alert certificate revoked
Error: Could not retrieve catalog from remote server: SSL_connect returned=1 errno=0 state=SSLv3 read server session ticket A: sslv3 alert certificate revoked
Warning: Not using cache on failed catalog
Error: Could not retrieve catalog; skipping run
Error: Could not send report: SSL_connect returned=1 errno=0 state=SSLv3 read server session ticket A: sslv3 alert certificate revoked
[vagrant@agentone ~]$
```

The agent sees that its certificate is revoked, and it does not run the catalog. It also does not try to request a new certificate.

Now, we'll use the `clean` command to remove the certificate. The old certificate is still in the **Certificate Revocation List** (**CRL**), however, so it's dead forever. We'll have to tell the master to remove the certificate from itself, and then force the agent to request a new certificate. It's a common mistake to try to issue a new certificate request before the old certificate is removed from the master, and this will fail.

Securing Puppet

On the master, issue the following command:

```
sudo puppet cert clean agentone.book.local
```

On the agent, go ahead and rerun Puppet. You will notice that the agent is still showing errors about the certificate being revoked. At this point, we need to manually remove the local certificate so that the agent requests a new certificate. We can do that by removing the SSL directory on the client with the following command:

```
sudo rm /var/lib/puppet/ssl -rf
```

Once this is complete, it should behave as if it were a new node, and we should be permitted to sign a certificate for the host again.

> Care needs to be taken when doing this on the master. It is possible that you accidentally remove all the downstream certificates. Though it's also possible to recover from this, it's not fun! I speak from experience as I have forgotten more than once that `puppet cert clean -all` doesn't only do requests.

Alternative SSL configurations

In addition to the normal mode of operation in which the Puppet Master serves as the CA, it also supports a mode where an external certificate authority is used. The setup of this particular mode is out of the scope of this book, as it requires an external web server to proxy requests. We will, however, discuss the various modes that can be utilized for SSL configuration.

When the external CA is set up, the external web server, usually Apache or Nginx, authenticates the client with the SSL certificate and uses certain headers in the request to indicate to Puppet that the client is authenticated, and it also specifies what the hostname of the client is.

In this case, you also have to manage getting the certificates on the client and the master manually. Puppet will not provide certificates in the external CA mode.

There are three possible modes to use in this setup. We'll cover them in increasing order of complexity.

The first method is simply an external root CA. This CA handles the issuing of all the certificates, that is, for both the master and the agents. In this mode, you copy the CA certs and the certificates to both the agent and the master. You then configure the web server on the master to use the CA certificate. No changes are required on the agent in this mode.

In the second and third methods, we introduce intermediate certificate authorities. These have their certificates signed by the root, and they issue the downstream certificates for the master and agents. In the second scenario, we use one intermediate authority to serve both the master and the agent. In the third scenario, which is the most complex scenario, we use a separate intermediate authority for the masters and the agents.

The server-side setup in this case is nearly identical. The only change is that you have to give the master the certificate bundle. On the client side, you also need to provide the certificate bundle consisting of the root and intermediate CA certificates.

> As was mentioned earlier, configuring Puppet in this manner is a very advanced operation. If you wish to read more about it or attempt it, more information can be found on the Puppet site at https://docs.puppetlabs.com/puppet/3.7/reference/config_ssl_external_ca.html.

Autosigning certificates

As your Puppet environment grows, manually signing certificates can become an issue. This is particularly true in cases where machines are being created automatically due to scaling, or because a cluster is expanding.

Puppet contains two primary methods to assist with this. They are basic autosign and policy-based autosign. In basic autosign, we give a list of hosts that we will sign certificates for. With policy-based autosign, we call an external script that allows us to determine whether a given certificate request is signed. We'll now cover these types of autosign methodologies and their potential use cases.

There exists a third type of autosign, which is used to simply tell the master to sign all certificates. It is known as naïve autosign. This should not be used except in certain test cases, so here, we'll cover only how to enable it. Besides, we're focusing on security, and in most cases, you can use at least basic autosign.

In these examples, we're going to need two agent machines to successfully demonstrate some concepts. To do so, we'll add a construct to our Vagrantfile, like this:

```
config.vm.define :agenttwo do |at|
  at.vm.box = "centos65-x64-puppet"
  at.vm.box_url = "http://puppet-vagrant-boxes.puppetlabs.com/centos-65-x64-virtualbox-puppet.box"
  at.vm.hostname = "agenttwo.book.local"
```

```
    at.vm.network "private_network", ip: "10.78.78.51", netmask:
"255.255.255.0"
    at.vm.provision "shell", inline: "yum update puppet -y"
  end
```

As before, do not wrap the box URL or the network type. If you need more assistance with this, refer back to the earlier example on the Puppet configuration. It has more details on how this should work.

Go ahead! Destroy and recreate your environment so that we can start afresh. To do so, issue the following commands:

vagrant destroy -f

vagrant up

This will reset the environment and allow us to start over, with fresh machines to practice autosigning.

Naïve autosign

Enabling naïve autosign is very simple. To do so, you edit the /etc/puppet/puppet.conf file and add the following to its master section:

```
autosign = true
```

Doing this will cause Puppet to automatically sign any certificate requests it receives.

As noted before, this has very significant security implications and should not be done without specific reasons to do so. It's usually only used in test environments to enable automated testing without the need to do more complex signing.

Basic autosign

Basic autosign has been around for a long time in the Puppet world. For a long time, it was the only real method to automatically sign certificates. This resulted in a number of third-party solutions to do this that policy-based autosign aims to supplement or replace.

To perform basic autosign, you need to configure the autosign file. By default, Puppet runs with autosign = $confdir/autosign.conf, which is /etc/puppet/autosign.conf on Red Hat based operating systems. This file should not be executable. In policy-based autosign, the autosign file is referenced in the configuration points to an executable script. If your autosign.conf file is executable, Puppet will attempt to run it as a policy-based autosign script.

The `autosign` file contains a list of hostnames or host expressions. In this case, host expressions are just hostnames beginning with an asterisk (*). It does not support more complex regular expressions.

Let's give it a try. On the master, let's create the `/etc/puppet/autosign.conf` file and add `agenttwo` to the file. It should contain this:

```
agenttwo.book.local
```

Once this is done, we can try to run Puppet on both agents. First, we'll do it on `agentone`. Run Puppet using the normal `sudo puppet agent -test` command. You should notice that the agent reports that it requested a certificate, and then exits, since `waitforcert` is disabled.

Now, run the same command on `agenttwo`. This is where the magic happens. The output should be similar to what is shown in the following screenshot:

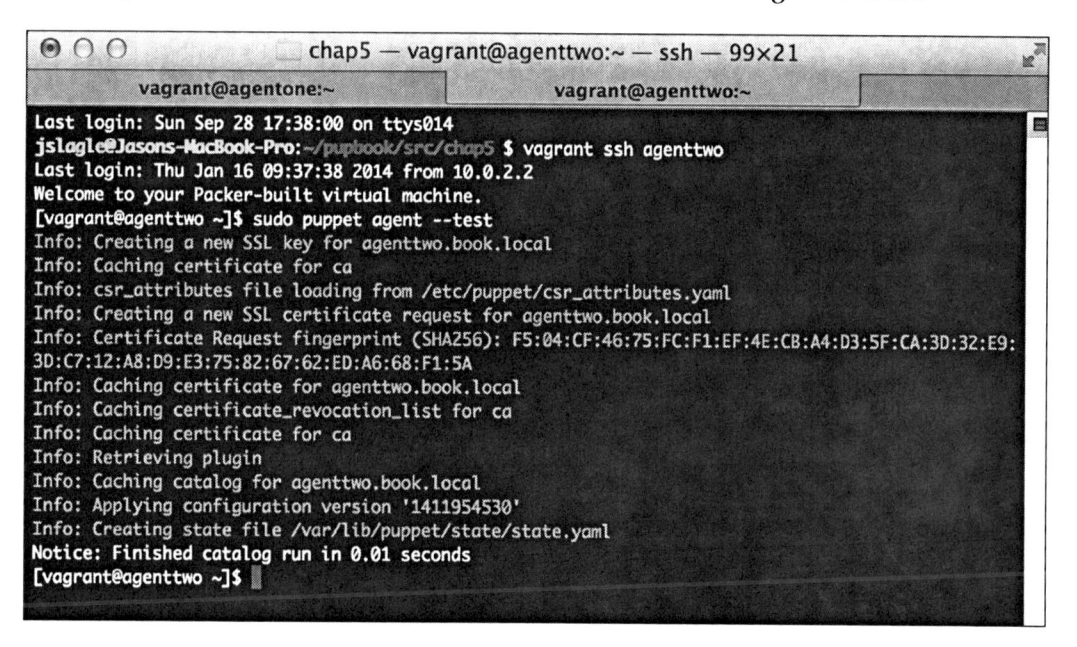

```
[vagrant@agenttwo ~]$ sudo puppet agent --test
Info: Creating a new SSL key for agenttwo.book.local
Info: Caching certificate for ca
Info: csr_attributes file loading from /etc/puppet/csr_attributes.yaml
Info: Creating a new SSL certificate request for agenttwo.book.local
Info: Certificate Request fingerprint (SHA256): F5:04:CF:46:75:FC:F1:EF:4E:CB:A4:D3:5F:CA:3D:32:E9:3D:C7:12:A8:D9:E3:75:82:67:62:ED:A6:68:F1:5A
Info: Caching certificate for agenttwo.book.local
Info: Caching certificate_revocation_list for ca
Info: Caching certificate for ca
Info: Retrieving plugin
Info: Caching catalog for agenttwo.book.local
Info: Applying configuration version '1411954530'
Info: Creating state file /var/lib/puppet/state/state.yaml
Notice: Finished catalog run in 0.01 seconds
[vagrant@agenttwo ~]$
```

As you can see, we've gone through an entire run here. We made a cert and it was accepted immediately. If you check out `/var/log/messages` on the master, you will see a request and then the immediate signing of the certificate.

Now, if you think about it for a second, you'll see a potential problem — no authentication took place. Therefore, a client can pretend to be any of the listed hosts and get a signed certificate and a compiled catalog. This can reveal information about the host.

This is somewhat mitigated if you use only full hostnames and remember to remove them when the hosts are deprovisioned. Alternatively, you can use policy-based autosigning. We'll cover that now.

Policy-based autosign

Policy-based autosign is a relatively new feature in Puppet, introduced in Puppet 3.4. It allows you to build a custom executable that Puppet will call each time it receives the CSR. That executable will receive the common name (usually the hostname) as an argument, and the CSR on standard input. The policy executable can then make a decision and return a piece of code to let the master know whether to autosign or not.

Configuring this requires a bit of work, but when done correctly, it can let you use special metadata to authenticate requests.

For this example, we're going to create a simple policy-based autosign script. We'll rely on our Vagrant provisioner to ensure that one of our hosts gets the necessary data and the other doesn't. This will allow us to see the behavior of the autosign process.

The first thing we need to do is to create our policy-based autosign script. This script needs to take the CSR, decode it, and look for any special data we've added. In the case of this script, we're going to be adding a special pre-shared key using a Puppet attribute. Then, on the master, we'll look for the presence of the key to indicate that the client is authenticated.

This is a simple key held in a file, which is the word `banana`.

Let's create our policy-based autosign script as `/etc/puppet/autosign-policy.rb`. Edit the file on the master by adding the following content:

```ruby
#!/usr/bin/env ruby

require "openssl"
include OpenSSL

csr = OpenSSL::X509::Request.new $stdin.read

atts = csr.attributes()

if atts.empty?
  exit 1
end

key = nil
```

```
atts.each do |a|
  if (a.oid=="extReq")
    val = a.value.value.first.value.first.value
    if val[0].value == "1.3.6.1.4.1.34380.1.1.4"
      key = val[1].value
    end
  end
end

if key == "banana"
  print "Match\n"
  exit 0
else
  print "No match\n"
  exit 1
end
```

Now let me give you a bit of explanation: the beginning of the script imports all the necessary pieces. Once that's done, we create an internal `openssl` object from `stdin`. Once we have that, we start the magic!

If our cert doesn't have any attributes, we exit. If it does, we search for an `extReq` attribute. Once we find that, we grab it using the giant string gathered via trial and error. I'm actually surprised that Ruby doesn't have any helper methods to get that data. The chained value and the first calls are really ugly!

Then we check whether our extension has the right object ID (`oid`). An `oid` is an element of the SSL certificate request that contains information. Every field is contained within an `oid`. In this case, it is one of the Puppet `oid` values that is used for a pre-shared key. We save it in a variable.

Finally, we compare that value to our secret key, `banana`, and exit with the exit code `0` if it matches. This tells Puppet to sign the certificate. Otherwise, we exit in a negative manner, which is by using any exit code other than zero; we use 1 in our case.

Now that we have a script, we need to configure our master to use it. To do so, edit the `Puppet.conf` file on the master. Add the following line under the `[master]` subsection:

    autosign = /etc/puppet/autosign-policy.rb

We also have to make the policy script executable. To do so, issue this:

sudo chmod a+x /etc/puppet/autosign-policy.rb

Securing Puppet

Now that we've set up the master, let's deal with some housekeeping. Rather than reprovision the master, we'll simply clean the certificates off the master and both of the agents. To do this, issue the following commands on the master:

```
sudo puppet cert clean agentone.book.local
sudo puppet cert clean agenttwo.book.local
sudo rm /var/lib/puppet/ssl/ca/requests/*
sudo service puppetmaster restart
```

One or more of these commands may throw an error. That's okay; we're just being thorough. Next, let's destroy the agents so that our provisioner can add the secret key to one of them. Issue the following commands on the host:

```
vagrant destroy agentone
vagrant destroy agenttwo
```

Now, we'll create the magic for the agent systems. In the Vagrant directory, create a file called `secret.yaml`, containing the following:

```
---
extension_requests:
  pp_preshared_key: banana
```

> More information on the SSL extensions supported by Puppet can be found at https://docs.puppetlabs.com/puppet/latest/reference/ssl_attributes_extensions.html#data-location-and-format.

We'll modify our Vagrant provisioner on one of our hosts to copy that file to the correct location on the agent system. To do so, modify the `agentone` (ao) section of the `Vagrantfile`, and add the following after the first shell provisioner:

```
ao.vm.provision "shell", inline: "cp /vagrant/secret.yaml /etc/puppet/csr_attributes.yaml"
```

Note that this should be on one line.

Go ahead and start `agentone` and `agenttwo` using the following commands:

```
vagrant up agentone
vagrant up agenttwo
```

Once they're up, we'll need to run Puppet on each of the nodes. When running on `agentone`, you should see a somewhat more interesting output than before. It should look something like this:

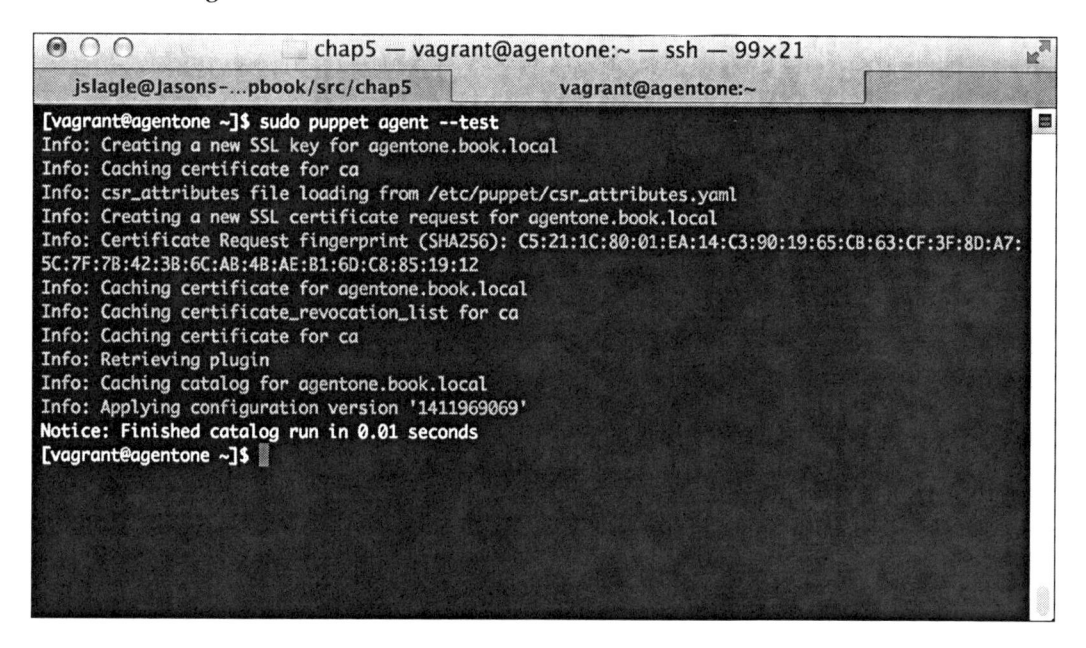

```
[vagrant@agentone ~]$ sudo puppet agent --test
Info: Creating a new SSL key for agentone.book.local
Info: Caching certificate for ca
Info: csr_attributes file loading from /etc/puppet/csr_attributes.yaml
Info: Creating a new SSL certificate request for agentone.book.local
Info: Certificate Request fingerprint (SHA256): C5:21:1C:80:01:EA:14:C3:90:19:65:CB:63:CF:3F:8D:A7:5C:7F:7B:42:3B:6C:AB:4B:AE:B1:6D:C8:85:19:12
Info: Caching certificate for agentone.book.local
Info: Caching certificate_revocation_list for ca
Info: Caching certificate for ca
Info: Retrieving plugin
Info: Caching catalog for agentone.book.local
Info: Applying configuration version '1411969069'
Notice: Finished catalog run in 0.01 seconds
[vagrant@agentone ~]$
```

As you can see, Puppet picked up our additional attributes. Once they were included, the agent signed the certificate.

Now, run the Puppet agent on `agenttwo`. You should see the old, familiar `waitforcert` message, as we did not install the extra attributes on `agenttwo`.

This is a somewhat simplistic example, but it shows all the building blocks used to build a policy-based signing system. The pre-shared key example can be extended to have multiple keys.

Additionally, you could check whether this is a valid instance on the cloud, for example. We could do this by having our policy script query our cloud provider's API to look for information on the instance requesting the certificate signing.

Summary

Since Puppet is so integral to the environment and has the ability to change the configuration of any system, it is vital that we protect it from potential attacks.

Luckily, the default out-of-the-box configuration is very secure. However, if we wish to approach advanced scenarios or extend Puppet, we might get into situations that warrant changing defaults.

Additionally, as our environment grows and becomes more complex, it makes sense to start to investigate ways to automate Puppet itself. Autosign has many tools available to make this easier for us.

Now that we've secured the Puppet Master software, in the next chapter, we'll move on to examine how community-contributed modules can help us with security, as well as getting us up to speed quicker. Then we'll move on to cover network security, which can be used to further restrict access to our Puppet master, thus further securing it.

6
Community Modules for Security

An open source tool is only as good as its community, and Puppet has a great one. Now that we've covered the basics and you have a functional Puppet setup, including reporting, we'll move on to how you can quickly improve that infrastructure. In many ways, the communities behind Puppet, right from the users to the vendors and sponsors, are what set Puppet apart from its competitors.

In this chapter, we will explore community-maintained modules that assist with security. There are a great number of modules available, so we'll try to focus on some that have good benefits or a module structure to model your own modules on. In particular, we'll cover the following in this chapter:

- The importance of the Puppet Forge
- The `augeasprovider` module by herculesteam, which allows you to use augeas to manage a variety of files in a native Puppet manner
- The `CIS` module by arildjensen, which allows you to apply most of the Center for Internet Security standards to a machine
- The `sudo` module by saz, used to manage `sudo`
- The `hiera-eyaml` gem, used to encrypt data in Hiera

By the end of this chapter, we should have a good toolkit to harden our hosts. Additionally, we'll have good understanding of where to go to look for modules.

The Puppet Forge

The Puppet Forge is a website run by Puppet Labs. It was born as a methodology for system administrators and developers using Puppet to share their Puppet modules with others. It can be found at `http://forge.puppetlabs.com`.

Over the years, the Forge has seen many improvements, in both its function as well as the number of modules available.

At the time of writing this book, there are more than 3,000 modules on the Forge. These modules include configuration of everything from MySQL to the Apache web server. Like many community projects, however, the quality and support of these modules varies.

In the early days of the Forge, it was like the wild west. Many modules were posted, but there were very lax standards on quality, and it was unknown whether a given module would work on your OS.

On the quality front, the community and Puppet Labs have done a great job at encouraging the community to adapt a set of standards and design patterns around modules. This allows things such as Hiera to work in a predictable manner, and the old habit of forking a module to make very minor changes is much less prevalent.

However, the problem of compatibility with both Puppet versions as well as various operating systems still existed. To solve that, the Puppet Forge introduced additional module metadata that can express those properties.

With the most recent modules on the Forge, you can quickly see which versions of Puppet and operating systems are supported.

We'll go on a brief tour of the Forge before looking at a few select modules. The Forge itself is pretty easy to use, so we'll keep this brief. The following screenshot shows the Forge home screen:

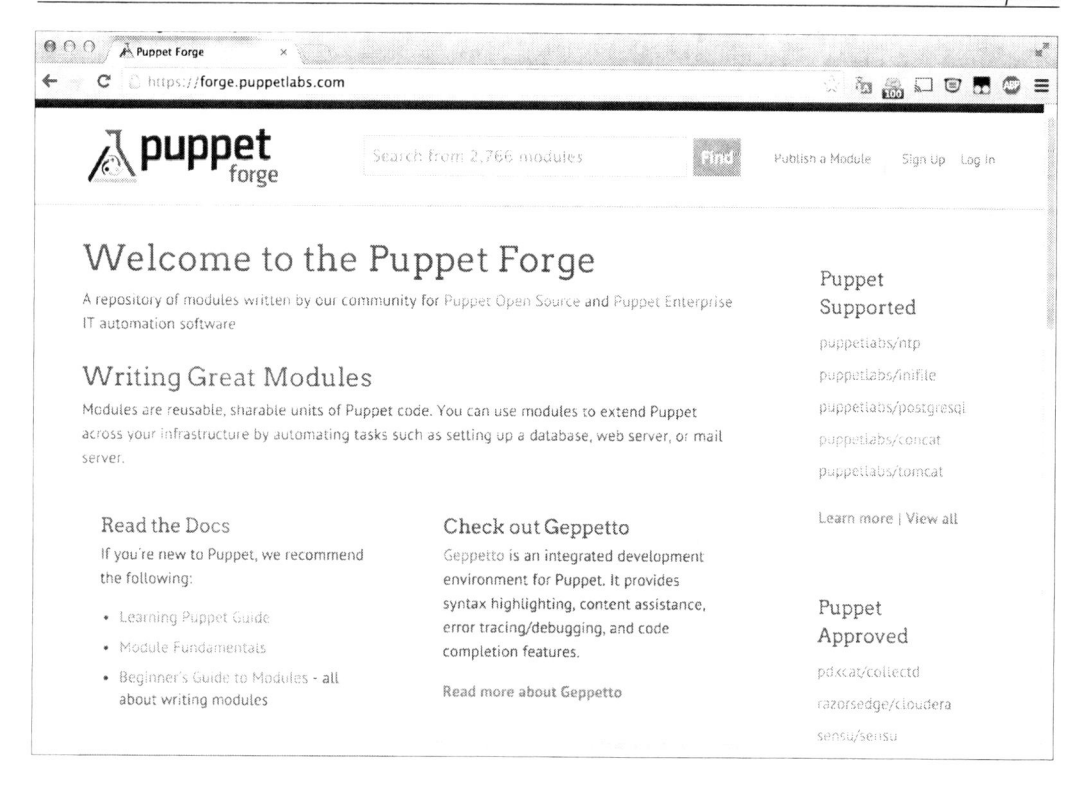

The preceding screenshot shows how the front page of the Forge currently looks. We'll include some additional features further down the page later, but this is the meat of the page.

At the top of the page, you'll see a search box. This allows you to perform searches based on keywords, authors, or metadata.

The main section of the page on the main site contains news and other information. At the time of writing this book, it contained documentation about how to write a good module. This contains some best practices and procedures used to produce reusable modules.

The section to the right contains two new areas. They are the **Puppet Supported** and **Puppet Approved** modules.

The **Puppet Supported** modules are all the modules that are maintained by Puppet Labs. These are fully supported under Puppet Enterprise. This means that when issues are found with these modules, you can use the Puppet Labs support resources to assist you with them.

Community Modules for Security

All of these modules have very good platform coverage, as well as good design patterns. Other than being great modules overall, they serve as a good place to get guidance on design for your own modules.

The **Puppet Approved** modules were announced at PuppetConf 2014. These are modules that are of exceptional quality, and while not officially supported, they are some of the best modules available. They tend to have good platform support and adhere to the current best practices.

At the bottom of the page are sections that contain information on recent releases as well as a leaderboard of the top contributors.

Once you search for modules, you'll receive a results screen that has some more options worth pointing out. An example of such a screen is shown here:

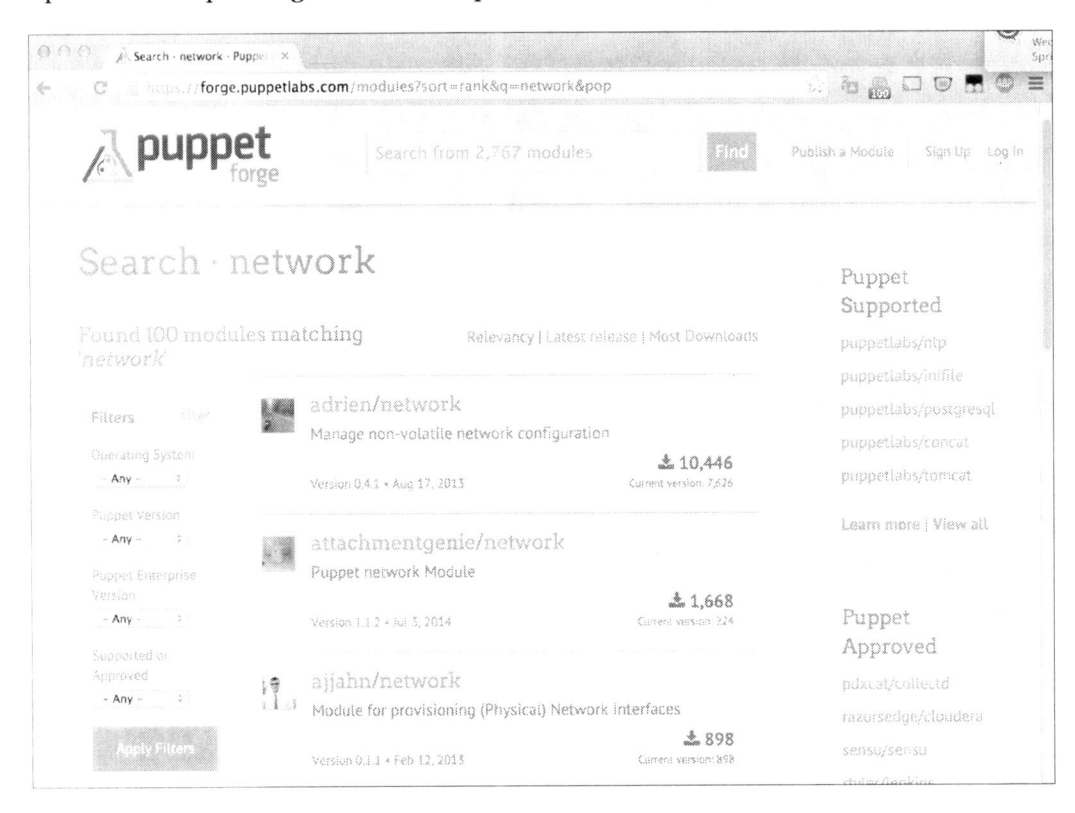

In the center of this section, you'll find the search results, but the real magic is to the left.

The filter area allows you to narrow down your search for modules. It currently works only with modules that provide metadata, but it allows you to filter by a number of options.

You can also search for modules using the `search` command in the modules' faces on the command line. To do this, we issue a command such as the following:

```
sudo puppet module search network
```

Replace `network` with whatever term you happen to be searching for. When we run this command, we'll see something similar to what is shown in the following screenshot, showing us some details about the modules:

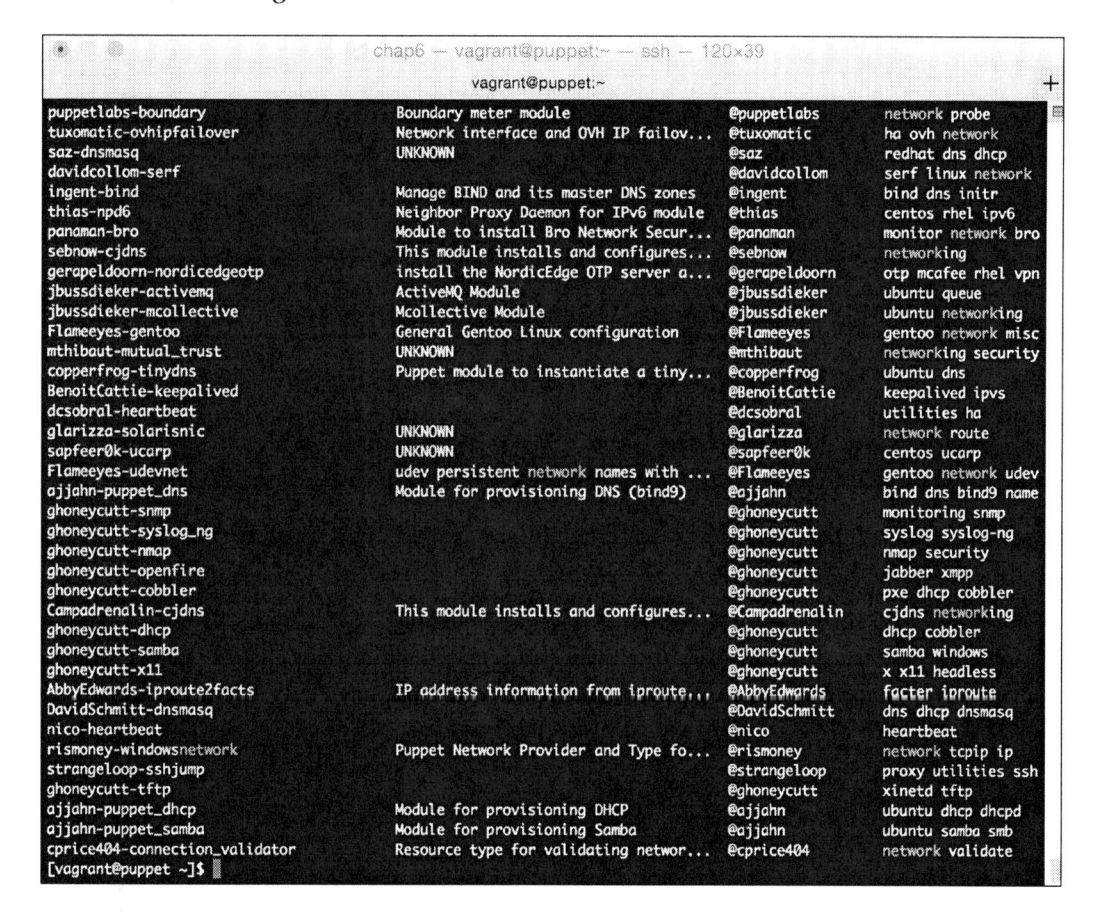

You can see that the output includes the name of the module, a short description, the name of the author, and a list of keywords that apply to the module.

Once you have identified a module, we can install it with the `puppet module` face. We've seen how to do this in previous chapters, and we'll show it later in this chapter. Additionally, instructions can also be found on any specific module page.

Now that we've explored the Forge, let's start looking at the modules we want to focus on. First up is the `augeasproviders` suite of modules.

The herculesteam/augeasproviders series of modules

The first module we'll explore is a swiss army knife of sorts. It started as a single module, but over time has become a series of modules. This is the `augeasproviders` module, originally by domcleal, but now maintained by herculesteam.

These modules use augeas to implement types and providers. Types and providers are the native Puppet interfaces for managing resources. They're written in Ruby and have considerably more power in how they manage the underlying resources compared to the built-in Puppet types they replace. They also add additional types for many other resources such as entries in the SSH configuration file, or management of the Apache web server configuration file.

Augeas is a configuration file editing tool. It parses configuration files into an internal tree and then allows you to use commands to manipulate that tree. Once changes are made, the file can then be written back out. This allows you to modify just part of a configuration file without internally parsing the entire file.

Once in augeas, there are a set of commands that can be used to modify the configuration in the file. Sections can be added, deleted, or even rearranged.

The advantage over the native method of managing these resources as entire files is that the augeas-based providers support editing a file by several different modules. Additionally, they will leave the structure and comments in the files intact, which can ease readability and preserve OS defaults that you may not intend to change in your module.

When managing a file such as the Puppet configuration file, if separate modules need to add configuration options, coordination between those modules can become difficult. The `file_line` resource and other resources aim to address some of that, but augeas is a perfect solution to those problems.

The `augeasproviders` modules implement types and providers for more than 15 different configuration formats. Some of the more important security-related ones are as follows:

Provider	Description
`kernel_parameter`	This manages passing kernel parameters to the `grub` or `grub2` configuration files
`pam`	This manages `pam` authentication configuration
`puppet_auth`	This manages the Puppet `auth.conf` file
`shellvar`	This allows management of any shell configuration file
`sshd_config`	This manages the `sshd_config` file sections
`sshd_config_subsystem`	This manages the SSH subsystems such as SFTP
`sysctl`	This allows Linux `sysctl` management
`syslog`	This allows management of the `syslog` configuration

These providers expose native Puppet types for the configuration in question. For instance, let's look at an example of using the `puppet_auth` type based on work performed in the last chapter. As you may recall, we added the following entry to `auth.conf`:

```
path ~ ^/file_(metadata|content)s?/agentone/
allow agentone.book.local
```

We can handle that using the `augeasproviders` type by adding a resource like the following to a Puppet manifest:

```
puppet_auth { 'Allow agentone':
  ensure          => present,
  path            => '^/file_(metadata|content)s?/agentone/',
  path_regex      => true,
  allow           => 'agentone.book.local',
  authenticated   => 'yes',
  ins_before      => 'path[allow][. = "/file"]',
}
```

By using these resources, you can build the authentication configuration in a much more automated fashion than managing the file as a whole. Using the power of exported resources, you could even have various modules register needed mount points.

This and many of the other modules in this series are very popular. Much more information can be found at the website of the module, http://augeasproviders.com.

Let's look at a more complete example for securing SSH.

Managing SSH with augeasproviders

Managing the SSH configuration of a host is often done with just a template or a flat file. However, as the configuration gets more complex, it makes sense to try to manage this in a more organized fashion.

This also has the advantage of being more flexible, as noted earlier. You could have a development server role that allows users to log in with passwords, while your main production server only allows for key-based login. Doing this with file-based management involves using facts and variables to determine this at the time the template would be written, which can be very difficult to do correctly.

To do this, we'll use the `sshd_config` type and provider from the `augeasproviders` module. We perform the following steps:

1. Let's go ahead and start up our VM. We can start where we left off at the end of the previous chapter, or use the code included with the book and follow along.
2. In either case, let's go ahead and use `vagrant up` to start our three VMs.
3. Now, we need to get the modules needed installed on the master. Let's go ahead and install the module. We'll only install the `sshd_config` module instead of the entire suite.
4. To do so, on the Puppet Master, issue the following command:

   ```
   sudo puppet module install herculesteam-augeasproviders_ssh
   ```

Once complete, the output is as follows:

```
Notice: Preparing to install into /etc/puppet/modules ...
Notice: Downloading from https://forgeapi.puppetlabs.com ...
Notice: Installing -- do not interrupt ...
/etc/puppet/modules
└─┬ herculesteam-augeasproviders_ssh (v2.0.0)
  └─┬ herculesteam-augeasproviders_core (v2.0.1)
    └── puppetlabs-stdlib (v4.3.2)
[vagrant@puppet ~]$
```

As you can see, it installed two additional modules. The first is the `augeasproviders_core` module, which contains some methods used by the other modules. It also includes `stdlib`, which much like the C standard library contains a series of useful utility functions, such as validation functions for parameters and various type conversion functions.

Once these modules are installed, we can start to configure our `sshd_config` module.

Remember way back in *Chapter 1, Puppet as a Security Tool*, we made some changes to the `sshd_config` file in order to prevent root login and set the maximum authentication attempts. We're going to re-implement these changes via this module. This allows us to more easily create per host configurations, and use methods such as exporting resources to manage the configuration.

To begin, let's dust off our old `openssh` module from *Chapter 1, Puppet as a Security Tool*. We'll modify that module to use the `augeasproviders` module instead of using the flat file.

First, let's go ahead and remove the `files` directory from that earlier module and start to modify the `init.pp` file to manage this. As previously mentioned, we'd usually use multiple files for the manifest. We will look at a complete example at the end of this section.

Go ahead and edit the `init.pp` file from that same module and delete the file-related sections of the module, leaving the content looking as follows:

```
class openssh {
  package { 'openssh-server':
    ensure => 'latest',
  }
  service { 'sshd':
    ensure => 'running',
  }
}
```

Now we can go ahead and start using the `augeasproviders` types to modify the existing configuration. Between the package and the service, let's add our commands to the manifest to manage just the SSH configuration settings we are concerned with.

Where the file section of the manifest was present, let's add the following:

```
sshd_config { 'PermitRootLogin':
  value   => 'no',
  notify  => Service['sshd'],
  require => Package['openssh-server'],
}

sshd_config { 'MaxAuthTries':
  value   => '3',
  notify  => Service['sshd'],
  require => Package['openssh-server'],
}
```

Notice how we also moved the dependency information into our configuration stanza. This eliminates the need to use the dependency chain we had in the file before, which is why it was removed in the preceding code.

Now, let's add it to our default manifest so it'll run on our agent nodes. Edit the `/etc/puppet/manifests/site.pp` file. Add the following lines:

```
node default {
  include openssh
}
```

Now, we need to run our code on one of our agent boxes. Connect to `agentone` and run Puppet. Remember to sign the certificate if necessary — see *Chapter 5, Securing Puppet*, if you need a reminder of how that works.

Once that is complete, you'll see a whole bunch of plugins get synced down to the client, and when it completes, the output will look like the following:

```
'{md5}094ac110ce9f7a5b16d0c80a0cf2243c'
Notice: /File[/var/lib/puppet/lib/puppet/provider/sshd_config]/ensure: created
Notice: /File[/var/lib/puppet/lib/puppet/provider/sshd_config/augeas.rb]/ensure: defined content as
 '{md5}ec5a1970f4f44e08e266d62d138f0e94'
Notice: /File[/var/lib/puppet/lib/puppet/parser/functions/getvar.rb]/ensure: defined content as '{m
d5}10bf744212947bc6a7bfd2c9836dbd23'
Notice: /File[/var/lib/puppet/lib/puppet/parser/functions/strftime.rb]/ensure: defined content as '
{md5}e02e01a598ca5d7d6eee0ba22440304a'
Notice: /File[/var/lib/puppet/lib/puppet/parser/functions/chop.rb]/ensure: defined content as '{md5
}4691a56e6064b792ed4575e4ad3f3d20'
Notice: /File[/var/lib/puppet/lib/puppet/parser/functions/is_float.rb]/ensure: defined content as '
{md5}10e0d3ecf75fac15e415aee79acf70dc'
Notice: /File[/var/lib/puppet/lib/puppet/parser/functions/parsejson.rb]/ensure: defined content as
'{md5}e7f968c34928107b84cd0860daf50ab1'
Notice: /File[/var/lib/puppet/lib/puppet/parser/functions/validate_cmd.rb]/ensure: defined content
as '{md5}78fd21cb3fc52efc3b53ba2b3301de18'
Info: Loading facts
Info: Caching catalog for agentone.book.local
Warning: The package type's allow_virtual parameter will be changing its default value from false t
o true in a future release. If you do not want to allow virtual packages, please explicitly set all
ow_virtual to false.
   (at /usr/lib/ruby/site_ruby/1.8/puppet/type/package.rb:430:in `default')
Info: Applying configuration version '1412816843'
Notice: /Stage[main]/Openssh/Sshd_config[MaxAuthTries]/ensure: created
Info: /Stage[main]/Openssh/Sshd_config[MaxAuthTries]: Scheduling refresh of Service[sshd]
Notice: /Stage[main]/Openssh/Sshd_config[PermitRootLogin]/ensure: created
Info: /Stage[main]/Openssh/Sshd_config[PermitRootLogin]: Scheduling refresh of Service[sshd]
Notice: /Stage[main]/Openssh/Service[sshd]: Triggered 'refresh' from 2 events
Info: Creating state file /var/lib/puppet/state/state.yaml
Notice: Finished catalog run in 1.25 seconds
[vagrant@agentone ~]$
```

As you can see, we've now made the changes to the configuration file. As a test, go ahead and modify one of the other configuration items in `/etc/ssh/sshd_config`. Additionally, change `MaxAuthTries` to a higher value such as `8`. Run Puppet again, and notice it only changes the one value back, like the following:

```
[vagrant@agentone ~]$ sudo puppet agent --test
Info: Retrieving plugin
Info: Loading facts
Info: Caching catalog for agentone.book.local
Warning: The package type's allow_virtual parameter will be changing its default value from false to true in a future release. If you do not want to allow virtual packages, please explicitly set allow_virtual to false.
   (at /usr/lib/ruby/site_ruby/1.8/puppet/type/package.rb:430:in `default')
Info: Applying configuration version '1412816843'
Notice: /Stage[main]/Openssh/Sshd_config[MaxAuthTries]/value: value changed ['8'] to '3'
Info: /Stage[main]/Openssh/Sshd_config[MaxAuthTries]: Scheduling refresh of Service[sshd]
Notice: /Stage[main]/Openssh/Service[sshd]: Triggered 'refresh' from 1 events
Notice: Finished catalog run in 0.66 seconds
[vagrant@agentone ~]$
```

As you can imagine, that's pretty powerful, since we can keep the OS level settings and just change what we need changed. You can also move logic relating to configuration into the module that uses it, as opposed to trying to centralize it in the module writing a monolithic configuration file. You can parameterize the values of the various pieces of the configuration using this method as well, either using the traditional approach of creating a parameter for each tunable, as I do in the module referenced in the following section, or using the newer `augeasproviders` instances class, which allows you to pass an entire hash of augeas configuration data into the module. More information on that can be found at the URL for augeas provided in the preceding section.

> For a more complete example of a module that manages this via `augeasproviders`, see https://github.com/jmslagle/jslagle-ssh.

The arildjensen/cis module

The next module we'll take a look at is the `cis` module by arildjensen. This module implements the Center for Internet Security benchmark standard for RHEL 6. In terms of support, this module lags a bit since it only supports Red Hat 6-based operating systems. However, it can serve as a great base for building your own module for another Unix-/Linux-like operating system.

The CIS benchmarks are a set of configuration standards that establish a baseline or benchmark for a secure system. It is a widely used and accepted set of standards, referenced in the PCI DSS standards and others.

The CIS benchmarks exist for a variety of operating systems and applications, including VMware, Apache Tomcat, and others.

> For more information on the CIS benchmarks, see `http://benchmarks.cisecurity.org/downloads/benchmarks/`.

The `arildjensen/cis` module implements the security benchmark for Red Hat 6 systems. It implements each of the individual controls as facts or manifests. We'll look at an example of its use.

Out of the box, the module contains a module that enables all of the controls. This module is called a composition module that merely includes all of the other needed classes to enable the controls in question. In many cases, this is sufficient, but it can also be used as a basis for creating a custom limited set of controls in your own composition module. This is just a normal Puppet module that includes the classes (in this case, the individual controls) we are concerned with.

We'll look at an example of doing that now. First we need to get the module installed. To do that, we use what should be a familiar process by now. Issue the following command on the Puppet Master:

```
sudo puppet module install arildjensen-cis
```

We'll see the familiar output:

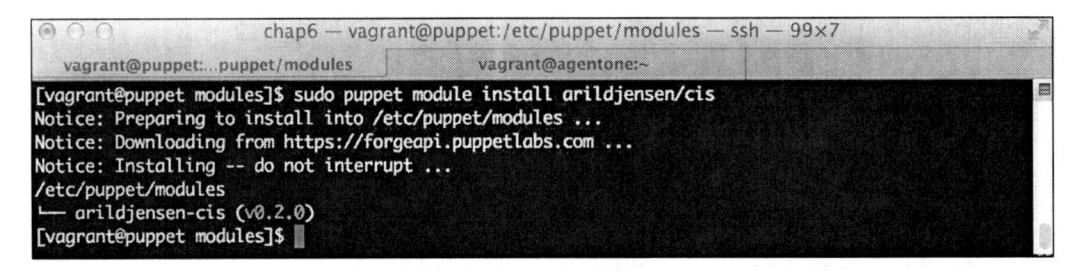

```
[vagrant@puppet modules]$ sudo puppet module install arildjensen/cis
Notice: Preparing to install into /etc/puppet/modules ...
Notice: Downloading from https://forgeapi.puppetlabs.com ...
Notice: Installing -- do not interrupt ...
/etc/puppet/modules
└── arildjensen-cis (v0.2.0)
[vagrant@puppet modules]$
```

Now that it's installed, we'll go ahead and build our own custom composition module using this module.

For our exercise, we'll choose just a small handful of the controls. There are nine different sections of the benchmark, each with a varying number of controls. Going through each one for our exercise here would easily take the rest of the chapter, so we'll build a small subset.

For our example, we'll configure the settings from section 2 and section 4.2 of the CIS benchmarks document. A link to that document is found later in the chapter. This will give us sufficient controls to see how the module works and see it in action. In production, you would want to review the CIS benchmarks and see which of the benchmarks you would apply.

We'll build our own module to do this. So, let's start by creating a module scaffold.

First, let's create the module. Issue the following command in the Vagrant home directory on the master to create a module scaffold:

`puppet module generate pupbook-ourcis`

You can accept the defaults for pretty much everything. You can add a description if you wish, and set the other fields to N/A.

Next, let's modify the metadata to add the dependency. Edit the metadata.json file and make the dependency section look like the following:

```
"dependencies": [
  {"version_requirement":">= 1.0.0","name":"puppetlabs-stdlib"},
  {"version_requirement":">= 0.2.0","name":"arildjensen-cis"}
]
```

Now, let's handle our init.pp file. In this case, it's just going to include all of the CIS module files that we need. When complete, it should look as follows:

```
class ourcis {
  include cis::el6::2_1_1    # Remove telnet server
  include cis::el6::2_1_2    # Remove telnet client
  include cis::el6::2_1_3    # Remove rsh server
  include cis::el6::2_1_4    # Remove rsh client
  include cis::el6::2_1_5    # Remove NFS client
  include cis::el6::2_1_6    # Remove NIS server
  include cis::el6::2_1_7    # Remove tftp
  include cis::el6::2_1_8    # Remove tftp server
  include cis::el6::2_1_9    # Remove talk
  include cis::el6::2_1_10   # Remove talk server
  include cis::el6::2_1_11   # Remove xinetd
  include cis::el6::2_1_12   # Disable chargen UDP
  include cis::el6::2_1_13   # Disable chargen TCP
  include cis::el6::2_1_14   # Disable daytime UDP
  include cis::el6::2_1_15   # Disable daytime TCP
  include cis::el6::2_1_16   # Disable echo UDP
  include cis::el6::2_1_17   # Disable echo TCP
  include cis::el6::2_1_18   # Disable tcpmux server
  include cis::el6::4_2_1    # Disable source routed packets
  include cis::el6::4_2_2    # Disable ICMP redirect
  include cis::el6::4_2_3    # Disable Seucure ICMP redirect
```

Community Modules for Security

```
        include cis::el6::4_2_4   # Log suspicious packets
        include cis::el6::4_2_5   # Ignore broadcasts
        include cis::el6::4_2_6   # Ignore bogus ICMP
        include cis::el6::4_2_7   # Enable source validation
        include cis::el6::4_2_8   # Enable SYN cookies
}
```

Save the file. The preceding code just includes the main module. Then, copy the entire module to the modules tree. Remember we'll need to rename it to just be `ourcis`. You can use the following command to do so:

```
sudo cp -a pupbook-ourcis /etc/puppet/modules/ourcis
```

And now let's apply it to our default node. Add an `include` line for our module there as follows:

```
include ourcis
```

Now for the big reveal. We'll go ahead and run Puppet on one of our agent nodes using `sudo puppet agent --test`. It will sync over a bunch of additional facts and then run. Once it completes, the output will look as follows:

```
-kernel.msgmax = 65536
-
-# Controls the maximum shared segment size, in bytes
-kernel.shmmax = 68719476736
-
-# Controls the maximum number of shared memory segments, in pages
-kernel.shmall = 4294967296
+fs.suid_dumpable = 0
+kernel.exec-shield = 1
+kernel.randomize_va_space = 2
+net.ipv4.conf.all.send_redirects=0
+net.ipv4.conf.default.send_redirects=0
+net.ipv4.conf.all.accept_source_route=0
+net.ipv4.conf.all.accept_redirects=0
+net.ipv4.conf.all.secure_redirects=0
+net.ipv4.conf.all.log_martians=1
+net.ipv4.conf.default.accept_redirects=0
+net.ipv4.conf.default.secure_redirects=0
+net.ipv4.icmp_echo_ignore_broadcasts=1
+net.ipv4.icmp_ignore_bogus_error_messages=1
+net.ipv4.conf.all.rp_filter=1
+net.ipv4.tcp_max_syn_backlog=4096

Info: Computing checksum on file /etc/sysctl.conf
Info: /Stage[main]/Cis::Linuxcontrols::C0015/File[/etc/sysctl.conf]: Filebucketed /etc/sysctl.conf to puppet with sum c97839af771c8447b9fc23090b4e8d0f
Notice: /Stage[main]/Cis::Linuxcontrols::C0015/File[/etc/sysctl.conf]/content: content changed '{md5}c97839af771c8447b9fc23090b4e8d0f' to '{md5}9b41067bf1924c1cd4df7fbe1f2c5100'
Notice: /Stage[main]/Cis::Linuxcontrols::C0015/File[/etc/sysctl.conf]/mode: mode changed '0644' to '0640'
Notice: Finished catalog run in 42.42 seconds
[vagrant@agentone ~]$
```

And ta-da! It has enforced the required parts of the CIS benchmarks.

This module makes it very quick to get a system up to speed with the benchmarks. It could fairly easily be extended to handle other operating systems using the generic Linux controls. The abstraction is a bit odd, so it'll take some work to untangle, but it's much easier than starting from scratch.

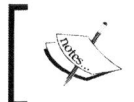

> For more information on the `puppet-cis` module, refer to the following link:
> https://forge.puppetlabs.com/arildjensen/cis

Now we'll take a look at the `sudo` module to handle configuring your `sudoers` file.

The saz/sudo module

The next module on our module examination journey is the `saz/sudo` module. This module presents a great methodology to manage the `sudoers` file. It is actually used by a large number of other modules for `sudoers` file management.

The module itself is fairly simple, so this section will be short as we go over it.

The `sudo` module manages all aspects of your `sudoers` configuration, which can catch some people by surprise. The module has options to leave the system configuration alone, as well as not purging unmanaged `sudoers` entries. The recommended path is to manage all the `sudoer` resources; however, the options are there if needed.

To install the `sudoers` module, we'll issue the following command:

```
sudo puppet module install saz-sudo
```

We'll now create a few simple rules. But, before we do so, we need to take a look at the `/etc/sudoers` file. If you look at it, at the very bottom, you'll see an entry for Vagrant. We must make sure we preserve this entry or we will cause Vagrant to stop working. This entry is what Vagrant uses to do system provisioning.

That being said, the most prudent course of action is to implement the current system rules before we add anything custom.

Community Modules for Security

This is another situation where normally we'd use a module. However, for simplicity, we're just going to add the rules into the `site.pp` file. This allows us to quickly model the desired configuration for the book. However, in production, that does not scale very far, so just don't do it. Your co-workers will thank you.

Let's edit our `site.pp` file and add rules that match the current `sudoers` file. We need to add a single rule since there is one non-default entry present in the `sudoers` file. The first entry is a default system entry that allows `root` to use `sudo`. The other is the custom entry that Vagrant uses. They are as follows:

```
root    ALL=(ALL)       ALL
vagrant ALL=(ALL)       NOPASSWD: ALL
```

In addition, the Vagrant configuration requires that we have the required TTY setting set to `false` for the Vagrant user using `sudo`. This is not the default on Red Hat-based systems because it can allow for unsafe practices if a user executes `sudo` over a non-interactive SSH session. However, since Vagrant is relying on passwordless `sudo` to do its provisioning, we must allow that user to use `sudo` with no TTY. We'll need to account for this in our configuration also.

Recreating this in the `sudo` module turns out to be fairly simple. Add the following to the `site.pp` file:

```
include sudo
sudo::conf { 'vagrant':
  content => "Defaults:vagrant !requiretty\nvagrant ALL=(ALL) NOPASSWD: ALL",
}
```

The Vagrant content line should be contained on a single line.

Once it's done, run Puppet. It will change a variety of files, and when complete, give output similar to the following:

```
# Preserving HOME has security implications since many programs
-# use it when searching for configuration files. Note that HOME
-# is already set when the the env_reset option is enabled, so
-# this option is only effective for configurations where either
-# env_reset is disabled or HOME is present in the env_keep list.
+# use it when searching for configuration files.
#
Defaults    always_set_home

@@ -116,4 +113,3 @@

## Read drop-in files from /etc/sudoers.d (the # here does not mean a comment)
#includedir /etc/sudoers.d
-vagrant      ALL=(ALL)      NOPASSWD: ALL

Info: Computing checksum on file /etc/sudoers
Info: /Stage[main]/Sudo/File[/etc/sudoers]: Filebucketed /etc/sudoers to puppet with sum 411c45100714188d6d40a3298a299bb3
Notice: /Stage[main]/Sudo/File[/etc/sudoers]/content: content changed '{md5}411c45100714188d6d40a3298a299bb3' to '{md5}4093e52552d97099d003c645f15f9372'
Notice: /Stage[main]/Main/Node[default]/Sudo::Conf[root]/File[10_root]/ensure: created
Info: /Stage[main]/Main/Node[default]/Sudo::Conf[root]/File[10_root]: Scheduling refresh of Exec[sudo-syntax-check for file /etc/sudoers.d/10_root]
Notice: /Stage[main]/Main/Node[default]/Sudo::Conf[vagrant]/File[10_vagrant]/ensure: created
Info: /Stage[main]/Main/Node[default]/Sudo::Conf[vagrant]/File[10_vagrant]: Scheduling refresh of Exec[sudo-syntax-check for file /etc/sudoers.d/10_vagrant]
Notice: /Stage[main]/Main/Node[default]/Sudo::Conf[vagrant]/Exec[sudo-syntax-check for file /etc/sudoers.d/10_vagrant]: Triggered 'refresh' from 1 events
Notice: /Stage[main]/Main/Node[default]/Sudo::Conf[root]/Exec[sudo-syntax-check for file /etc/sudoers.d/10_root]: Triggered 'refresh' from 1 events
Notice: Finished catalog run in 1.81 seconds
[vagrant@agentone ~]$
```

Notice that the Vagrant entry was removed from the file (see the - entry); however, we added a new file called `10_vagrant`. This contained the rule we created in the preceding manifest.

It's worth noting that we could have used the `config_file_replace` option in the `sudoers` class to tell the module to not replace the default configuration file. In this case, adding our entry for Vagrant would have been unnecessary. Replacing the file has the advantage of ensuring that this important security-related file is consistent on all of your systems.

Now that we have the base down, we'll add one more `sudo` rule to the file. In this case, we'll allow the Puppet user to run `puppet agent -test` without a password. We might use this rule in the case of having an automated system that populates the Puppet repository once tests pass. In this case, you would want to be able to force a Puppet run on a child system. The `sudo` rule to do this looks like the following:

```
puppet ALL=NOPASSWD: /usr/bin/puppet, /usr/local/bin/puppet
```

To translate that to a `sudo` manifest item, the content just becomes the preceding code. As such, you end up with the following:

```
sudo::conf { 'puppet_puppet':
  content => 'puppet ALL=NOPASSWD: /usr/bin/puppet, /usr/local/bin/puppet',
}
```

Note that the content line should be one line.

When you run it, you will see the appropriate file appear under the `/etc/sudoers.d/` directory.

Using that methodology, we can pragmatically manage our `sudoers` files to ensure the records we want on a host are present, and in most cases, only those items. This is a huge benefit from a compliance standpoint. Even if someone adds an entry, it will be removed at the next Puppet run.

> If you want more information on this module, it can be found at https://forge.puppetlabs.com/saz/sudo. It contains documentation on the module as well as some examples.

The hiera-eyaml gem

The last module we're going to look at in this chapter is not a module at all. It's actually a gem that installs an extension for Hiera.

As you recall from earlier, Hiera is a hierarchical data store which allows us to separate our data from our code. For instance, it lets us move the NTP servers we're using out of the manifests.

It supports a wide variety of methods to create a hierarchy, which allows us to supplement or override configuration data needed by various modules.

In fact, several of the modules we've looked at earlier in this chapter have great Hiera bindings. Modules with strong Hiera bindings are constructed in a manner that allows the configuration of the main class to be passed in as parameters. Puppet can query Hiera to get the values of these parameters, allowing us to override them without changing Puppet code.

Of the modules covered in this chapter, CIS can use Hiera to configure items such as log servers or NTP servers. The `sudo` module allows configuration of the `sudoers` file completely within Hiera by overriding and extending certain values.

One of the downfalls of Hiera out of the box is that it does not present a good way to handle secure data as the value is stored in files unencrypted. A compromise of that data store, which is likely present in version control, could lead to a compromise of sensitive data such as keys.

There have been a couple of attempts to solve the secret data problem. The first was `hiera-gpg`. It allows you to GPG encrypt an entire Hiera data file.

While this solved the secret data problem, it came with manageability issues. Without decrypting the file, you couldn't easily tell what keys were present in the file. It also made tracking changes difficult. Finally, it was tricky to set up and use, involving getting GPG set up and working and manually encrypting files. Additionally, since all of the entries were encrypted, it was not easy to separate our duties. If you had access to decrypt the file to edit it, you would be able to edit every entry in the file.

The `hiera-eyaml` module was created to address some of these issues. It uses an inline encryption algorithm that allows the non-secret parts of the files to stay in plain text. It also comes with utility commands to decrypt the file and launch an editor. For these reasons, it is much easier to use than `gpg-yaml`.

We'll show a short example of its use here, but to do so we need to set up Hiera first.

Since Puppet 3, Hiera has become a built-in default for Puppet data. Therefore, to use it, we only need to create the appropriate data file.

To do so, let's create the directory where we'll store our data files. Run the following command:

```
sudo mkdir /etc/puppet/hieradata
```

Now, we'll create the configuration file. To do so, we'll edit `/etc/puppet/hiera.yaml` and add the following contents:

```
---
:backends:
  - yaml
:yaml:
  :datadir: /etc/puppet/hieradata
:hierarchy:
  - "%{::fqdn}"
  - common
```

This will configure Puppet to use the directory we created previously as the data directory, and enable two levels of the hierarchy: they are the FQDN of the host and then a common file. We now need to restart the Puppet Master with `sudo service puppetmaster restart`.

Community Modules for Security

To demonstrate Hiera's use, let's make a quick module that takes a single parameter. To keep it brief, we'll just show the command and then the edits.

First run the following:

```
puppet module generate pupbook-hieraexample
```

In this case, we can accept all the defaults. We'll edit the `init.pp` file and make it look as follows:

```
class hieraexample($secret = 'nope' {
  file { '/tmp/secret':
    ensure  => present,
    content => $secret,
  }
}
```

This will simply write a file with the content out. Copy the module into the `/etc/puppet/modules` directory named `hieraexample`. Now we need to add it to our `site.pp` file. Edit the `/etc/puppet/manifests/site.pp` file and include the new module with `include hieraexample`.

Let's run it on the master and see what happens. Since we've not run on the master yet, you'll see a bunch of things run when you run it. Once complete, if you check the content of the `/tmp/secret` file, it should contain our default, the word `nope`.

Now, let's make a Hiera common data file to contain a more appropriate value. Edit `/etc/puppet/data/common.yaml` and make it look like this:

```
---
hieraexample::secret: "yup"
```

Now, rerun Puppet again and you should see that it changed a file. The contents of the file will now also contain the word `yup`. This is really cool, as now we don't need to keep that data in our manifests or modules.

Moving on, we now need to install the `hiera-eyaml` plugin and configure it for use. Let's start by installing the gem on our Puppet Master machine. We'll use Puppet to install the gem for us, additionally demonstrating that Puppet has the ability to handle package installation via gem. To do so, issue the following:

```
sudo puppet resource package hiera-eyaml ensure=installed provider=gem
```

Here we used the Puppet `resource` face to create a command-line-based resource for our package, passing the arguments we needed to get it installed. This can be useful as it can abstract away package installation if you handle a variety of operating systems such as Solaris and Linux. As long as you know the package name, and it's present in a default repository, Puppet can install it.

When complete, this will output information on the package, which should show the version that was installed.

We need to do some key generation. Let's go ahead and do that using the following commands:

```
eyaml createkeys
sudo cp -a keys /etc/puppet/
sudo chown -R puppet:puppet /etc/puppet/keys
sudo chmod 0400 /etc/puppet/keys/*.pem
sudo chmod 0500 /etc/puppet/keys
```

This will copy the keys to a suitable location and then secure them. If you were using version control, you would want to exclude the keys directory from being added to version control to protect the private key.

Now we need to make our Hiera setup use our new super fancy encrypted backend. To do so, edit `/etc/puppet/hiera.yaml` and make it look as follows:

```
---
:backends:
  - eyaml
  - yaml
:yaml:
  :datadir: /etc/puppet/data
:eyaml:
  :datadir: /etc/puppet/data
  :pkcs7_private_key: /etc/puppet/keys/private_key.pkcs7.pem
  :pkcs7_public_key: /etc/puppet/keys/public_key.pkcs7.pem
  :extension: 'yaml'
:hierarchy:
  - "%{::fqdn}"
  - common
```

The changes we made here were to include the backend. Then we configured it to use the data `datadir` as the other backend, and to use the `yaml` extension. We also had to point it at our private key.

Community Modules for Security

Now, remember we need to bounce the Puppet Master since we made changes to the `hiera.yaml` file. To do that, issue `sudo service puppetmaster restart`.

So now let's edit an encrypted Hiera data file for one of our hosts. We'll do this in our directory then copy it in.

The Hiera editor doesn't seem to support handling empty files, so first let's just use `echo` to get a header on the file, then edit it with `eyaml` by doing the following:

```
echo "---" >agentone.book.local.yaml
eyaml edit agentone.book.local.yaml
```

Now, in this file, let's edit the content to look as follows:

```
---
hieraexample::secret: DEC::PKCS7[sup3rs3kr37]!
```

Notice how we have the `DEC::PKCS7` line with brackets. The `eyaml` backend will encrypt anything present in those brackets. In this case, we're using the static text `sup3rs3kr37`.

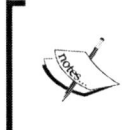

> YAML and `hiera-eyaml` also support multiline data. More information on YAML formatting, in particular how to handle multiline data, can be found at `http://www.yaml.org/spec/1.2/spec.html#id2760844`.

Once you complete editing the file, take a look at the contents. They should look similar to the following code (but they are different since we have differing keys):

```
---
hieraexample::secret:
ENC[PKCS7,MIIBeQYJKoZIhvcNAQcDoIIBajCCAWYCAQAxggEhMIIBHQIBADAFMAAC
AQEwDQYJKoZIhvcNAQEBBQAEggEAarwvO6zbXQm+8q0L5XLpkffqikvnWHGHTeynEV
NiXy/Yf8FpiMItfYPm0TDJ1AB/L6tOxBngN3Wxg0gG6OYwkNhVKi5OOUudOdKP5GNZ
aU3RcCAuJlRvcwlyZ+jCGQ9V0W7/nfiQTJ6S2muuq1CoAuqvA9GfaZLkAEUUXGSfu3
XYt5k0/adngsQxLShtn5atWgnBW9zUVmI7l2BL750svc3UUUwWPgpzfmINT4up/OyI
kFNG2ykFP0AHcdhLQt2/ALPZUDTOI68wOOOBfPFA5wkwDPyDZb1PP1hfyzfBfmZztz
mB6RNiOaUevsSI12H3HKb8vNHBCWfvPxqMRBF9HjA8BgkqhkiG9w0BBwEwHQYJYIZI
AWUDBAEqBBB98Wid9hcLrsFTbXlth47XgBDmiWtMUMlHo/DG7CS2eLVU]
```

Notice how the `DEC` part has become `ENC`, and the value has become much longer. This is the encrypted version of our preceding key.

Now, copy the file into `/etc/puppet/data`.

Let's rerun the Puppet agent on the master to see what happens. There should be no changes to the file since it's still pulling its data from the common Hiera data file.

However, when you run Puppet on `agentone` and check the contents of the `/tmp/secret` file, they should contain our secret word.

As you can see, `hiera-eyaml` presents a good solution to handle any data you don't want publicly visible. You can use it to store things like passwords and keys that you do not want publicly visible in your code repository.

> If you want more information on Hiera, please see https://docs.puppetlabs.com/hiera/1/.
> More information on `hiera-eyaml` can be found at https://github.com/TomPoulton/hiera-eyaml.

Summary

The Puppet community is a wonderful resource that can make your life much easier. When looking to automate a given piece of your infrastructure, it makes perfect sense to go look at the Forge to see if someone else has made a module to configure the application or infrastructure piece you are looking to automate.

Even if the module does not support your operating system, concentrating work on extending an existing module to support more operating systems or features betters the community as a whole.

Picking modules to review here was actually really difficult. There are so many good modules to choose from on the Forge.

To summarize, in this chapter, we explored modules that provided types and providers for use in configuring files. These modules allow us to manage things we would previously have managed as files using native Puppet types.

We then looked at the `cis` module to harden Red Hat 6 systems. This module is an example of some of the things we can use Puppet to harden on our systems.

After that, we used the `sudo` module to manage your `sudoers` files, centralizing configuration of the security-related `sudo` data.

Finally, we saw how to use the `hiera-eyaml` gem to store encrypted data on your Puppet Master.

In the next chapter, we'll look at using Puppet to handle your network security needs. We'll see you then!

Network Security and Puppet

One of the most important things to be done on a system, security-wise, is to ensure that it is safe from network-based attacks.

Ensuring that your system only listens on expected ports and controls access to services at the network level is a tedious, repetitive process. What if services could automatically open the necessary firewall rules? What if the systems running a cluster application could learn about one another and open access to just the other nodes?

With Puppet, all this is possible. We'll cover some of these cases in this chapter. We'll cover the following topics:

- Basic information in the firewall module
- The firewall type
- The firewall chain type
- Pre and post rules—what they are and how they're used
- Adding firewall rules to your own modules in an extensible way

Let's get rolling with our first topic!

Introducing the firewall module

The puppetlabs/firewall module is one of the supported modules from Puppet Labs. This means that if you run Puppet Enterprise, you can officially get support on the module on operating systems it will currently run on. At present, this includes Linux distributions. For this reason, this module is one of the best examples of modules available.

The module happens to also be one of the older ones. The current incarnation of this module dates back to early 2011. It also contains the code from an earlier iptables module that dates all the way back to 2007.

The module manages firewall rules on your host. In its current form, it can manage iptables firewalls for IPv4 and IPv6 as well as **ebtables** for Ethernet bridging and filtering support. In this chapter, we'll cover the iptables IPv4 aspects of the module, although the concepts will apply to all of the other types as well.

Iptables is the primary firewall interface on Linux hosts since kernel Version 2.4. It will eventually be replaced by nftables, having been merged into the main Linux kernel with kernel Version 3.13. However, for the moment, iptables is the primary method of implementing host-level firewall services on the Linux kernel.

We could spend the rest of the book covering iptables and host-based firewalls. Instead, we're going to cover just enough information to get you started using Puppet to manage your host base solution. More information on iptables can be found at http://netfilter.org/. There are also a number of books available on the subject, including *Designing and Implementing Linux Firewalls and QoS using netfilter, iproute2, NAT and l7-filter*, which can be found at https://www.packtpub.com/networking-and-servers/designing-and-implementing-linux-firewalls-and-qos-using-netfilter-iproute2-n.

The firewall consists of a series of chains. Each of these chains contains rules with actions. The various rules may match packets based on a variety of factors. These can be things like source and destination address or port, or even things like TCP flags. Once a packet matches a rule, an action is applied to it. These actions are things like forwarding or dropping the packet.

The puppetlabs-firewall module provides you with a series of Puppet types and providers around the firewall concept.

If you remember, Puppet types are native Ruby implementations of functionality in the Puppet core. These are extensible using custom types, of which the firewall module provides two. These two types are the firewall and firewallchain types.

Providers are particular implementations of a type. The Puppet firewall module types for firewall and firewall chains in turn have providers that implement the firewall types for both iptables and ip6tables.

These types and providers enable you to manage their firewall configuration using native puppet resources as opposed to using files and exec resources, which was previously required. This increases the flexibility of managing the firewall over using the exec type or managing files with the saved iptables rules. With types and providers, you do not need to centralize your rules or use exported resources. You can instead embed the firewall logic into the modules that need ports open.

Let's take a look at the specific types along with some examples of their use.

The firewall type

The primary type provided and used in the firewall module is the firewall type. This type contains a whole slew of parameters that allow you to configure every aspect of the firewall rules. This is necessary because the base iptables software has many options that you can pass to rules. To model rules successfully, the underlying type and provider needs to support all of the features that you can do on the command line. This results in a very large parameter set. A summary of some of the most commonly used parameters as of Version 1.2.0 are described in the following table:

Parameter	Description
action	This provides the action to be taken on the packet. This can be one of the accept parameter that allows the packets, the reject parameter that denies the packet and ends an ICMP unreachable code, or the drop parameter that silently drops the packet. These options are lowercase unlike in iptables where they are uppercase.
chain	This is the iptables chain that this rule applies to. This is only relevant to the iptables provider and requires this feature.
destination	This specifies the destination address to be matched. This can contain a CIDR range. You can negate the range by prefixing it with an exclamation point (!).
dport	This contains the destination port to match. This can also be a range or array of ports.
dst_range	This specifies the destination range. This is in x.x.x.x-y.y.y.y format, such as 10.20.20.10-10.20.20.40.
ensure	This specifies whether the given resource is present or absent. It defaults to present.
jump	For iptables, this attribute specifies the jump value. This can be LOG, QUEUE, RETURN, DNAT, SNAT, MASQUERADE, REDIRECT, or MARK. The values ACCEPT, DROP, and REJECT are used with the action parameter, not with jump in this module.
name	This provides the name of the rule. When rules are inserted, they are sorted by name. As such, they must be prepended with numbers to ensure proper ordering. For instance, rule 10-Allow_ssh will be applied before rule 20-Deny_all.
port	This specifies the port or range of ports to match. This can also be a range or array of ports. This will match both the source and destination port.

Parameter	Description
proto	This specifies the protocol to match. The default value is TCP, however, UDP. ICMP and many other protocols are supported. All can also be used to match all the protocols. For more information, see the documentation at the link mentioned later in this section. These must be lowercase in the manifest.
reject	This is used to set the ICMP type that the packet is rejected with when the action is reject.
source	This specifies the source address of the packet to match. It can be a single IP or a CIDR range.
sport	This specifies the source port. It can be a port, a range of ports, or an array of ports to match.
src_range	This specifies a source IP range in x.x.x.x-y.y.y.y format. For example, 10.30.40.1-10.30.41.23.
state	This matches the state of a connection. It can be ESTABLISHED, INVALID, NEW, or RELATED.
tcp_flags	This matches the TCP Flags set on a packet. These can be any valid TCP flags such as SYN, ACK, PSH, and so on. See the documentation for more values.

> The preceding attributes are just a subset of the available parameters that are most commonly used. A full documentation on all of the parameters can be found at https://forge.puppetlabs.com/puppetlabs/firewall.

As previously mentioned under the name parameter, the rules are ordered based on the name before being applied. The typical application of the ruleset is that names are prepended with a number. This allows you to ensure that the rules are applied in the order that is desired.

This module is somewhat dangerous compared to some of the others we looked at also. If you misuse it, it is easy to lock yourself out of a host. Care should be taken to test all the changes thoroughly before applying them to the production hosts.

Let's go through an example using the firewall module. We'll do a very simplistic example that logs all the connections to our host via SSH.

For now, we'll create a separate module to manage our base firewall configuration and add our rules there. Later in this chapter, we'll discuss how to add rules to your modules.

To begin, let's go ahead and create our firewall module. In this case, I'm not going to use the name firewall to avoid problems with namespaces (it's possible to do so, but if we name it something else, we can avoid it completely).

To do this, run the following command in your home directory on the master. We'll copy it over like we previously have:

```
puppet module generate pupbook-fw
```

Go ahead and answer all the questions or accept the defaults, and we'll move on to define some content for this module.

In this case, we're going to start by adding a firewall rule that logs `ssh`. We won't add any additional rules or purge existing rules. We'll cover the functionality in the pre and post rules sections since it requires a fair amount of configuration, and we have a full section that will cover these topics.

For the moment, let's make our `pupbook-fw/manifests/init.pp` file look like the following:

```
class fw {

  include ::firewall

  firewall { '050 log all ssh':
    ensure => present,
    proto  => 'tcp',
    port   => '22',
    jump   => 'LOG',
  }
}
```

The preceding code contains our rule to `log all ssh` traffic. The only other line in the module is an `include` of the `firewall` class. The purpose of this class is to ensure that all the prerequisites needed to use iptables are met. On RHEL 6, this handles installation of the `iptables-persistent` package, which ensures that firewall rules are persisted across reboots.

We'll be applying this class to just one of our nodes to test it. So, add the following command to the `/etc/puppet/manifests/site.pp` file:

```
node 'agentone.book.local' {
  include fw
}
```

Network Security and Puppet

Before we use the firewall module, we obviously need to install it. Use the following command to do this:

```
sudo puppet module install puppetlabs-firewall
```

Now we need to test it. Remember that you'll need to sign the certificate if these are new VMs. You can refer to *Chapter 5, Securing Puppet*, for a refresher.

When that's completed, we can go ahead and run Puppet on the `agentone` VM. When you finish, you should get the output as follows:

```
[vagrant@agentone ~]$ sudo puppet agent --test
Info: Retrieving plugin
Notice: /File[/var/lib/puppet/lib/puppet]/ensure: created
Notice: /File[/var/lib/puppet/lib/puppet/provider]/ensure: created
Notice: /File[/var/lib/puppet/lib/puppet/util]/ensure: created
Notice: /File[/var/lib/puppet/lib/puppet/util/ipcidr.rb]/ensure: defined content as '{md5}
e1160dfd6e73fc5ef2bb8abc291f6fd5'
Notice: /File[/var/lib/puppet/lib/puppet/provider/firewall.rb]/ensure: defined content as
'{md5}32d2f5e5dcc082986b82ef26a119038b'
Notice: /File[/var/lib/puppet/lib/puppet/provider/firewallchain]/ensure: created
Notice: /File[/var/lib/puppet/lib/puppet/provider/firewall]/ensure: created
Notice: /File[/var/lib/puppet/lib/puppet/provider/firewall/iptables.rb]/ensure: defined co
ntent as '{md5}b50a64e46a8b6cf10063ac4bb3d4ad41'
Notice: /File[/var/lib/puppet/lib/puppet/type]/ensure: created
Notice: /File[/var/lib/puppet/lib/puppet/type/firewallchain.rb]/ensure: defined content as
 '{md5}548676cc7da53598eb24268ebac38a0d'
Notice: /File[/var/lib/puppet/lib/puppet/type/firewall.rb]/ensure: defined content as '{md
5}88739d191642568aab222bca3fb79b8a'
Notice: /File[/var/lib/puppet/lib/puppet/provider/firewallchain/iptables_chain.rb]/ensure:
 defined content as '{md5}98ac7c8a44014681a243da2391b09de6'
Notice: /File[/var/lib/puppet/lib/facter]/ensure: created
Notice: /File[/var/lib/puppet/lib/facter/ip6tables_version.rb]/ensure: defined content as
'{md5}091123ad703f1706686bca4398c5b06f'
Notice: /File[/var/lib/puppet/lib/facter/iptables_persistent_version.rb]/ensure: defined c
ontent as '{md5}b7a47827cd3d3bb1acbd526a31da3acb'
Notice: /File[/var/lib/puppet/lib/facter/iptables_version.rb]/ensure: defined content as '
{md5}facbd760223f236538b731c1d1f6cf8f'
Notice: /File[/var/lib/puppet/lib/puppet/provider/firewall/ip6tables.rb]/ensure: defined c
ontent as '{md5}6b9a9e99a50ae6cc278337483aa7ba0f'
Notice: /File[/var/lib/puppet/lib/puppet/util/firewall.rb]/ensure: defined content as '{md
5}6f7667742d9f6d192cd202be0014dd85'
Info: Loading facts
Info: Caching catalog for agentone.book.local
Info: Applying configuration version '1414331277'
Notice: /Stage[main]/Fw/Firewall[050 log all ssh]/ensure: created
Info: Creating state file /var/lib/puppet/state/state.yaml
Notice: Finished catalog run in 0.66 seconds
[vagrant@agentone ~]$
```

As you can see, the type and provider got synced over to our virtual machine and the rule got created. We can confirm this by running the following command:

```
sudo iptables -L
```

When you run this, you should see the output like the following:

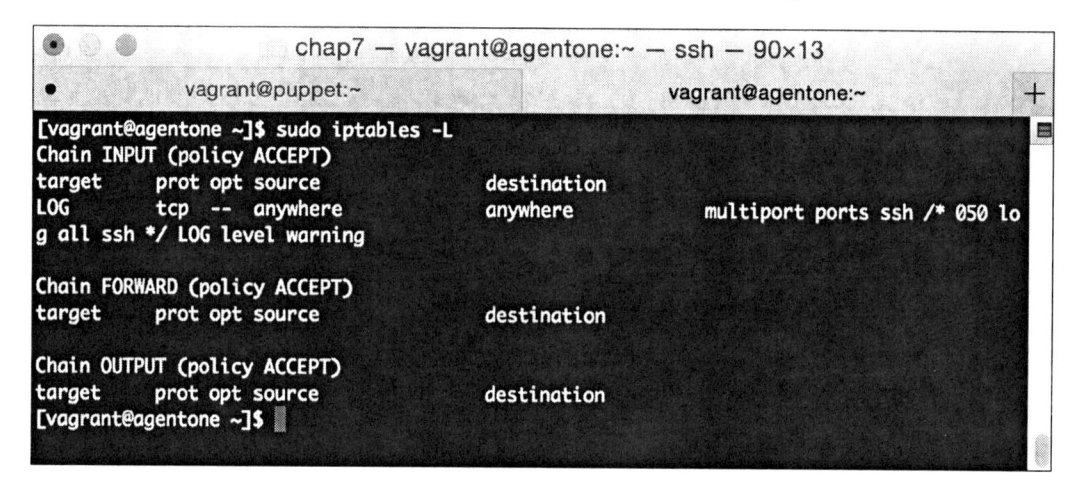

```
[vagrant@agentone ~]$ sudo iptables -L
Chain INPUT (policy ACCEPT)
target     prot opt source               destination
LOG        tcp  --  anywhere             anywhere             multiport ports ssh /* 050 lo
g all ssh */ LOG level warning

Chain FORWARD (policy ACCEPT)
target     prot opt source               destination

Chain OUTPUT (policy ACCEPT)
target     prot opt source               destination
[vagrant@agentone ~]$
```

You can see our rule in the iptables configuration. Now let's open a second SSH connection and see what the logs say. Open another terminal and run a second `vagrant ssh agentone` command to get on agentone. Then, we'll take a look at the log file in `/var/log/messages`.

You should see lots of messages, such as the following:

```
Oct 26 07:41:57 localhost kernel: IN=eth0 OUT= MAC=08:00:27:73:bf:
1c:52:54:00:12:35:02:08:00 SRC=10.0.2.2 DST=10.0.2.15 LEN=40 TOS=0x00
PREC=0x00 TTL=64 ID=17892 PROTO=TCP SPT=64974 DPT=22 WINDOW=65535
RES=0x00 ACK URGP=0
Oct 26 07:41:58 localhost kernel: IN=eth0 OUT= MAC=08:00:27:73:bf:
1c:52:54:00:12:35:02:08:00 SRC=10.0.2.2 DST=10.0.2.15 LEN=72 TOS=0x00
PREC=0x00 TTL=64 ID=17893 PROTO=TCP SPT=64974 DPT=22 WINDOW=65535
RES=0x00 ACK PSH URGP=0
```

Right away, we can see an improvement we want to make to the module. Right now, it's logging `ALL` SSH packets. This will very quickly result in a large number of log messages. To deal with this, we'll add some more options to our rule in our module.

To do this, edit your `pupbook-fw/manigests/init.pp` file again, and in the parameters, add the following:

```
state => 'NEW',
```

This will make the rule only match new packets.

Once this is done, rerun Puppet. You should receive an output that indicates it's updated your rule and now state matches new. The iptables output will now look like the following:

```
[vagrant@agentone ~]$ sudo iptables -L
Chain INPUT (policy ACCEPT)
target     prot opt source               destination
LOG        tcp  --  anywhere             anywhere             multiport ports ssh /* 050 lo
g all ssh */ state NEW LOG level warning

Chain FORWARD (policy ACCEPT)
target     prot opt source               destination

Chain OUTPUT (policy ACCEPT)
target     prot opt source               destination
[vagrant@agentone ~]$
```

You will also see that the log messages have reduced to just initial SSH connections.

The example shows something else. Building Puppet modules is often an iterative process. In this case, we created a module using what we knew we wanted—we wanted to log SSH traffic. However, once it was built, it was determined that this wasn't quite what we wanted. What we actually wanted was to log NEW SSH connections. Therefore, we iterated on the module and improved it to meet the actual goal.

This shows the importance of testing your changes. When dealing with the firewall module in particular, it is very possible to lock yourself out of a machine. Therefore, you should always test your changes prior to them going to production.

Fortunately, if you've been following along, you have a GREAT method to test your changes using Vagrant. In *Appendix, Going Forward*, we'll explore some other resources, such as rspec-puppet, that can be used to help test.

For now, let's take a look at the other firewall module type.

The firewallchain type

The firewallchain type is something that some people may never use. It allows you to manage the firewall chains themselves under iptables.

If you recall from the earlier section, the firewall rules are contained in chains. Firewall chains are groupings of related rules. By default, the filter table, which handles packet filtering, contains three chains `INPUT`, `OUTPUT`, and `FORWARD`. These chains filter packet input when they are forwarded and on output. There are other default chains present in other tables.

It is possible to add your own chain to better organize your firewall rules. You can then use the jump rule to send packets into your new chain.

You can use this type if you want to change some default parameters about a chain you created.

The parameters available to the firewall chain type are as follows:

Parameter	Description
`ensure`	What happens to the chain? The valid values are `present` and `absent`.
`ignore`	This allows the user to specify rules to be ignored when purging rules. It can be used to ignore rules added by other services dynamically. It takes a regular expression or an array of regular expressions that matches the `iptables-save` output.
`name`	This contains the name of the chain. It should be in chain:table:protocol format, such as `MYCHAIN:filter:IPv4`.
`policy`	This specifies the default policy of the chain. This must be one of `accept`, `drop`, `queue`, and `return`. See the iptables documentation for more details. The value here must be in lowercase.
`provider`	This is the provider of the type. Usually, it is not set. Currently, only the `iptables_chain` command is supported.
`purge`	This is the boolean value indicating whether rules unmanaged by Puppet in the chain are dropped.

The most common parameters used here are the `ignore`, `policy`, and `purge` parameters. These can be used as an alternative method of purging rules from what we will see later in the chapter. One can also set the policy to drop, for instance, as opposed to adding an explicit drop at the bottom of your rule set.

Now we'll explore a common pattern for implementing these types.

Creating pre and post rules

Over the years, a good pattern to deal with firewall rules has emerged. This pattern uses the concept of a class that is applied before and after all other firewall rules. This allows us to set up rules that are in place before any other—allowing local packets, and so on. We can also add our default rule to the post rules.

If you follow the directions on the puppetlabs/firewall website at `https://forge.puppetlabs.com/puppetlabs/firewall`, it instructs you on how to set up pre and post rules. We'll be using a modified version of this procedure since we're not going to be managing every resource on our system.

The module instructions assume that you want the module applied to all hosts. As such, they will purge firewall rules off all hosts that run Puppet. In a perfect world, we'd reach a point where our entire infrastructure is Puppetized and this could be the case. This is where we aim to get with our Puppet deployments as it means all of our resources can be tracked and audited. It also makes systems easy to rebuild. However, as this book is targeted at users just starting with Puppet, we're going to assume that you're retrofitting an existing environment and will not add these default rules. In our case, we will only manage firewall rules on a host we explicitly apply our firewall module to.

To create this pattern, we will need to create two more classes. These classes will also be in our firewall module, and we'll call them `pre` and `post`.

The `pre` class will contain all of the firewall rules we want to be applied before any other rules. We'll use this to set up things like allowing established connections, permitting connections to a localhost, and so on.

We'll use the internal features of Puppet to ensure ordering. To make this somewhat easier, we'll use resource defaults to set them up, so we don't need to add them to each rule.

In our `pre` class, we'll do the things we previously mentioned, for example, allow connections to a localhost. Allow ICMP and established connections. To do this, we'll make the `pre` class look like the following:

```
class fw::pre {
  Firewall {
    require => undef, # Undo require
  }

  firewall { '000 Allow localhost':
    proto   => 'all',
    iniface => 'lo',
    action  => 'accept',
  } ->
  firewall { '001 Allow established':
    proto  => 'all',
    state  => ['RELATED', 'ESTABLISHED'],
    action => 'accept',
  } ->
```

```
    firewall { '002 Allow ICMP':
      proto  => 'icmp',
      action => 'accept',
    }
  }
```

In this class, we set a default that unsets the `require` parameter. Later on in the main firewall class, we'll set the default we're overriding here.

We will go on to create a series of default rules. These are modeled off by some of the defaults that CentOS uses in its default configuration. They are also similar to the rules in the documentation for the module, although they have been reordered to an order that I think makes more sense, such as moving rules that are commonly hit in the list.

Next, we'll move on to the post class. As a reminder, this will be applied after all the other rules.

The `post` class should look like the following:

```
  class fw::post {
    firewall { '999 accept all':
      proto  => 'all',
      action => 'accept',
      before => undef,
    }
  }
```

In a production environment, this should be the `deny` value with log and not the `accept` value. In our test case, we'll accept all for demonstration purposes.

This should seem pretty familiar by now. The only thing to note here is that we're overriding the `before` parameter to be `undef` in the resource so that it gets applied after the other rules.

Now we'll revisit our main module and use it to pull all this together. Let's go ahead and open the `init.pp` file again. We'll edit it. The final contents would look like the following:

```
  class fw {

    Firewall {
      before  => Class['fw::post'],
      require => Class['fw::pre'],
    }

    include fw::pre
```

```
      include fw::post
      require ::firewall

      firewall { '050 log all ssh':
        ensure => present,
        proto  => 'tcp',
        port   => '22',
        jump   => 'LOG',
        state  => 'NEW',
      }
    }
```

Our SSH rule is still in there. We just filled in some things around it. Notice at the top we used class defaults as mentioned earlier. In this class, every rule will have the before and require lines applied to it. This ensures that the ordering is applied correctly, and you don't accidentally lose connection while things are applied. Then, we have to include our `pre` and `post` classes. The remainder of the class is as it was earlier.

Let's go ahead and copy it back into its place and run it on our agentone node.

Once this is done, your output should be as follows:

```
[vagrant@agentone ~]$ sudo puppet agent --test
Info: Retrieving plugin
Info: Loading facts
Info: Caching catalog for agentone.book.local
Warning: The package type's allow_virtual parameter will be changing its default value fro
m false to true in a future release. If you do not want to allow virtual packages, please
explicitly set allow_virtual to false.
   (at /usr/lib/ruby/site_ruby/1.8/puppet/type/package.rb:430:in `default')
Info: Applying configuration version '1414369387'
Notice: /Stage[main]/Fw::Pre/Firewall[000 Allow localhost]/ensure: created
Notice: /Stage[main]/Fw::Pre/Firewall[001 Allow established]/ensure: created
Notice: /Stage[main]/Fw::Pre/Firewall[002 Allow ICMP]/ensure: created
Notice: /Stage[main]/Fw::Post/Firewall[999 accept all]/ensure: created
Notice: Finished catalog run in 0.95 seconds
[vagrant@agentone ~]$
```

Running the `sudo iptables -L` command will show the following ouput:

```
[vagrant@agentone ~]$ sudo iptables -L
Chain INPUT (policy ACCEPT)
target     prot opt source               destination
ACCEPT     all  --  anywhere             anywhere             /* 000 Allow localhost */
ACCEPT     all  --  anywhere             anywhere             /* 001 Allow established */ s
tate RELATED,ESTABLISHED
ACCEPT     icmp --  anywhere             anywhere             /* 002 Allow ICMP */
LOG        tcp  --  anywhere             anywhere             multiport ports ssh /* 050 lo
g all ssh */ state NEW LOG level warning
ACCEPT     all  --  anywhere             anywhere             /* 999 accept all */

Chain FORWARD (policy ACCEPT)
target     prot opt source               destination

Chain OUTPUT (policy ACCEPT)
target     prot opt source               destination
[vagrant@agentone ~]$
```

And success! You can see that our rules were applied in the order we expected.

Now that we understand the basics of the firewall module, we'll explore how you might add it to the modules you write.

Adding firewall rules to other modules

So far, we concentrated on using a single firewall utility class. While this is useful for site or organization wide rules, it quickly becomes unwieldy to manage if there are specific exceptions for given hosts or applications. As such, there must be a better way to manage firewall rules close to the applications we're installing via Puppet.

This section will also serve to introduce another common pattern that is being applied in the Puppet world. This is the roles and profiles pattern.

The concept of the roles and profiles pattern is that we have utility modules. These modules are responsible for being generic enough to configure an underlying system. Consider modules to configure Apache or Samba. These modules will likely not contain any site-specific implementation. They are also the modules that will be reused.

From these modules, we build profiles. These profiles use the underlying utility modules to build more complete services. For instance, this is where you would use the Apache module to define a given website or to define a web server. You might also create a profile to create a given set of `samba` mounts using the Samba module.

Finally, there are the roles. These roles become a collection of profiles that build complete systems. The role may be a specific website. It includes profiles for the various websites. Perhaps it also includes a database server, or a particular version of Nginx to use for proxying. The profiles would configure these pieces, and the roles would bring them together into a complete system.

This pattern was first introduced by Craig Dunn in a blog post in 2012. Since then, it has gained a lot of popularity in the Puppet world. The original blog post and more information can be found at http://www.craigdunn.org/2012/05/239/.

The profile would tend to be where you would define the firewall ruleset. It is really difficult for the underlying module to do it in a way that is correct for all users. As such, many modules include no firewall support or only very basic support. When you add the firewall configuration in the profile, you can include the correct class logic to ensure that your ordering is right, and the specific configuration you want is in place.

To demonstrate this, we'll use the profile pattern and the puppetlabs/ntp module to create an **Network Time Protocol** (**NTP**) server profile. We'll also create a role for it even though it will contain only one class.

Let's start by installing the `ntp` module. To do so, run the following command on the master:

```
sudo puppet module install puppetlabs-ntp
```

Now that we've done this, we need to create two modules—one will hold our roles, and the other will hold our profiles. The commands to do these are as follows:

```
puppet module generate pupbook-roles
puppet module generate pupbook-profiles
```

Go ahead and accept the defaults for these, and add a description as you see fit.

First, we'll configure the role. The role we're going to create is for an NTP server, so we'll call it `ntpserver`. Let's edit the `manifests/ntpserver.pp` file inside our profiles module. We want it to look as follows:

```
class profiles::ntpserver {

  include ::ntp

  include ::fw

  firewall { '060 allow ntp':
    proto    => 'udp',
```

```
    port    => '123',
    action  => 'accept',
    before  => [Class['::fw::post'], Class['::ntp']],
    require => Class['::fw::pre'],
  } }
}
```

Is allowing all to NTP dangerous?

For many years, it was common practice to allow anything to talk to NTP, and indeed the default configuration of most NTP servers would serve time to any client. However, there has been a recent rash of amplification attacks utilizing a deficiency in the default configuration of many servers. This attack has generated multi-gigabit attacks against a variety of targets. As such, it is best to now lock down NTP serving to the client networks you wish to provide time to.

This is a really simplistic profile because we're implementing a simple service. We include the ntp module with default options (although they could be overriden by Hiera, as in the last chapter). We then include the proper firewall configuration to ensure that port 123 / UDP is open.

The role will be even simpler and will look as follows:

```
class roles::ntpserver {
  include profiles::ntpserver
}
```

The ntpserver role only contains the ntpserver profile. In a more complex service, you'd see it include more. Perhaps you have a management server role that also serves as an NTP server. You'd also normally include a common profile that includes everything common to all systems, such as SSH rules.

Now, copy the modules into the module directory and we'll test them.

Let's apply the ntpserver role to agentone and test it. To do so, we'll include the ntpserver role on the node definition. It should now look as follows:

```
node 'agentone.book.local' {
  include roles::ntpserver
}
```

Network Security and Puppet

Now, let's run Puppet on agentone. When complete, you should get the output like the following:

```
-# Specify the key identifier to use with the ntpq utility.
-#controlkey 8
+# Driftfile.
+driftfile /var/lib/ntp/drift
+
-# Enable writing of statistics records.
-#statistics clockstats cryptostats loopstats peerstats

Info: Computing checksum on file /etc/ntp.conf
Info: /Stage[main]/Ntp::Config/File[/etc/ntp.conf]: Filebucketed /etc/ntp.conf to puppet w
ith sum 7fda24f62b1c7ae951db0f746dc6e0cc
Notice: /Stage[main]/Ntp::Config/File[/etc/ntp.conf]/content: content changed '{md5}7fda24
f62b1c7ae951db0f746dc6e0cc' to '{md5}c9d83653966c1e9b8dfbca77b97ff356'
Info: Class[Ntp::Config]: Scheduling refresh of Class[Ntp::Service]
Info: Class[Ntp::Service]: Scheduling refresh of Service[ntp]
Notice: /Stage[main]/Ntp::Service/Service[ntp]/ensure: ensure changed 'stopped' to 'runnin
g'
Info: /Stage[main]/Ntp::Service/Service[ntp]: Unscheduling refresh on Service[ntp]
Notice: /Stage[main]/Profiles::Ntpserver/Firewall[060 allow ntp]/ensure: created
Notice: Finished catalog run in 0.66 seconds
[vagrant@agentone ~]$
```

Once again, we'll examine the iptables output and see that the rule was applied:

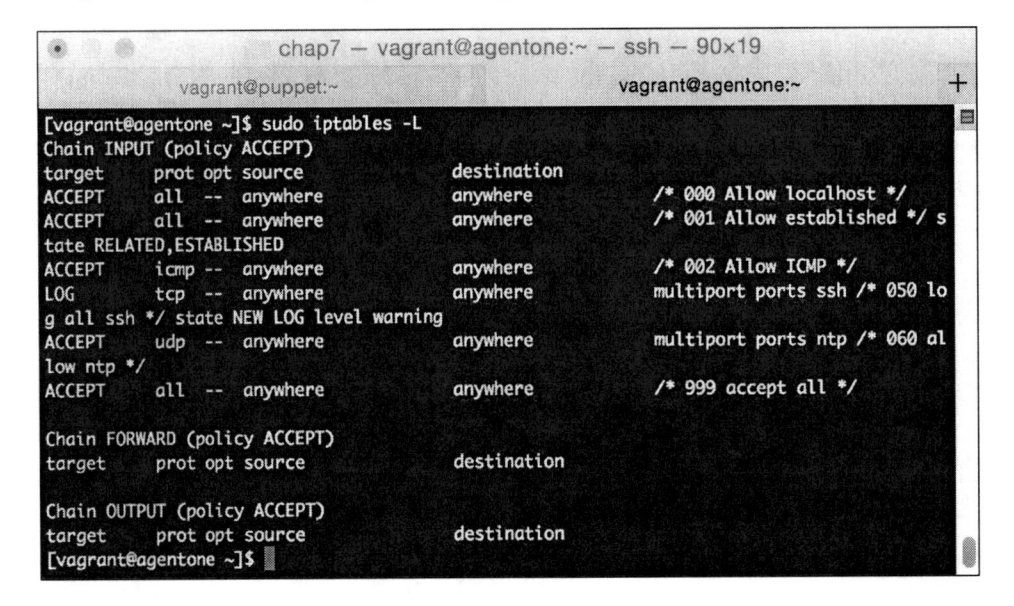

```
[vagrant@agentone ~]$ sudo iptables -L
Chain INPUT (policy ACCEPT)
target     prot opt source               destination
ACCEPT     all  --  anywhere             anywhere             /* 000 Allow localhost */
ACCEPT     all  --  anywhere             anywhere             /* 001 Allow established */ s
tate RELATED,ESTABLISHED
ACCEPT     icmp --  anywhere             anywhere             /* 002 Allow ICMP */
LOG        tcp  --  anywhere             anywhere             multiport ports ssh /* 050 lo
g all ssh */ state NEW LOG level warning
ACCEPT     udp  --  anywhere             anywhere             multiport ports ntp /* 060 al
low ntp */
ACCEPT     all  --  anywhere             anywhere             /* 999 accept all */

Chain FORWARD (policy ACCEPT)
target     prot opt source               destination

Chain OUTPUT (policy ACCEPT)
target     prot opt source               destination
[vagrant@agentone ~]$
```

You can see the rule in the table.

Using this pattern, you can create a complex system and have the firewall rules follow the profiles that require them. It also keeps site-specific logic away from modules that implement functionality, which promotes module reusability.

Summary

Managing system firewalls is a repetitive and an error prone task. These sorts of tasks are great for management by Puppet. Using the puppetlabs/firewall module, we can implement system level firewall services with ease and with configuration, that is easily read and audited.

In this last chapter, we learned how to use the firewall type to manage our firewalls. Using the parameters of the type, we can manage all the aspects of the iptables configuration.

We then learned a design pattern that allowed us to ensure that our rules got applied in a consistent order, and also ensure that common rules are applied to all hosts in our environment.

Finally, we learned a pattern that allowed us to build reusable modules and attach the firewall configuration needed for services to the service definitions.

In the next chapter, we'll explore centralized logging, which is very important to utilize in a secure environment. We'll see you there!

Centralized Logging

As a security professional, one of the key requirements is that you centralize logging so it can be analyzed. This allows you to maintain a single point where all logs are processed and acted upon.

Even those not in the security profession can benefit from this. Gathering all application logs benefits operations as well as development professionals.

There are a large number of products on the market, both open source and commercial, that can be used to tackle this problem.

On the commercial side, we have offerings such as **Splunk** or **Loggly** that can be used to gather your logs and provide analysis on them. These are both great products that can be Puppetized.

On the open source side, the most common solution seems to be converging around **Logstash**, written by Jordan Sissel and now maintained by Elasticsearch.

In this chapter, we'll cover the installation of the Logstash environment using Puppet. Some of the concepts are similar to those used by some of the commercial products. However, these products tend to be harder to test. As such, we'll focus on the open source tools. In particular, we will cover the following topics:

- What Logstash is
- Installing Logstash and its prerequisites with Puppet
- Using Kibana to report on log data
- Configuring hosts using Puppet to ship log data to Logstash

When we're complete, you should be able to implement a fairly complete centralized logging host using what we've covered in this chapter.

Let's get to it!

Welcome to logging happiness

As previously mentioned, logging presents a challenge to many organizations. Gathering and processing log files is required for a number of reasons. It is used to watch for anomalous behavior as well as look for unauthorized activity.

For many years, a centralized syslog host was the most common method used to implement centralized logging. All of the hosts would ship their logs to one place and analysis was done there.

This worked OK for systems that used syslog for all logging. However, syslog has some drawbacks. It lacks a good way to deal with multiline records. Additionally, it only has a limited number of granularity levels so everything ended up logged in several giant log files. Attempts were made with various syslog agents to overcome some of these challenges, but there had to be a more complete way to handle the problem.

Enter Logstash. Logstash is nothing more than a system that takes input from multiple sources, parses it, and stores that output elsewhere. However, this simplicity is what gives it so much power. It can parse data from any number of sources, including syslog, files, or other Logstash instances. It can also write to a variety of places, including files, Elasticsearch, or even systems such as Nagios. This is not in any way a comprehensive list of inputs or outputs either. There are dozens of them available for various scenarios.

Logstash alone is a neat product, but the real power presents itself in what is called the **Elasticsearch, Logstash, and Kibana (ELK) and stack**. This stack consists of Elasticsearch on the backend for searching, Logstash for log processing, and Kibana for analytics.

When used together, these projects create a full log management solution, complete with quick and powerful searching as well as a web interface to interact with your logs. Using Kibana, you can even create dashboards to allow you to graph certain events over time, plot them on a map, or other useful things.

Installing Logstash is simple; however, the agent or the forwarder must be installed on all hosts. Additionally, for optimal performance, several of the components that run with Logstash are best run on their own instances.

We'll quickly stand up Logstash in demo mode to show you some of its power, then we'll approach using Puppet to configure your Logstash environment.

Installing the ELK stack

To install the ELK stack, we'll use the RPM-based downloads for both Elasticsearch and Logstash. Then, we'll manually install Kibana since it does not yet have a package.

Packages for these can be downloaded from Elasticsearch at http://www.elasticsearch.org/overview/elkdownloads/. We'll download the latest version of Elasticsearch, Logstash, and Kibana. At the time this book was written, those are 1.4.0, 1.4.2, and 3.1.2 respectively.

We'll do this work on our agentone VM, as we should work to keep our puppetmaster standalone. First, fire up the agentone VM. If you need a reminder on how to do this using Vagrant, refer to *Chapter 1, Puppet as a Security Tool*, to get a quick refresher course.

Once it's up, go ahead and SSH to agentone. Once it's booted, run the following commands to install Elasticsearch and Logstash on the machine:

```
sudo yum install https://download.elasticsearch.org/elasticsearch/
elasticsearch/elasticsearch-1.4.0.noarch.rpm
```

```
sudo yum install https://download.elasticsearch.org/logstash/logstash/
packages/centos/logstash-1.4.2-1_2c0f5a1.noarch.rpm
```

You may need to adjust the versions to the ones you got previously from the downloads page.

Logstash will pull in Java as it's needed for the application to run. Once it's installed, we'll quickly configure it to consume our syslog data on localhost just for testing purposes.

Once that's installed, let's set about configuring Logstash and Elasticsearch. Elasticsearch contains a large number of configuration parameters, but for our simple example, the default configuration will suffice. As such, we'll simply enable it and start it. To do so, run the following commands:

```
sudo chkconfig elasticsearch on
```

```
sudo /sbin/service elasticsearch start
```

Now we'll move on to Logstash. We'll configure Logstash to read our messages file and send it to Elasticsearch for us to use in Kibana.

To do so, edit the /etc/logstash/conf.d/logstash-example.conf file to contain the following:

```
input {
  file {
    path => "/var/log/messages"
```

```
            start_position => "beginning"
            type => "syslog"
        }
    }

    filter {
      if [type] == "syslog" {
        grok {
          match => { "message" => "%{SYSLOGTIMESTAMP:syslog_timestamp}
%{SYSLOGHOST:syslog_hostname} %{DATA:syslog_program}(?:\
[%{POSINT:syslog_pid}\])?: %{GREEDYDATA:syslog_message}" }
          add_field => [ "received_at", "%{@timestamp}" ]
          add_field => [ "received_from", "%{host}" ]
        }
        syslog_pri { }
        date {
          match => [ "syslog_timestamp", "MMM  d HH:mm:ss", "MMM dd
HH:mm:ss" ]
        }
      }
    }

    output {
      elasticsearch { host => localhost }
    }
```

We'll save this. This configuration file will read the `syslog` data from the `/var/log/messages` file and process it into `elasticsearch`. It will read some metadata from the `syslog_message` parameter to create the `timestamp` and add a `host` parameter. This is straight out of the Logstash documentation with some modifications to read the `syslog` data from a file instead of `syslog`. One thing worth noting is that in its default configuration, Logstash does not run as `root`. Therefore, it will not be able to read the messages file that is readable only by `root`. A simple solution is to add the Logstash user to the `root` group and make the file `group` readable; however, for simplicity's sake, we'll run the following command to make it readable by all:

sudo chmod 644 /var/log/messages

> You should be careful to not do the preceding actions in production. This was applied on a test system where shortcuts can be taken to keep the examples to a reasonable length. This book presumes you have the knowledge to properly configure the mode and ownership of your log files so that the Logstash user can pick them up. More information on permissions can be found at https://en.wikipedia.org/wiki/File_system_permissions.

Save this file and let's start Logstash. To do this, run the following command:

```
sudo chkconfig logstash on
sudo /sbin/service logstash start
```

Give it a few minutes to come up and index some events. You should be able to see that it has events processed by running the following command:

```
curl 'http://localhost:9200/_search?pretty'
```

If it has successfully indexed events, you should see something similar to the following:

```
        "_type" : "syslog",
        "_id" : "GYVej3UqR4GiK81wyybLYg",
        "_score" : 1.0,
        "_source":{"message":"Jan 16 04:36:03 localhost kernel: (7 early reservations) ==> boo
tmem [0000000000 - 001fff0000]","@version":"1","@timestamp":"2014-01-16T12:36:03.000Z","type
":"syslog","host":"agentone.book.local","path":"/var/log/messages","syslog_timestamp":"Jan 1
6 04:36:03","syslog_hostname":"localhost","syslog_program":"kernel","syslog_message":"(7 ear
ly reservations) ==> bootmem [0000000000 - 001fff0000]","received_at":"2014-11-09 20:41:13 U
TC","received_from":"agentone.book.local","syslog_severity_code":5,"syslog_facility_code":1,
"syslog_facility":"user-level","syslog_severity":"notice"}
        }, {
        "_index" : "logstash-2014.01.16",
        "_type" : "syslog",
        "_id" : "bM_joklrRYi49Nt_k2anTg",
        "_score" : 1.0,
        "_source":{"message":"Jan 16 04:36:03 localhost kernel:  #0 [0000000000 - 0000001000]
    BIOS data page ==> [0000000000 - 0000001000]","@version":"1","@timestamp":"2014-01-16T12:3
6:03.000Z","type":"syslog","host":"agentone.book.local","path":"/var/log/messages","syslog_t
imestamp":"Jan 16 04:36:03","syslog_hostname":"localhost","syslog_program":"kernel","syslog_
message":" #0 [0000000000 - 0000001000]    BIOS data page ==> [0000000000 - 0000001000]","rec
eived_at":"2014-11-09 20:41:13 UTC","received_from":"agentone.book.local","syslog_severity_c
ode":5,"syslog_facility_code":1,"syslog_facility":"user-level","syslog_severity":"notice"}
        }, {
        "_index" : "logstash-2014.01.16",
        "_type" : "syslog",
        "_id" : "p2pr_lDuRwuX05CWADE_-A",
        "_score" : 1.0,
        "_source":{"message":"Jan 16 04:36:03 localhost kernel:  #4 [000009fc00 - 0000100000]
    BIOS reserved ==> [000009fc00 - 0000100000]","@version":"1","@timestamp":"2014-01-16T12:3
6:03.000Z","type":"syslog","host":"agentone.book.local","path":"/var/log/messages","syslog_t
imestamp":"Jan 16 04:36:03","syslog_hostname":"localhost","syslog_program":"kernel","syslog_
message":" #4 [000009fc00 - 0000100000]    BIOS reserved ==> [000009fc00 - 0000100000]","rec
eived_at":"2014-11-09 20:41:19 UTC","received_from":"agentone.book.local","syslog_severity_c
ode":5,"syslog_facility_code":1,"syslog_facility":"user-level","syslog_severity":"notice"}
        } ]
    }
}
[vagrant@agentone ~]$
```

Centralized Logging

Now that we have some data, we'll concentrate on getting Kibana working so that we can see what it looks like.

To run Kibana in its current form (Version 3), we will need a web server. We'll use Apache in this example since it ships with Red Hat and has good Puppet support. Let's go ahead and install it.

To do so, run the following command:

`sudo yum install httpd -y` Once this is done, we'll download and unpack Kibana. First, download it with the following command:

`cd /tmp && wget https://download.elasticsearch.org/kibana/kibana/kibana-3.1.2.tar.gz`

You may need to adjust the preceding file.

> Kibana is in between versions. As of time of this writing, it is on Version 3, but Version 4 is in beta. Version 4 contains a built-in web server, so its setup will vary slightly.

Next, we'll unpack it into the root of our HTML tree. To do so, run the following command:

`cd /var/www/html && sudo tar zxvf /tmp/kibana-3.1.2.tar.gz`

Finally, we can start Apache and configure it to start at boot by running the following two commands:

`sudo chkconfig httpd on`

`sudo /sbin/service httpd start`

We'll also need to adjust some settings on Elasticsearch to allow Kibana to connect. Edit the `/etc/elasticsearch/elasticsearch.yml` file and add the following two lines at the bottom:

```
http.cors.enabled: true
http.cors.allow-origin: http://10.78.78.50
```

Now, restart `elasticsearch` by running the `sudo service elasticsearch restart` command.

Now, Kibana is running on our VM server. We should be able to hit it using the IP we have for private hosts; in this case, it is `http://10.78.78.50/kibana-3.1.2`.

You should be greeted with a screen that looks like the following:

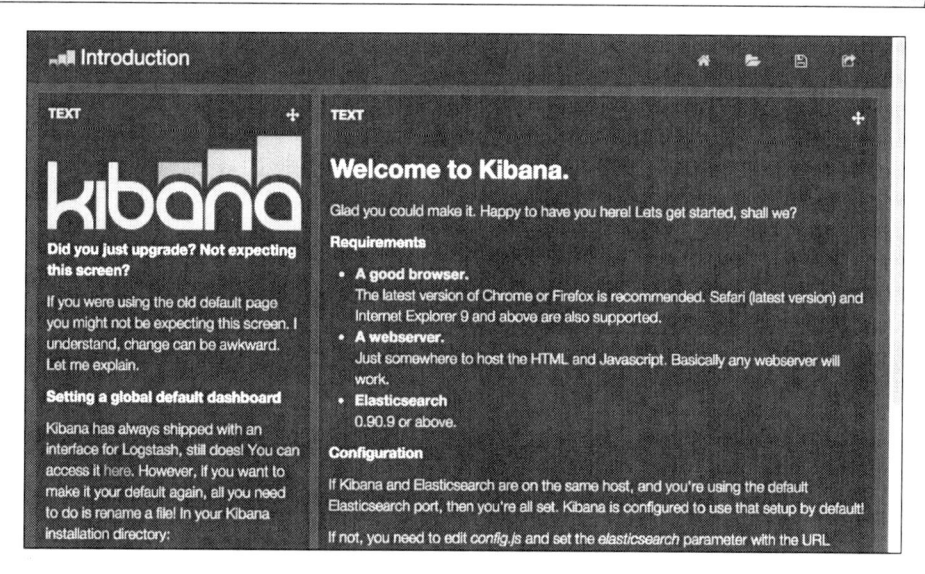

If you scroll down, you'll see a Logstash dashboard. Go ahead and click on it. It'll give you a nice starting point to configure a dashboard. This screen looks like the following screenshot:

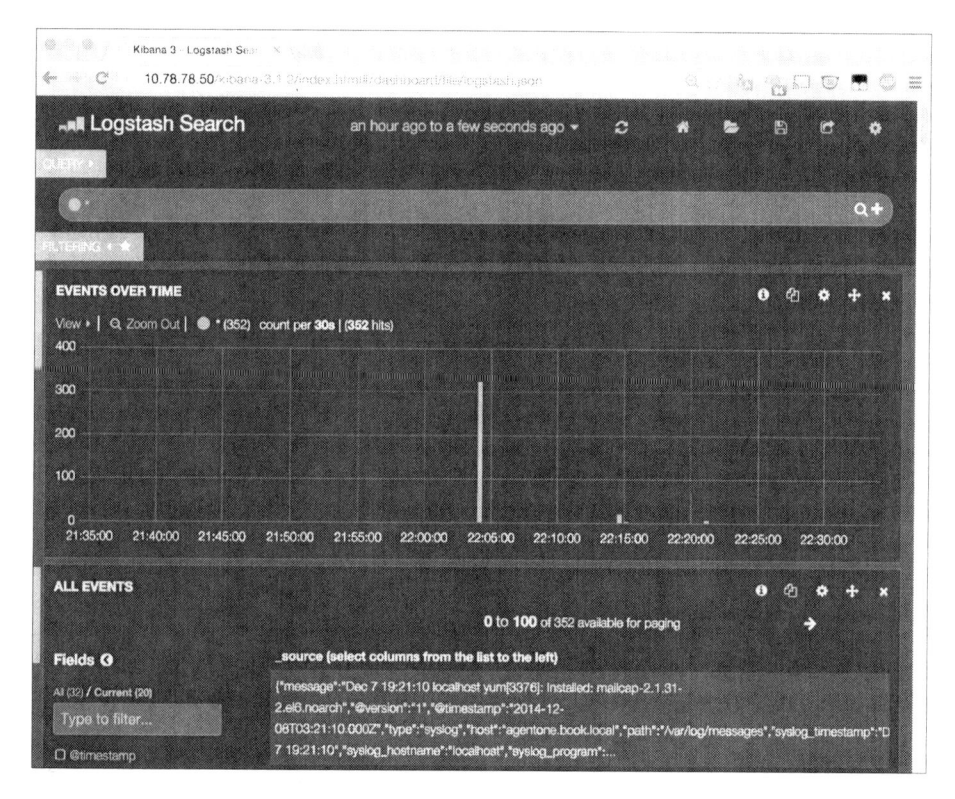

On this main screen, we can see several sections. At the top of the page, there is a query bar. If you type in that box, you can search all of the following events. For instance, typing `yum` will let you search for any event that contains `yum`.

The middle box contains a time series histogram of events. It just shows how many events occurred in a given bucket of time. You can zoom in and out with your mouse and update the bottom pane.

The bottom pane contains all of the raw events in a paginated format. Additionally, it contains a box on the left that is intended to help you quickly filter data. I encourage you to explore and play with this interface. It's fairly easy to use and the documentation is good.

Kibana and Logstash are complex enough that one could write a book about just them (and indeed, at least one does exist). The purpose of this section was to give you enough of an introduction to know why you would want to use them, and what you can do with them. Now we'll move on to managing them with Puppet.

Logstash and Puppet

When configuring any service, especially a service that is present on many host, one should look to Puppet for help. In the case of Logstash, we can configure all of its components using Puppet, and we can configure our hosts to report data as well. In this section, we'll see how to install the base Logstash components using Puppet. Depending on the desired configuration, this could be repeated for each host, or you could use another system to transport logs, one of which we'll see in a later section.

We'll be extending the roles and profiles concept we introduced in the previous chapter to configure these services. As such, make sure you still have these modules available.

Let's begin with Elasticsearch.

Installing Elasticsearch

Elasticsearch has a large variety of supported installation configurations. It can be installed as a cluster that shares data and allows searches to be split. It can also be installed in a single node configuration. In each configuration, there are a number of knobs that can be tuned to set things, such as the node name, instance name, and so on.

Elasticsearch provides an official Puppet module to manage this installation. This module is one of the new Puppet approved modules. This means the module has good support and is well designed.

Chapter 8

In our test case, we'll be accepting most of the defaults for the installation. In fact, we'll essentially be duplicating what we did previously where we collocated the `elasticsearch` server with the `logstash` host. There will only be a single node in this cluster that holds the data.

In a production situation, you might wish to run multiple nodes in your cluster or, depending on your usage, even multiple clusters. Fortunately, using facts, this is a fairly easy operation.

To use the module, we first have to install it. To do so, run the following on the master:

```
sudo puppet module install elasticsearch/elasticsearch
```

Now that we have the module installed, we'll create a profile for it. As you can recall, we use profiles to combine the utility module (in this case, the Elasticsearch module) into a module we can use locally. As such, let's create a `logstash-elasticsearch` profile that creates an `elasticsearch` instance for our Logstash installation. To do so, go to the module directory for our profiles module, and create a new file called `manifests/logstash-elasticsearch.pp`. We want the contents to look like the following:

```
class profiles::logstash-elasticsearch {
  include elasticsearch

  elasticsearch::instance { "${hostname}-ls-es01":
    config => {
      'http.cors.enabled'      => 'true',
      'http.cors.allow-origin' => "http://${ipaddress_eth1}",
    }
  }
}
```

Once that's done, we'll create a role that uses this profile. We'll call the `logstash-server` role. In production, we'd likely have a separate `logstash-elasticsearch` role we'd apply to multiple hosts, but for our simple test (Or if you have a smaller environment—less than 50 or so hosts), we can create it all on a single host.

One of the nice things about Puppetizing all of this is that we can parameterize this in such a way that adding an additional Elasticsearch node becomes simple, and reshaping the cluster is also easy.

For now, let's get our role created and test it out.

Centralized Logging

To do so, let's create our role in the roles module under `manifests/logstash-server.pp`. We want the content to be as follows:

```
class roles::logstash-server {
  include profiles::logstash-elasticsearch
}
```

Finally, let's apply the role to our `agentone` node by inserting the following into the `/etc/puppet/manifests/site.pp` file:

```
node 'agentone.book.local' {
  include roles::logstash-server
}
```

Now go ahead and run Puppet on agentone. Remember that we're going to have to sign the certificate if you restarted the VM. Once complete, you should see output such as the following:

If you now check the process table with `ps auxww|grep` elastic, you'll see that we have two instances of `elasticsearch` started now. This is because we've created a new instance of `elasticsearch` with our given name. At this point, we should stop the old `elasticsearch` service and disable it. To do so, run the following commands:

```
sudo chkconfig elasticsearch off
sudo /sbin/service elasticsearch stop
```

We also then want to restart our current cluster so it gets the right port. This is optional, but it sure makes our lives easier in the future. To do so, run the following command:

```
sudo /sbin/service elasticsearch-agentone-ls-es01 restart
```

Once complete, let's test it using `curl` and move on. Run the command `curl localhost:9200` and you should see output like the following:

```
{
  "status" : 200,
  "name" : "agentone-agentone-ls-es01",
  "cluster_name" : "elasticsearch",
  "version" : {
    "number" : "1.4.0",
    "build_hash" : "bc94bd81298f81c656893ab1ddddd30a99356066",
    "build_timestamp" : "2014-11-05T14:26:12Z",
    "build_snapshot" : false,
    "lucene_version" : "4.10.2"
  },
  "tagline" : "You Know, for Search"
}
```

You can see our new cluster name, so we know all is good. It appended our hostname to the instance name, so it's present twice, but that is the price we pay for the instance in Puppet being named well.

Now let's work on Logstash.

Installing Logstash

Much like the `elasticsearch` module, the `logstash` module is provided by Elasticsearch. This module is fairly mature but is not part of the Puppet Approved program.

Centralized Logging

There is a fairly tight coupling between the version of the module and the version of Logstash it manages. In this case, we will want a Version > 0.5.0 since we're managing Logstash 1.4. This is the latest version at the time this book was written, so we can simply install it. If there are newer versions, the install commands would need to be adjusted accordingly to match the version you wish to work with.

To install the module on the master, run the following command:

```
sudo puppet module install elasticsearch-logstash
```

This will get the module installed and should be second nature by now.

The `logstash` module uses a concept of configuration file snippets to perform its work. It's used to rely on a fairly robust set of defines to do the work, however, as configurations became more complex, creating a system of types and plugins to manage all possibilities became more difficult. As such, the project reverted to using file snippets that expose all of the possible configuration functionalities in the `logstash` module.

As mentioned previously, we'll define a profile, and then we'll define a role to use that.

First, let's create our configuration snippets. Basically, we're going to slice up the configuration file we used in the first section into three pieces. We'll then configure Logstash to use these pieces in a configuration.

Let's create the input from the messages file. To do this, we'll take the input section of the configuration file from earlier and put it in a file in the module path. We can then use the `logstash::configfile` method to include it.

Before we can do that, we need to create the file directory in our module. Inside the profiles module, run the `mkdir files` command to create the directory to hold static files served by the master.

Then, let's edit the `files/messages-input.conf` file and add the following contents:

```
input {
  file {
    path => "/var/log/messages"
    start_position => "beginning"
    type => "syslog"
  }
}
```

This should look familiar from earlier. We're creating a file input that will pick up the messages file and classify it as syslog. It'll also pick up the entire file through the first pass.

Now, let's add the second configuration file snippet. We'll call this file `files/syslog-filter.conf`. It should look as follows:

```
filter {
  if [type] == "syslog" {
    grok {
      match => { "message" => "%{SYSLOGTIMESTAMP:syslog_timestamp} %{SYSLOGHOST:syslog_hostn
      add_field => [ "received_at", "%{@timestamp}" ]
      add_field => [ "received_from", "%{host}" ]
    }
    syslog_pri { }
    date {
      match => [ "syslog_timestamp", "MMM  d HH:mm:ss", "MMM dd HH:mm:ss" ]
    }
  }
}
```

Note that the first match line was wrapped. This should also be reviewed as it's the same match line as the earlier one. It takes anything with a syslog type and applies three filters. The first one is a grok filter that splits the message into parts. The second is a filter that can parse the syslog priority. The final one is a filter that parses the syslog type's date to set the event timestamp for Logstash internally.

Finally, let's configure our output file. We'll put this one in the `files/elasticsearch-output.conf` file. The contents are as follows:

```
output {
  elasticsearch { cluster => "Elasticsearch" }
}
```

In this case, we're sending the output to the elasticsearch cluster. This is a bit different than earlier the one, as it uses discovery instead of pointing to a static host. Your use of this depends on your paranoia. If your network is well controlled, it is safe to use discovery. If you are worried about unknown hosts joining the cluster, you should statically set the hosts to connect to using a template.

Now that we have our files in place, we can go ahead and create our profile. We'll create it as the `manifests/logstash.pp` profile. We'll create the contents to look as follows:

```
class profiles::logstash {

  class { '::logstash':
    manage_repo     => true,
    repo_version    => '1.4',
    purge_configdir => true,
  }

  logstash::configfile { 'messages-input':
    order  => 100,
    source => 'puppet:///modules/profiles/messages-input.conf',
  }
  logstash::configfile { 'syslog-filter':
    order  => 200,
    source => 'puppet:///modules/profiles/syslog-filter.conf',
  }
  logstash::configfile { 'elasticsearch-output':
    order  => 900,
    source => 'puppet:///modules/profiles/elasticsearch-output.conf',
  }

}
```

Note that the last source line was wrapped.

This profile will install Logstash, telling it to manage the repository on the system and purge unmanaged configuration files. It then goes on to create three configuration file resources for our snippets. We set the order to ensure that they get added in the proper order, using numbers with `100` to allow us plenty of room to expand in the future.

Now we add it to our `logstash-server` role in our roles profile, which should now look like the following:

```
class roles::logstash-server {
  include profiles::logstash-elasticsearch
  include profiles::logstash
}
```

Once that's done, we can go ahead and run Puppet on agentone again and observe the output. It should look as follows:

```
[vagrant@agentone ~]$ sudo puppet agent --test
Info: Retrieving plugin
Info: Loading facts
Info: Caching catalog for agentone.book.local
Warning: The package type's allow_virtual parameter will be changing its default value from false to true in a future release. If you do not want to allow virtual packages, please explicitly set allow_virtual to false.
   (at /usr/lib/ruby/site_ruby/1.8/puppet/type/package.rb:430:in `default')
Info: Applying configuration version '1415598077'
Notice: /Stage[main]/Logstash::Repo/Yumrepo[logstash]/ensure: created
Info: changing mode of /etc/yum.repos.d/logstash.repo from 600 to 644
Notice: /Stage[main]/Logstash::Config/File[/etc/logstash/patterns]/ensure: created
Notice: /Stage[main]/Logstash::Config/File[/etc/logstash/plugins]/ensure: created
Notice: /Stage[main]/Logstash::Config/File[/etc/logstash/plugins/logstash]/ensure: created
Notice: /Stage[main]/Logstash::Config/File[/etc/logstash/plugins/logstash/filters]/ensure: created
Notice: /Stage[main]/Logstash::Config/File[/etc/logstash/plugins/logstash/codecs]/ensure: created
Notice: /Stage[main]/Logstash::Config/File[/etc/logstash/plugins/logstash/inputs]/ensure: created
Notice: /Stage[main]/Logstash::Config/File[/etc/logstash/plugins/logstash/outputs]/ensure: created
Notice: /Stage[main]/Logstash::Config/File_concat[ls-config]/ensure: created
Info: /Stage[main]/Logstash::Config/File_concat[ls-config]: Scheduling refresh of Class[Logstash::Service]
Info: Class[Logstash::Service]: Scheduling refresh of Logstash::Service::Init[logstash]
Info: Logstash::Service::Init[logstash]: Scheduling refresh of Service[logstash]
Notice: /Service[logstash]: Triggered 'refresh' from 1 events
Notice: Finished catalog run in 2.51 seconds
```

Once this completes, run the curl command from the first section. It is as follows:

`curl 'http://localhost:9200/_search?pretty'`

You should see the results returned, so on to Kibana!

Reporting on log data

As we saw earlier, Kibana is the graphical dashboard frontend in the ELK stack. It provides a rich interface that allows you to turn normal boring log data (or any data in Elasticsearch actually), into colorful dashboards that contain operational data. We'll go over to install Kibana via Puppet here. Since in Version 3 this is just a web application, this is a fairly straightforward procedure.

Installing Kibana

Since Kibana is just a web application running as static HTML, we'll configure it using a local web server as we did in the first section. Much like in that section we'll be using Apache to handle the installation of Kibana.

This will vary a bit from how we've handled the past installations. We're going to create an end-to-end module to handle this instead of relying on a community module.

The first step is to create our module to do it. We'll call it the `pupbook-kibana` module. We're doing this because none of the community modules present solve exactly what we're looking to do, and because it's a good exercise in a complete functioning module. To get started, run the following command to generate our module template:

```
puppet module generate pupbook-kibana
```

Now, we'll start flushing our module out. First, we'll create a class to install Kibana. We'll call it the `kibana::install` class. To do so, let's edit the `manifests/install.pp` file and add the following content:

```
class kibana::install (
  $version = "3.1.2",
  $site = "https://github.com/elasticsearch/kibana/archive/",
  $target = "/var/www/kibana",
  $archtarget = "/opt/",
) {
  validate_string($version)
  validate_string($site)

  $archive = "v${version}.tar.gz"
  $downloadurl = "${site}/${archive}"

  file { $archtarget:
    ensure => directory,
  }

  file { $target:
    ensure => directory,
  }

  # We use curl to download
  package { 'curl':
    ensure => present,
  }
```

```
  exec { 'download-kibana':
    command => "curl -L -s -S -k -o ${archtarget}/${archive}
${downloadurl}",
    path    => "/bin:/usr/bin",
    creates => "${archtarget}/${archive}",
    require => [Package['curl'], File[$archtarget], File[$target]],
    notify  => Exec['extract-kibana'],
  }

  exec { 'extract-kibana':
    command     => "tar --strip-components=1 -zxf
${archtarget}/${archive} -C ${target}",
    path        => "/bin:/usr/bin",
    refreshonly => true,
  }

}
```

Be aware that a few of the preceding lines were wrapped. They should be obvious, but if you have questions, see the code included with the book.

This is a fairly complete example complete with some validation. We're allowing parameters to be passed to the class to change what version we download, or where we install.

First, we set some variables to make our lives a bit easier, containing things like our archive name and the full URL we're downloading from.

Then, we go on to ensure that the directories we need are present, and the curl package we use to download software is installed.

Finally, we hit the interesting parts. We have two exec resources here that do the meat of the work. The first one sets up a download of the kibana source to a temporary location (the /opt location by default). This downloads the file from GitHub by default. It then notifies the other exec that will extract the archive contents to our target directory.

Ideally, we'd like all the software to be distributed by package, and we could easily use a tool to create the RPM. We would then need a repository infrastructure to hold it, and so on. This is a great goal if you have multiple packages you're dealing with, but if it ends up simply being a single package, this method will work. There are even utility modules on the forge that can assist. Use the search term archive to find them.

Once this install method runs, we will have a fully installed and working copy of Kibana. We now need to configure Apache to serve it. To do this, we'll use the puppetlabs/apache module.

Centralized Logging

First, we need to install it with our now super familiar command on the Puppet Master:

```
sudo puppet module install puppetlabs/apache
```

Now that it's installed, we'll create the necessary glue in our `kibana` module to use it to serve the pages.

We can do this in our profile for Kibana, since that's what the profile is normally for. However, I find that since Kibana requires a web server to operate, it's a reasonable choice to go ahead and configure it in that module. The only reason you may not want to is if you were to create a reusable module where the end user may wish to use a different web server to serve up `kibana`.

Let's edit the `manifests/apache.pp` file in our `kibana` module, and we'll make it look as follows:

```
class kibana::apache {
  class { '::apache':
    default_vhost => false,
  }

  apache::vhost { 'kibana':
    docroot => '/var/www/kibana/src/',
    port    => '80',
    require => Class['kibana::install'],
  }
}
```

This fairly simple class creates the `apache::vhost` for our Kibana configuration. If we had to interact with other `apache::vhost`, we'd need a more flexible way to handle this (unless we wanted Kibana to be the default `vhost`), but we shouldn't be mixing services that are unrelated anyway. A perfectly reasonable thing to do is to run this interface on one of the `logstash` hosts as it is very lightweight.

We can create one last class that handles configuring Kibana. However, in this case, the default configuration will suffice as it did earlier.

Let's glue it all together by adding it to the `init.pp` file. Edit the `manifests/init.pp` file and add the following:

```
class kibana {
  include kibana::install
  include kibana::apache
}
```

Continuing on this journey, we'll add this class directly to the role. Since it's specific to the site, we can skip the profile setup here and add it straight to the role. Edit the `roles/manifests/logstash-server.pp` file to make it look as follows:

```
class roles::logstash-server {
  include profiles::logstash-elasticsearch
  include profiles::logstash
  include kibana
}
```

Whew! That was a lot of work to get the entire stack up. None of it was difficult, but since we created an entire module from scratch it had some more steps.

We've already applied the role to our host, so it's just a matter of running Puppet on the agentone host now to see the results. When you do so, the output should be similar to the following screenshot:

Now, hit `http://10.78.78.50` with a browser. You should be greeted with the Kibana welcome page we saw in the first section of the chapter.

Now that we've got the entire ELK stack Puppetized, let's take a look at how we can use Puppet to automate collecting data from each of our hosts.

Configuring hosts to report log data

Now that we've been through the work of Puppetizing the host infrastructure for Logstash, let's take a look at how to Puppetize the collection on our hosts. There are a large number of ways to do this that contain various tradeoffs on things such as local parsing and the size of the shipping solution.

For this exercise, we'll use Redis as a message queue. This is the recommended configuration if you wish to use a message queue based system, if you wish to use a message queue and do not have one installed. It has the downside of having added complexity due to needing Redis installed. However, our Redis installation in this example is quite simple using a community module.

This is a well-supported and tested configuration. There are other possible message queues one could use instead of Redis, so if your environment has one set up, by all means use that one.

The first step is to get Redis installed. There are a stack of community modules that can do this. We'll be using the most popular one in terms of downloads, which is the `thomasvandoren/redis` command. To do this, first we must get it installed. The all too familiar following command does it:

```
sudo puppet module install thomasvandoren/redis
```

Now, we'll add a new profile for a Redis server. This will use a very default configuration, so it will be rather small. In our roles module, create the `manifests/logstash-redis.pp` file. The contents are as follows:

```
class profiles::logstash-redis {
  include redis
}
```

It's that simple. We'll use all of the default `redis` configuration, including the password. In production, you'd likely want to set authentication up for these purposes.

Now, we'll create a new `redis` input for our indexer. To do this, let's first create the configuration file snippet for the input in the profiles module. To do this, edit the `files/redis-input.conf` file and add the following contents:

```
input {
  redis {
```

```
            host => "localhost"
            data_type => "list"
            key => "logstash"
            type => "redis-input"
        }
    }
```

This tells Elasticsearch that we want a `redis-input` listening on `localhost`. We'll use the `list` data type, which is one of the methods Redis has to move data. We'll set our `key` or `queue` to `logstash`, and the type (if not specified on the shipper) to `redis-input`.

Now, we can go ahead and configure our profile for `logstash` to use this. To do this, we'll add a new stanza to the `manifests/logstash.pp` file to include our `redis` configuration file. We'll place it right after our messages input and it should look as follows:

```
    logstash::configfile { 'redis-input':
        order  => 101,
        source => 'puppet:///modules/profiles/redis-input.conf',
    }
```

Additionally, we'll add our new `logstash-redis` profile to our `logstash-server` role. To do this, edit the `manifests/logstash-server.pp` file in our roles module and make it look as follows:

```
    class roles::logstash-server {
      include profiles::logstash-elasticsearch
      include profiles::logstash
      include kibana
      include redis
    }
```

Once done, go ahead and run Puppet on agentone. You should see it install Redis and reconfigure Logstash. This may take some time as the module we're using actually compiles and installs Redis. We're going to omit the screenshot of the output for brevity (we've seen plenty of such outputs by now).

Now that we have that we can focus on the shipper side. To do this, we'll create a new profile called `logstash-shipper`. We'll base it on the `logstash` profile.

> There is an opportunity for improvement here by bringing the common pieces of this configuration together. This is a good opportunity for you to practice what you've learned.

Centralized Logging

First, let's make our `redis-input` file. For this example, we'll hardcode the IP to send to. We'd want to do this via a template in a bigger environment, likely obtained from Hiera. However, we're once again trying to keep these examples shorter and more simple. Edit the `files/redis-output.conf` file under the profiles module and add the following content:

```
output {
  redis {
    host => '10.78.78.50'
    data_type => 'list'
    key => 'logstash'
  }
}
```

This looks very much like our input, but in this case, we're statically setting the host to our Redis master.

Now, let's create the profile. Edit the `manifests/logstash-shipper.pp` file and include the following content:

```
class profiles::logstash-shipper {

  class { '::logstash':
    manage_repo     => true,
    repo_version    => '1.4',
    purge_configdir => true,
  }

  logstash::configfile { 'messages-input':
    order  => 100,
    source => 'puppet:///modules/profiles/messages-input.conf',
  }
  logstash::configfile { 'syslog-filter':
    order  => 200,
    source => 'puppet:///modules/profiles/syslog-filter.conf',
  }
  logstash::configfile { 'redis-output':
    order  => 900,
    source => 'puppet:///modules/profiles/redis-output.conf',
  }

}
```

This is very close to our `logstash` profile, with only the output changing to use the new configuration we've put in place. Now, we can create a `logstash-shipper` role by creating the `manifests/logstash-shipper.pp` file under the roles module, as shown in the following code:

```
class roles::logstash-shipper {
```

```
        include profiles::logstash-shipper
}
```

This is another case where the role ends up being very short and only contains the single module.

Now, let's add this as a default configuration in our `site.pp` file. Under the `/etc/puppet/manifests/site.pp` code, add the following default node definition:

```
node default {
    include roles::logstash-shipper
}
```

Finally, we're ready to go. On the master, run the `sudo chmod 644 /var/log/messages` command to make our messages file readable by Logstash, then run Puppet.

Now, let's return to our Kibana installation and see what we see there. We'll take a short cut straight to the Logstash dashboard by going to `http://10.78.78.50/index.html#/dashboard/file/logstash.json`. Once there scroll down to the filter section on the left-hand side and click on the host. You should see the output as follows:

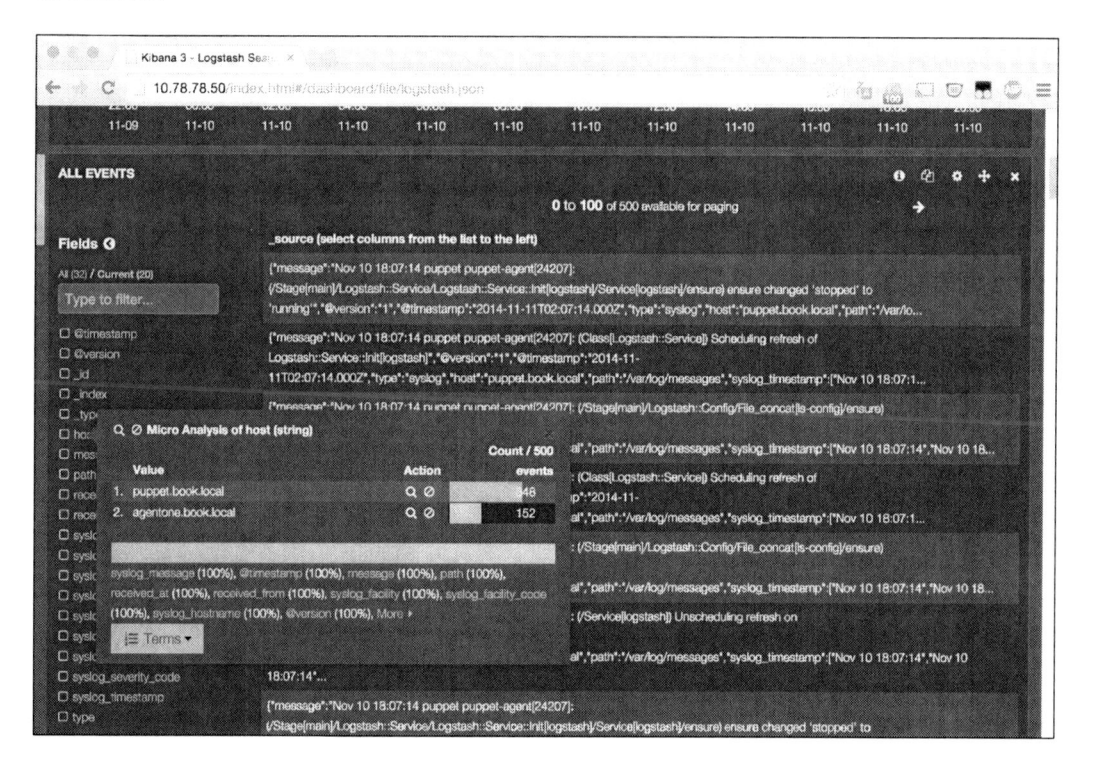

You can see that we now have data from both our Puppet master as well as agentone. If you start up agenttwo, sign its certificate, and run Puppet, you would see logs from that host also.

Using this method, we can now ship logs from all of our hosts to our single centralized Logstash server and analyze them using Kibana.

Summary

In this chapter, we explored centralized logging. We've seen why one might want to implement it and what the benefits are.

We then looked at the Logstash environment and the ELK stack. This includes Elasticsearch, Logstash, and Kibana that provide a complete log management solution that can scale to many hosts.

After doing this, we explored how to install all of these pieces using Puppet. We went through the acts of installing Elasticsearch, Logstash, and then Kibana using Puppet to automate the system.

Finally, we explored how to use Puppet to manage your other hosts to ship logs to this centralized logging solution and do this in a repeatable manner.

By doing all this, we saw many examples of how to implement solutions in Puppet. The building block of tools available to you continues to grow. While we didn't explore how to bring every log into this solution, we've given you enough knowledge to expand what we've learned to be used in other situations.

More information on the ELK stack can be found at `http://www.elasticsearch.org/overview/`.

In the next chapter, we'll cover how to use Puppet to help manage SELinux and audited configurations.

Puppet and OS Security Tools

We learned a lot so far about using Puppet to secure your systems as, well as how to use it to make groups of systems more secure. However, in all of that, we've not yet covered some of the basic OS-level functions that are available to secure a system. In this chapter, we'll review several of those functions.

SELinux is a powerful tool in the security arsenal. Most administrators experience with it, is along the lines of "how can I turn that off ?" This is born out of frustration with the poor documentation about the tool, as well as the tedious nature of the configuration.

While Puppet cannot help you with the documentation (which is getting better all the time), it can help you with some of the other challenges that SELinux can bring. That is, ensuring that the proper contexts and policies are in place on the systems being managed.

In this chapter, we'll cover the following topics related to OS-level security tools:

- A brief introduction to SELinux and auditd
- The built-in Puppet support for SELinux
- Community modules for SELinux
- Community modules for auditd

At the end of this chapter, you should have enough skills so that you no longer need to disable SELinux. However, if you still need to do so, it is certainly possible to do via the modules presented here.

Introducing SELinux and auditd

During the course of this chapter, we'll explore the SELinux framework for Linux and see how to automate it using Puppet. As part of the process, we'll also review auditd, the logging and auditing framework for Linux. Using Puppet, we can automate the configuration of these often-neglected security tools, and even move the configuration of these tools for various services to the modules that configure those services.

The SELinux framework

SELinux is a security system for Linux originally developed by the United States **National Security Agency (NSA)**. It is an in-kernel protection mechanism designed to provide **Mandatory Access Controls (MACs)** to the Linux kernel.

SELinux isn't the only MAC framework for Linux. AppArmor is an alternative MAC framework included in the Linux kernel since Version 2.6.30. We choose to implement SELinux; since it is the default framework used under Red Hat Linux, which we're using for our examples.

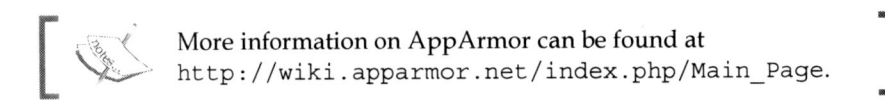

> More information on AppArmor can be found at `http://wiki.apparmor.net/index.php/Main_Page`.

These access controls work by confining processes to the minimal amount of files and network access that the processes require to run. By doing this, the controls limit the amount of collateral damage that can be done by a process, which becomes compromised.

SELinux was first merged to the Linux mainline kernel for the 2.6.0 release. It was introduced into Red Hat Enterprise Linux with Version 4, and into Ubuntu in Version 8.04. With each successive release of the operating systems, support for SELinux grows, and it becomes easier to use.

SELinux has a couple of core concepts that we need to understand to properly configure it. The first are the concepts of **types** and **contexts**. A type in SELinux is a grouping of similar things. Files used by Apache may be `httpd_sys_content_t`, for instance, which is a type that all content served by HTTP would have. The `httpd` process itself is of type `httpd_t`. These types are applied to **objects**, which represent discrete things, such as files and ports, and become part of the context of that object. The context of an object represents the object's user, role, type, and optionally data on multilevel security. For this discussion, the type is the most important component of the context.

Using a policy, we grant access from the **subject**, which represents a running process, to various objects that represent files, network ports, memory, and so on. We do that by creating a policy that allows a subject to have access to the types it requires to function.

SELinux has three modes that it can operate in. The first of these modes is disabled. As the name implies, the disabled mode runs without any SELinux enforcement. The second mode is called permissive. In permissive mode, SELinux will log any access violations, but will not act on them. This is a good way to get an idea of where you need to modify your policy, or tune Booleans to get proper system operations. The final mode, enforcing, will deny actions that do not have a policy in place. Under Red Hat Linux variants, this is the default SELinux mode. By default, Red Hat 6 runs SELinux with a targeted policy in enforcing mode. This means, that for the targeted daemons, SELinux will enforce its policy by default.

An example is in order here, to explain this well.

So far, we've been operating with SELinux disabled on our hosts. The first step in experimenting with SELinux is to turn it on. We'll set it to permissive mode at first, while we gather some information. To do this, after starting our master VM, we'll need to modify the SELinux configuration and reboot. While it's possible to change from enforcing mode to either permissive or disabled mode without a reboot, going back requires us to reboot.

Let's edit the `/etc/sysconfig/selinux` file and set the `SELINUX` variable to permissive on our puppetmaster. Remember to start the vagrant machine and SSH in as it is necessary. Once this is done, the file should look as follows:

```
# This file controls the state of SELinux on the system.
# SELINUX= can take one of these three values:
#       enforcing - SELinux security policy is enforced.
#       permissive - SELinux prints warnings instead of enforcing.
#       disabled - SELinux is fully disabled.
SELINUX=permissive
# SELINUXTYPE= type of policy in use. Possible values are:
#       targeted - Only targeted network daemons are protected.
#       strict - Full SELinux protection.
SELINUXTYPE=targeted
```

Once this is complete, we need to reboot. To do so, run the following command:

```
sudo shutdown -r now
```

Wait for the system to come back online.

Once the machine is back up and you SSH back into it, run the `getenforce` command. It should return permissive, which means SELinux is running, but not enforced.

Now, we can make sure our master is running and take a look at its context. If it's not running, you can start the service with the `sudo service puppetmaster start` command. Now, we'll use the `-Z` flag on the `ps` command to examine the SELinux flag. Many commands, such as `ps` and `ls` use the `-Z` flag to view the SELinux data. We'll go ahead and run the following command to view the SELinux data for the running puppetmaster:

```
ps -efZ|grep puppet
```

When you do this, you'll see a Linux output, such as follows:

```
unconfined_u:system_r:initrc_t:s0 puppet   1463     1  1 11:41 ? 00:00:29 /usr/bin/ruby /usr/bin/puppet master
```

If you take a look at the first part of the output line, you'll see that Puppet is running in the `unconfined_u:system_r:initrc_t` context. This is actually somewhat of a bug and a result of the Puppet policy on CentOS 6 being out of date. We should actually be running under the `system_u:system_r:puppetmaster_t:s0` context, but the policy is for a much older version of Puppet, so it runs unconfined.

Let's take a look at the `sshd` process to see what it looks like also. To do so, we'll just `grep` for `sshd` instead:

```
ps -efZ|grep sshd
```

The output is as follows:

```
system_u:system_r:sshd_t:s0-s0:c0.c1023 root 1206   1  0 11:40 ? 00:00:00 /usr/sbin/sshd
```

This is a more traditional output one would expect. The `sshd` process is running under the `system_u:system_r:sshd_t` context. This actually corresponds to the system user, the system role, and the `sshd` type.

The user and role are SELinux constructs that help you allow role-based access controls. The users do not map to system users, but allow us to set a policy based on the SELinux user object. This allows role-based access control, based on the SELinux user. Previously the `unconfined` user was a user that will not be enforced.

Now, we can take a look at some objects. Doing a `ls -lZ /etc/ssh` command results in the following:

```
[vagrant@puppet ~]$ ls -lZ /etc/ssh
-rw-------. root root system_u:object_r:etc_t:s0       moduli
-rw-r--r--. root root system_u:object_r:etc_t:s0       ssh_config
-rw-------. root root system_u:object_r:etc_t:s0       sshd_config
-rw-------. root root system_u:object_r:sshd_key_t:s0  ssh_host_dsa_key
-rw-r--r--. root root system_u:object_r:sshd_key_t:s0  ssh_host_dsa_key.pub
-rw-------. root root system_u:object_r:sshd_key_t:s0  ssh_host_key
-rw-r--r--. root root system_u:object_r:sshd_key_t:s0  ssh_host_key.pub
-rw-------. root root system_u:object_r:sshd_key_t:s0  ssh_host_rsa_key
-rw-r--r--. root root system_u:object_r:sshd_key_t:s0  ssh_host_rsa_key.pub
[vagrant@puppet ~]$
```

As you can see, each of the files belongs to a context that includes the system user, as well as the object role. They are split among the `etc` type for configuration files and the `sshd_key` type for keys.

The SSH policy allows the `sshd` process to read both of these file types. Other policies, say, for NTP, would potentially allow the `ntpd` process to read the `etc` types, but it would not be able to read the `sshd_key` files.

This very fine-grained control is the power of SELinux. However, with great power comes very complex configuration. Configuration can be confusing to set up, if it doesn't happen correctly. For instance, with Puppet, the wrong type can potentially impact the system if not dealt with.

Fortunately, in permissive mode, we will log data that we can use to assist us with this. This leads us into the second half of the system that we wish to discuss, which is auditd.

> In the meantime, there is a bunch of information on SELinux available on its website at http://selinuxproject.org/page/Main_Page. There's also a very funny, but informative, resource available describing SELinux at https://people.redhat.com/duffy/selinux/selinux-coloring-book_A4-Stapled.pdf.

The auditd framework for audit logging

SELinux does a great job at limiting access to system components; however, reporting what enforcement took place was not one of its objectives.

Enter the auditd. The auditd is an auditing framework developed by Red Hat. It is a complete auditing system using rules to indicate what to audit. This can be used to log SELinux events, as well as much more.

Under the hood, auditd has hooks into the kernel to watch system calls and other processes. Using the rules, you can configure logging for any of these events. For instance, you can create a rule that monitors writes to the /etc/passwd file. This would allow you to see if any users were added to the system. We can also add monitoring of files, such as `lastlog` and `wtmp` to monitor the login activity. We'll explore this example later when we configure auditd.

To quickly see how a rule works, we'll manually configure a quick rule that will log the time when the `wtmp` file was edited. This will add some system logging around users logging in.

To do this, let's edit the /etc/audit/audit.rules file to add a rule to monitor this. Edit the file and add the following lines:

```
-w /var/log/wtmp -p wa -k logins
-w /etc/passwd -p wa -k password
```

We'll take a look at what the preceding lines do. These lines both start with the `-w` clauses. These indicate the files that we are monitoring. Second, we have the `-p` clauses. This lets you set what file operations we monitor. In this case, it is `write` and `append` operations. Finally, with the the `-k` entries, we're setting a keyword that is logged and can be filtered on.

This should go at the end of the file. Once it's done, reload auditd with the following command:

```
sudo service auditd restart
```

Once this is complete, go ahead and log another `ssh` session in. Once you can simply log, back out. Once this is done, take a look at the /var/log/audit/audit.log file. You should see the content like the following:

```
type=SYSCALL msg=audit(1416795396.816:482): arch=c000003e syscall=2
success=yes exit=8 a0=7fa983c446aa a1=1 a2=2 a3=7fff3f7a6590 items=1
ppid=1206 pid=2202 auid=500 uid=0 gid=0 euid=0 suid=0 fsuid=0 egid=0
sgid=0 fsgid=0 tty=(none) ses=51 comm="sshd" exe="/usr/sbin/sshd"
subj=system_u:system_r:sshd_t:s0-s0:c0.c1023 key="logins"
```

```
type=SYSCALL msg=audit(1416795420.057:485): arch=c000003e syscall=2
success=yes exit=7 a0=7fa983c446aa a1=1 a2=2 a3=8 items=1 ppid=1206
pid=2202 auid=500 uid=0 gid=0 euid=0 suid=0 fsuid=0 egid=0 sgid=0
fsgid=0 tty=(none) ses=51 comm="sshd" exe="/usr/sbin/sshd"
subj=system_u:system_r:sshd_t:s0-s0:c0.c1023 key="logins"
```

There are tons of fields in this output, including the SELinux context, the userID, and so on. Of interest is the `auid`, which is the audit user ID. On commands run via the `sudo` command, this will still contain the user ID of the user who called `sudo`. This is a great way to log commands performed via `sudo`.

Auditd also logs SELinux failures. They get logged under the type AVC. These `access vector cache` logs will be placed in the `auditd` log file when a SELinux violation occurs.

> Much like SELinux, auditd is somewhat complicated. The intricacies of it are beyond the scope of this book. You can get more information at http://people.redhat.com/sgrubb/audit/.

SELinux and Puppet

Puppet has direct support for several features of SELinux. There are two native Puppet types for SELinux: **selboolean** and **selmodule**. These types support setting SELinux Booleans and installing SELinux policy modules.

SELinux Booleans are variables that impact on how SELinux behaves. They are set to allow various functions to be permitted. For instance, you set a SELinux Boolean to true to allow the `httpd` process to access network ports.

SELinux modules are groupings of policies. They allow policies to be loaded in a more granular way. The Puppet selmodule type allows Puppet to load these modules.

Additionally, there is support in the file type for setting the SELinux data on files, as you may recall from an earlier chapter.

The selboolean type

The targeted SELinux policy that most distributions use is based on the SELinux reference policy. One of the features of this policy is the use of Boolean variables that control actions of the policy.

Puppet and OS Security Tools

There are over 200 of these Booleans on a Red Hat 6-based machine. We can investigate them by installing the `policycoreutils-python` package on the operating system. You can do this by executing the following command:

```
sudo yum install policycoreutils-python
```

Once installed, we can run the `semanage boolean -l` command to get a list of the Boolean values, along with their descriptions. The output of this will look as follows:

```
sanlock_use_samba                   (off  ,  off) Allow sanlock to manage cifs files
allow_execmod                       (on   ,  on)  Allow all unconfined executables to use libraries requiring text relocatio
n that are not labeled textrel_shlib_t)
awstats_purge_apache_log_files (off ,  off) Determine whether awstats can purge httpd log files.
allow_guest_exec_content            (off  ,  off) allow_guest_exec_content
allow_gssd_read_tmp                 (on   ,  on)  Allow gssd to read temp directory.  For access to kerberos tgt.
webadm_manage_user_files            (off  ,  off) Allow webadm to manage files in users home directories
allow_rsync_anon_write              (off  ,  off) Allow rsync to modify public files used for public file transfer services.
   Files/Directories must be labeled public_content_rw_t.
git_session_bind_all_unreserved_ports (off , off) Determine whether Git session daemon can bind TCP sockets to all un
reserved ports.
httpd_ssi_exec                      (off  ,  off) Allow HTTPD to run SSI executables in the same domain as system CGI script
s.
httpd_use_openstack                 (off  ,  off) Allow httpd to access openstack ports
puppet_manage_all_files             (off  ,  off) Allow Puppet client to manage all file types.
httpd_enable_ftp_server             (off  ,  off) Allow httpd to act as a FTP server by listening on the ftp port.
fcron_crond                         (off  ,  off) Enable extra rules in the cron domain to support fcron.
virt_use_fusefs                     (off  ,  off) Allow virt to read fuse files
allow_domain_fd_use                 (on   ,  on)  Allow all domains to use other domains file descriptors
authlogin_radius                    (off  ,  off) Allow users to login using a radius server
ssh_chroot_full_access              (off  ,  off) Allow ssh with chroot env to manage all files
httpd_setrlimit                     (off  ,  off) Allow httpd daemon to change system limits
squid_connect_any                   (on   ,  on)  Allow squid to connect to all ports, not just HTTP, FTP, and Gopher ports.
virt_use_samba                      (off  ,  off) Allow virt to manage cifs files
cluster_use_execmem                 (off  ,  off) Allow cluster administrative cluster domains memcheck-amd64- to use execut
able memory
named_write_master_zones            (off  ,  off) Allow BIND to write the master zone files. Generally this is used for dyna
mic DNS or zone transfers.
exim_manage_user_files              (off  ,  off) Allow exim to create, read, write, and delete unprivileged user files.
logging_syslog_can_read_tmp         (off  ,  off) Allow syslogd daemon to read user tmp content
cron_can_relabel                    (off  ,  off) Allow system cron jobs to relabel filesystem for restoring file contexts.
git_system_use_cifs                 (off  ,  off) Determine whether Git system daemon can access cifs file systems.
[vagrant@puppet ~]$
```

As you can see, there exists a very large number of settings that can be reconfigured, simply by setting the appropriate Boolean value.

The selboolean Puppet type supports managing these Boolean values. The provider is fairly simple, accepting the following values:

Parameter	Description
name	This contains the name of the Boolean to be set. It defaults to the title.
persistent	This checks whether to write the value to disk for the next boot.
provider	This is the provider for the type. Usually, the default getsetsebool value is accepted.
value	This contains the value of the Boolean, true or false.

Usage of this type is rather simple. We'll show an example that will set the `puppetmaster_use_db parameter` to `true` value. If we are using the SELinux Puppet policy, this would allow the master to talk to a database. For our use, it's a simple unused variable that we can use for demonstration purposes.

As a reminder, the SElinux policy for Puppet on CentOS 6 is outdated, so setting the Boolean does not impact the version of Puppet we're running. It does, however, serve to show how a Boolean is set.

To do this, we'll create a sample role and profile for our puppetmaster. This is something that would likely exist in a production environment to manage the configuration of the master. In this example, we'll simply build a small profile and role for the master.

Let's start with the profile. Copy over the profiles module we've slowly been building up, and let's add a `puppetmaster.pp` profile. To do so, edit the `profiles/manifests/puppetmaster.pp` file and make it look as follows:

```
class profiles::puppetmaster {
  selboolean { 'puppetmaster_use_db':
    value      => on,
    persistent => true,
  }
}
```

Then, we'll move on to the role. Copy the roles, and edit the `roles/manifests/puppetmaster.pp` file there and make it look as follows:

```
class roles::puppetmaster {
  include profiles::puppetmaster
}
```

Once this is done, we can apply it to our host. Edit the `/etc/puppet/manifests/site.pp` file. We'll apply the `puppetmaster` role to the puppetmaster machine, as follows:

```
node 'puppet.book.local' {
  include roles::puppetmaster
}
```

Now, we'll run Puppet and get the output as follows:

```
[vagrant@puppet modules]$ sudo puppet agent --test
Info: Retrieving plugin
Info: Caching catalog for puppet.book.local
Info: Applying configuration version '1416805803'
Notice: /Stage[main]/Profiles::Puppetmaster/Selboolean[puppetmaster_use_db]/value: value changed 'off' to 'on'
Notice: Finished catalog run in 22.70 seconds
[vagrant@puppet modules]$
```

As you can see, it set the value to on when run. Using this method, we can set any of the SELinux Boolean values we need for our system to operate properly.

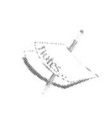

> More information on SELinux Booleans with information on how to obtain a list of them can be found at https://access.redhat.com/documentation/en-US/Red_Hat_Enterprise_Linux/6/html/Security-Enhanced_Linux/sect-Security-Enhanced_Linux-Working_with_SELinux-Booleans.html.

The selmodule type

The other native type inside Puppet is a type to manage the SELinux modules. Modules are compiled collections of the SELinux policy. They're loaded into the kernel using the `selmodule` command. This Puppet type provides support for this mechanism.

The available parameters are as follows:

Parameter	Description
name	This contains the name of the module – it defaults to the title
ensure	This is the desired state – present or absent
provider	This specifies the provider for the type – it should be selmodule
selmoduledir	This is the directory that contains the module to be installed
selmodulepath	This provides the complete path to the module to be installed if not present in selmoduledir
syncversion	This checks whether to resync the module if a new version is found, such as ensure => latest

Using the module, we can take our compiled module and serve it onto the system with Puppet. We can then use the module to ensure that it gets installed on the system. This lets us centrally manage the module with Puppet.

The community module that we'll be using to manage SELinux in a later section uses this type to load the module into Puppet. We'll see an example where this module compiles a policy and then installs it, so we won't show a specific example here. Instead, we'll move on to talk about the last SELinux-related component in Puppet.

File parameters for SELinux

The final internal support for SELinux types comes in the form of the file type. We covered these options briefly in an earlier chapter, but really didn't add any details, so we'll do so here.

The file type parameters are as follows:

Parameter	Description
selinux_ignore_defaults	By default, Puppet will use the matchpathcon function to set the context of a file. This overrides that behavior if set to true value.
Selrange	This sets the SELinux range component. We've not really covered this. It's not used in most mainstream distributions at the time this book was written.
Selrole	This sets the SELinux role on the file.
seltype	This sets the SELinux type on the file.
seluser	This sets the SELinux role on the file.

Usually, if you place files in the correct location (the expected location for a service) on the filesystem, Puppet will get the SELinux properties correct via its use of the matchpathcon function. This function (which also has a matching utility) applies a default context based on the policy settings. Setting the context manually is used in cases where you're storing data outside the normal location. For instance, you might be storing web data under the /opt file.

The preceding types and providers provide the basics that allow you to manage SELinux on a system. We'll now take a look at a couple of community modules that build on these types and create a more in-depth solution.

Configuring SELinux with community modules

We now looked at how to get a system up and working using SELinux under Puppet. We can go ahead and build a module to manage our policies by hand, but why not use a module someone else has invested time into. We're better off contributing work back to make an existing module better if it can be made to work for us.

In this section, we'll be looking at the spiette/selinux module that contains a more complete solution to manage SELinux on Puppet.

This module can handle setting SELinux to any of the three modes (disabled, permissive, and enforcing). It can also handle compiling SELinux policy modules and installing them on hosts. This allows you to track the more easily handled plain text versions of the files in version control with your Puppet data, instead of the binary compiled policy modules.

Creating a full policy is out of the context of this book, so for our example purposes, we'll first use the default policy shipped with the module. Then, we'll create a very simple policy module. I have used the *SELinux Cookbook, Sven Vermeulen, Packt Publishing*, at the Packt Publishing website as a reference for creating an example module for our use.

Let's get moving! First, we need to, as usual, install the module for our use. To do so, run the following command on the master:

```
sudo puppet module install spiette-selinux
```

Now that it's installed, let's make a profile to handle our resources. Under our profiles module, let's create a manifest called `profiles/manifests/selinuxtest.pp`. We'll use this as the content to begin with:

```
class profiles::selinuxtest {
  class { 'selinux':
    mode => 'permissive',
  }

  selinux::module { 'rsynclocal':
    ensure => 'present',
  }

}
```

These class and defined types are largely out of the module documentation for the SELinux module, but we'll explore what they do. The first declares the main `selinux` class. We can pass one of two parameters in, and accept the defaults with just an `include` or `require` parameter on the class. The first parameter is the `mode` parameter. It specifies the mode we want SELinux to be set to. In this case, it's `'permissive'` mode. If changing the mode requires a reboot, it will log as such in your manifest at each run.

The second parameter is `installmake`. This indicates if `make` should be installed by this module, or if it is installed with another module. One of the downsides of compiling this locally is that it requires `make` to be installed. In many cases, this will be set to `true` value, which is the default value. If you happen to manage your compiler tools in another manifest, you can set this to `false` value here.

The second thing present in this manifest is a `selinux::module` defined resource. This define is what sets the system up to compile and load a module. In this case, we're going to load the default example `rsynclocal` module that ships with the `selinux` module. This define accepts the following parameters:

Parameter	Description
ensure	This contains one of `present`, `enabled`, `disabled`, or `absent` values. This sets the state of the module on the target system.
modules_dir	This specifies the directory on the target system that modules are stored in. The default is under the Puppet `var` directory in a directory called `selinux`.
source	This is the source directory to the module. Defaults to `puppet:///modules/selinux/${name}`.
ignore	This contains any files that you want ignored in the preceding directory. It is useful for excluding things, such as `swap` files, VCS resources, and so on.

Now, let's create our role to hold our profile. Edit the `roles/manifests/selinuxtest.pp` file under our roles module and set the content to the following:

```
class roles::selinuxtest {
  include profiles::selinuxtest
}
```

Puppet and OS Security Tools

They say repetition is the key to learning, and by now the roles and profiles pattern have become a second nature. Now, let's make sure the modules are present on our system, and we'll include the module on our master as a test. We'll edit our `/etc/puppet/manifests/site.pp` file and add the new role to it, as follows:

```
node 'puppet.book.local' {
  include roles::puppetmaster
  include roles::selinuxtest
}
```

Now, let's run Puppet and see what happens! If you need a refresher here on how to do this, you can refer to any of the previous chapters. The output should be something similar to the following screenshot:

```
-#       targeted - Only targeted network daemons are protected.
-#       strict - Full SELinux protection.
-SELINUXTYPE=targeted
+# SELINUXTYPE= can take one of these two values:
+#       targeted - Targeted processes are protected,
+#       minimum - Modification of targeted policy. Only selected processes are protected.
+#       mls - Multi Level Security protection.
+SELINUXTYPE=targeted

Info: Computing checksum on file /etc/selinux/config
Info: FileBucket got a duplicate file {md5}b073d595403cb0c382a432ddc86bd46f
Info: /Stage[main]/Selinux::Config/File[/etc/selinux/config]: Filebucketed /etc/selinux/conf
ig to puppet with sum b073d595403cb0c382a432ddc86bd46f
Notice: /Stage[main]/Selinux::Config/File[/etc/selinux/config]/content: content changed '{md
5}b073d595403cb0c382a432ddc86bd46f' to '{md5}6b0ca1ae134409744a0d5f5d354e35da'
Notice: /Stage[main]/Profiles::Selinuxtest/Selinux::Module[rsynclocal]/File[/var/lib/puppet/
selinux/rsynclocal]/ensure: created
Notice: /Stage[main]/Profiles::Selinuxtest/Selinux::Module[rsynclocal]/File[/var/lib/puppet/
selinux/rsynclocal/rsynclocal.te]/ensure: defined content as '{md5}3def84b0012434040742c96e0
0e63b66'
Info: /Stage[main]/Profiles::Selinuxtest/Selinux::Module[rsynclocal]/File[/var/lib/puppet/se
linux/rsynclocal/rsynclocal.te]: Scheduling refresh of Exec[rsynclocal-makemod]
Notice: /Stage[main]/Profiles::Selinuxtest/Selinux::Module[rsynclocal]/Exec[rsynclocal-makem
od]: Triggered 'refresh' from 1 events
Notice: /Stage[main]/Profiles::Selinuxtest/Selinux::Module[rsynclocal]/Selmodule[rsynclocal]
/ensure: created
Notice: Finished catalog run in 25.60 seconds
[vagrant@puppet ~]$
```

Notice that it did quite a bit. We can now run the following command and see that our policy module is loaded:

```
sudo semodule -l|grep rsynclocal
```

You should see that the `rsynclocal` module is installed.

We'll now quickly create a small policy module that we can use for a test to show that it works. To do this, we're going to create essentially an empty module – we'll define types but give them no permissions. We'll then quickly be able to see that it fails and it gets logged as expected.

To do so, create a `selinuxtest` directory under the `profiles/files` directory. From the root of the `profiles` module, we can run the following command to do this:

`mkdir -p files/selinuxtest`

Inside this directory, we'll create our `files/selinuxtest/selinuxtest.te` module file. Edit this file and make the contents look as follows:

```
policy_module(selinuxtest, 0.1)

gen_require(`
  type unconfined_t;
  class process transition;
')

type selinuxtest_t;
type selinuxtest_exec_t;

role unconfined_r types selinuxtest_t;
userdom_user_application_domain(selinuxtest_t, selinuxtest_exec_t)
```

> A good high-level tutorial of writing a policy can be found at http://billauer.co.il/selinux-policy-module-howto.html. It explains what the preceding command does.

This essentially creates a blank type and exec type with no permissions. Once done, let's add it to our `profiles` manifest, which should now look as follows:

```
class profiles::selinuxtest {
  class { 'selinux':
    mode => 'permissive',
  }

  selinux::module { 'rsynclocal':
    ensure => 'present',
  }

  selinux::module { 'selinuxtest':
    ensure => 'present',
    source => 'puppet:///modules/profiles/selinuxtest/',
  }

}
```

Puppet and OS Security Tools

Do notice how in our new module, we specified the source inside our profile. The ability to do this allows us to keep the `selinux` module as a utility module with no local changes.

Now, if we run Puppet again, we should see the output like we did previously, that indicated our module was compiled and installed.

Now, to test it, we'll just change the context of a binary to our new `selinuxtest_t` type and try to run it. To do this, run the following command:

```
sudo chcon -t selinuxtest_t /bin/nano
```

Now, start `nano` and exit it. It'll run since we're in `permissive` mode. Then, we'll `grep nano` from the audit log to see what happened:

```
[vagrant@puppet ~]$ sudo grep nano /var/log/audit/audit.log
type=AVC msg=audit(1417232446.274:5124): avc:  denied  { relabelto } for  pid=8170 comm="chcon" name="nano" dev=dm-0 ino=271960 scontext=unconfined_u:unconfined_r:unconfined_t:s0-s0:c0.c1023 tcontext=system_u:object_r:selinuxtest_t:s0 tclass=file
type=AVC msg=audit(1417232446.274:5124): avc:  denied  { associate } for  pid=8170 comm="chcon" name="nano" dev=dm-0 ino=271960 scontext=system_u:object_r:selinuxtest_t:s0 tcontext=system_u:object_r:fs_t:s0 tclass=filesystem
type=PATH msg=audit(1417232446.274:5124): item=0 name="/bin/nano" inode=271960 dev=fd:00 mode=0100755 ouid=0 ogid=0 rdev=00:00 obj=system_u:object_r:bin_t:s0 nametype=NORMAL
type=AVC msg=audit(1417232469.435:5127): avc:  denied  { execute } for  pid=6532 comm="bash" name="nano" dev=dm-0 ino=271960 scontext=unconfined_u:unconfined_r:unconfined_t:s0-s0:c0.c1023 tcontext=system_u:object_r:selinuxtest_t:s0 tclass=file
type=PATH msg=audit(1417232469.435:5127): item=0 name="/bin/nano" inode=271960 dev=fd:00 mode=0100755 ouid=0 ogid=0 rdev=00:00 obj=system_u:object_r:selinuxtest_t:s0 nametype=NORMAL
type=AVC msg=audit(1417232469.435:5128): avc:  denied  { execute_no_trans } for  pid=8171 comm="bash" path="/bin/nano" dev=dm-0 ino=271960 scontext=unconfined_u:unconfined_r:unconfined_t:s0-s0:c0.c1023 tcontext=system_u:object_r:selinuxtest_t:s0 tclass=file
type=SYSCALL msg=audit(1417232469.435:5128): arch=c000003e syscall=59 success=yes exit=0 a0=1df4a30 a1=1dd85e0 a2=1dda1a0 a3=7fff68e13810 items=2 ppid=6532 pid=8171 auid=500 uid=500 gid=500 euid=500 suid=500 fsuid=500 egid=500 sgid=500 fsgid=500 tty=pts0 ses=679 comm="nano" exe="/bin/nano" subj=unconfined_u:unconfined_r:unconfined_t:s0-s0:c0.c1023 key=(null)
type=EXECVE msg=audit(1417232469.435:5128): argc=1 a0="nano"
type=PATH msg=audit(1417232469.435:5128): item=0 name="/bin/nano" inode=271960 dev=fd:00 mode=0100755 ouid=0 ogid=0 rdev=00:00 obj=system_u:object_r:selinuxtest_t:s0 nametype=NORMAL
[vagrant@puppet ~]$
```

You'll note that SELinux would have actually denied our attempt to use the `chcon` parameter. However, you can also see that there are several AVC denies on `nano` itself.

As you can see, this provides a handy method to handle installation of your own custom SELinux policy modules.

> More information on this module can be found on its GitHub page at https://forge.puppetlabs.com/spiette/selinux.

Configuring auditd with community modules

Auditd has many less available community modules. This is likely due to its very simple nature—configuring can be done with a simple file module and a couple of packages in most cases. Nonetheless, let's take a look at a community module that will manage your configuration for you. It even provides a decent base ruleset and contains very powerful customization options.

We'll be looking at the evenup/auditd module here. As mentioned previously, it has most of the auditd options exposed and provides a decent default ruleset with the option to override. We'll start by installing it:

```
sudo puppet module install evenup-auditd
```

The module contains a single entry point, the main `auditd` class that accepts four parameters. They are as follows:

Parameter	Description
logagent	The module supports using Beaver to process `auditd` log files (Beaver is a log shipper for Logstash). It can be `beaver` or `null`.
rules	This is the path to the rules file – defaults to `puppet:///modules/auditd/auditd`
config_override	This is a hash that contains values to override the default `config`. It is explained later in the chapter.
package_name	The `auditd` package name. Usually, it is determined automatically.

This module uses a different pattern for configuration, where you can supply a `config` hash to override the settings. This is as opposed to exposing the 24 different values as parameters. The names of these configuration variables can be found in the `init.pp` file, as they aren't documented very well. Submitting a better documentation is an easy way new users can give back to community modules.

For our example, we'll simply accept all of the defaults. In this case, they're sufficient, so customizing the parameters is less important.

You might ask why when we've not customized the rules we pass `auditd` at all. As it happens, the rule set that comes with the auditd module is fairly comprehensive, and includes the rules that we used in our previous example and many more. If we wished to customize the ruleset that got applied, we would do so by setting the rules parameter to the module to a new file. This would likely be present in our profiles module as to avoid modifying the base module. We would then pass this using either Hiera or a specific class declaration that contains it.

We'll create our profile and our role and then apply it to the master.

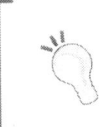

> We've been creating roles for most profiles. In reality, many of these things, such as auditd would likely go in a common role to get applied everywhere. That's where the roles pattern shows its real power.

To do so, let's create the `profiles/manifests/auditd.pp` file inside our profiles module with the following content:

```
class profiles::auditd {
   include ::auditd
}
```

We use the `::` here to stop the circular dependency caused by how classes are resolved.

If we want to pass in a custom rule set, let's say in our profiles module, in the `profiles/files/etc/auditd/auditd.rules` file, it would look like the following:

```
class profiles::auditd {
  class { 'auditd':
    rules => 'puppet:///modules/profiles/etc/audit/auditd.rules',
  }
}
```

Either way, the next step would be as follows:

Then, we'll create the role. In the `roles/manifests/auditd.pp` file in our roles, add the following:

```
class roles::auditd {
   include profiles::auditd
}
```

Finally, add the `auditd` role to the master in the `/etc/puppet/manifests/site.pp` file:

```
node 'puppet.book.local' {
  include roles::puppetmaster
  include roles::selinuxtest
  include roles::auditd
}
```

Now, we'll run Puppet and see what happens. It should look like the following:

```
+# Files and programs deleted by the user (successful and unsuccessful)
+-a always,exit -F arch=b64 -S unlink -S unlinkat -S rename -S renameat -F auid>=500 -F auid !=4294967295 -k delete
+
+# Make the configuration immutable - reboot is required to change audit rules
+# 0 disable
+# 1 enable
+# 2 imutable - reboot required to change config
+-e 1

Info: Computing checksum on file /etc/audit/audit.rules
Info: /Stage[main]/Auditd::Config/File[/etc/audit/audit.rules]: Filebucketed /etc/audit/audit.rules to puppet with sum 6317ac90125b85387f74ee4848c0276d
Notice: /Stage[main]/Auditd::Config/File[/etc/audit/audit.rules]/content: content changed '{md5}6317ac90125b85387f74ee4848c0276d' to '{md5}f1da231ed56d51cc15edcee87597677c'
Notice: /Stage[main]/Auditd::Config/File[/etc/audit/audit.rules]/mode: mode changed '0640' to '0440'
Info: /Stage[main]/Auditd::Config/File[/etc/audit/audit.rules]: Scheduling refresh of Class[Auditd::Service]
Info: /Stage[main]/Auditd::Config/File[/etc/audit/audit.rules]: Scheduling refresh of Class[Auditd::Service]
Info: Class[Auditd::Service]: Scheduling refresh of Service[auditd]
Notice: /Stage[main]/Auditd::Service/Service[auditd]: Triggered 'refresh' from 1 events
Notice: Finished catalog run in 38.43 seconds
[vagrant@puppet ~]$
```

You can see that it updated the rules and reloaded auditd. It added a lot of rules, so the Puppet run itself should have triggered some of them. Look at the `/var/log/audit/audit.log` file, and look for the word `key`. Our new rules used keywords, so you can find them easily. You should see the output like the following:

```
type=SYSCALL msg=audit(1417268692.615:5661): arch=c000003e syscall=87 success=yes exit=0 a0=
50dfb10 a1=0 a2=c a3=617461635f746e65 items=2 ppid=9038 pid=9039
auid=500 uid=0 gid=0 euid=0
 suid=0 fsuid=0 egid=0 sgid=0 fsgid=0 tty=pts0 ses=679 comm="puppet"
exe="/usr/bin/ruby" sub
j=unconfined_u:unconfined_r:unconfined_t:s0-s0:c0.c1023 key="delete"
```

You can see that it contains the `auid`, which is the user who did the sudo command. It's a great way to log that, as was mentioned earlier.

By applying a module like this to all your hosts, you can quickly get auditd working everywhere. Combine this with Logstash from the last chapter, and you have an excellent way to manage audit logging.

Summary

This chapter set out to demystify some of the repetitiveness of configuring SELinux and auditd on Linux hosts. While it's not possible to explain all of the intricacies of them in a book on Puppet, we hope that there was enough information to get you started and perhaps, reverse the trend of just setting it to disabled or permissive.

First, we looked at what SELinux and auditd were, and gave a brief example of how they can be used. We looked at what they can do, and how they can be used to secure your systems.

After this, we looked at the specific support for SELinux in Puppet. We looked at the two built-in types to support it, as well as the parameters on the file type.

Then, we took a look at one of the several community modules for managing SELinux. Using this module, we can store the policies as text instead of compiled blobs.

Finally, we looked at a community module to manage auditd. While auditd is simple to configure, using a module saves the work of creating your own. Contributing back is a good way to support open source.

Now, we'll move on and wrap up our time together, and review what we learned and see where to go from here.

Going Forward

We've finally reached the end of our journey. It's time to examine where you'll go from here as you continue to expand your experience with Puppet. There exists a number of resources to further your education. In this chapter, we'll cover the following topics:

- Where to get more information on developing good modules
- A brief discussion of Puppet device management
- Other useful reporting tools
- Some other useful Puppet tools
- A brief discussion of the Puppet community
- Some general thoughts on moving forward

What we've learned

We've covered a lot in our time together. In everything that we've covered, we learned some useful patterns that will serve you, as you expand your skill base. Specific examples were shown that are useful in themselves, but the underlying concepts being taught will assist you, as you build your own Puppet infrastructure.

Just as importantly, we learned that tools exist to make our lives easier. As security professionals, often times, change can be viewed as the enemy. However, with the right controls and processes in place, change can actually be a positive thing. Change drives business values. A company that is not moving forward is falling behind. Tools, such as Puppet and the others introduced in this book can help manage that change and still satisfy the regulatory, and other, requirements that are present in our jobs.

Where to go next

Puppet is a diverse ecosystem. The core Puppet tool itself is just a single tool in that system. When combined with tools, such as Hiera, PuppetDB, and others, the real power begins to shine. There are plenty of resources that will help you with these tools. In this section, we'll briefly explore where to go next, as you continue to delve into the Puppet ecosystem.

Writing and testing Puppet modules

We've written our fair share of Puppet modules during this book. We even explored some good patterns to use in doing so. However, there are several things we just touched on that should be explored further, such as testing. Additionally, we'll point out some other general resources that will help you on your way.

Puppet modules and data in Hiera should be considered code, just as any other part of your system. As such, they should be tested thoroughly to ensure that they operate properly. The prevailing method of doing that is using rspec with a number of plugins.

The first project is `rspec-puppet`. We use `rspec-puppet` to create behavior-driven tests of our Puppet manifests. These test the catalog to ensure that the things we are expecting to happen end up in the catalog. This also has a pleasant side effect of compiling the catalog when we run them, so it catches any silly syntax errors. More information on rspec can be found at http://rspec.info/, and on `rspec-puppet` at http://rspec-puppet.com/.

The second useful project for testing is beaker and the `beaker-rspec` gem. Beaker is an acceptance testing system that can use Vagrant or any number of other systems to provision systems for testing. Along with the `beaker-rspec` plugin, beaker can be used to write rspec tests that describe the state of the system. That is, Puppet runs and then rspec validates it. It actually did what you expected it to do on the system. This can sometimes vary from what you thought Puppet was going to do in the catalog.

In addition to testing, there are a handful of patterns that are considered useful when developing modules. We already covered several patterns earlier in the book, such as the roles and profiles pattern. The Puppet Labs documentation contains a wealth of good resources on good module development. For more information on this, see https://docs.puppetlabs.com/guides/module_guides/bgtm.html.

Finally, there are a number of good books available on Puppet, and especially module writing. *Extending Puppet* (https://www.packtpub.com/networking-and-servers/extending-puppet), *Alessandro Franceschi, Packt Publishing* is a resource written by a very experienced community member with a large amount of experience writing reusable modules that are available to the public.

Puppet device management

In the past handful of years, there have been a number of initiatives to use Puppet on devices other than actual computers. The first iteration of this came back in 2011 with the release of support for managing F5 load balancers. Additional community support exists for a variety of devices, such as Cisco switches and routers. With some work, this model can even be extended to managing firewalls. Imagine getting all of the same auditing benefits from Puppet being applied to your network devices.

The device management solution uses the concept of a proxy host that serves as an intermediary between the host systems and the devices being managed. This proxy host turns the device configuration into resources and then sends the changes back to the device to keep them in sync. The proxy host could be the Puppet Master, or any node managed by Puppet and does not require additional software.

More information for the base device information can be found at https://docs.puppetlabs.com/references/latest/man/device.html, as well as for the f5 module at https://forge.puppetlabs.com/puppetlabs/f5 and for Cisco switch management at https://forge.puppetlabs.com/mburger/networkdevice.

The growing trend, however, seems to be running Puppet natively on the devices. Cisco and Juniper both support some methods of running the Puppet agent on devices for at least some of their lines. Cisco uses a container that runs Puppet and can communicate with the host, while Juniper has native packages for their routers running newer versions of Junos.

This has the advantage of being a simpler configuration, since it does not require the proxy hosts. Additionally, since the agent is tightly coupled with the device, there is better support for that specific device in the agent.

A brief introduction to the Cisco method of on-device management can be found in the PuppetConf talk at http://puppetlabs.com/presentations/managing-cisco-devices-using-puppet. Information on using Puppet on Junos can be found at http://puppetlabs.com/solutions/juniper-networks.

Additional reporting resources

We dedicated a chapter to explore reporting in Puppet, but largely focused on internal tools that can help you do reporting.

There exists a good reference book for reporting in Puppet specifically, which is *Puppet Reporting and Monitoring* at `https://www.packtpub.com/networking-and-servers/puppet-reporting-and-monitoring` by *Michael Duffy* (full disclosure—I was a technical reviewer of this book). It covers many of the Puppet reporting topics in much greater detail than we can afford to do here.

We will, however, point out a couple of resources available that can help with reporting out of the box. These resources are Puppetboard and The Foreman.

Puppetboard is a web-based user interface that replaces the Puppet Dashboard, which was officially moved to community support. It provides an interface into the status of your Puppet runs, as well as a nice browser that lets you browse facts on your hosts and other such things. We wrote the custom code to provide reporting solutions for several of the problems in the reporting chapter, which can be run natively in Puppetboard.

Puppetboard relies on PuppetDB being installed as it uses it as the data backend. It uses data from PuppetDB to build rich dashboards with information about your systems.

More information on Puppetboard can be found at `https://github.com/puppet-community/puppetboard`.

Another good reporting-related tool for one to review is The Foreman. The Foreman is more than just a reporting tool. It aims to be a complete life cycle management tool that provisions your systems and then works with Puppet to configure them. It can even serve as an external node classifier that holds information about what classes get applied to a node.

In addition to this, The Foreman contains reporting features on nodes similar to those of Puppetboard. It can show trends in systems by type, show systems not completing Puppet runs, and so on.

More information on The Foreman can be found at `http://theforeman.org/`.

These are not the only reporting engines available for Puppet. Other options, such as Puppet Explorer exist at `https://github.com/spotify/puppetexplorer` and more are added everyday.

Finally, don't forget Kibana. By bringing your log data into Logstash, you can use Kibana to create reports. You can even configure Logstash to send certain events straight to an alerting system to alert on certain values. This can be used to build reporting, as well as any of the previously mentioned software packages.

Other Puppet resources

There are a few other Puppet-related tools that don't really fit elsewhere, so we're going to talk about them briefly here.

The first such tool is Puppet Enterprise. In a security role, it may be important for you to have certified supported configurations for the tools managing your environment. Puppet Enterprise offers this, as well as additional features and capabilities not present in the base open source system.

Puppet Enterprise contains prebuilt, self-contained, packages for a large variety of operating systems. This includes all of the expected Linux variants, as well as other operating systems, such as AIX and Solaris. This can make it much easier to deploy Puppet on systems that it might otherwise be difficult to get a modern version of Ruby on.

On top of that, Puppet Enterprise contains a powerful dashboard that permits reporting, as well as system configuration. It serves as a node classifier, so if you use the roles and profiles pattern, for instance, you can apply profiles to the system straight from the Puppet Enterprise management dashboard.

More information on Puppet Enterprise can be found at `http://puppetlabs.com/puppet/puppet-enterprise`.

Another new item of the Puppet community is Puppet Server. This is a new rewrite of the Puppet Master in Clojure that runs on the JVM. The system then uses JRuby to run all of the existing Puppet code. This allows you to continue to write your types in providers in Ruby, while using the proven power of the JVM to increase the performance. This allows the Puppet Master to take advantage of things, such as multithreading and a much better garbage collection system. It also simplifies the configuration over the old method of using Apache and Passenger.

This, of course, comes at the cost of running the master in the JVM. That may give a certain amount of people cause for concern as they have previous bad experiences with Java-based applications. However, from a security standpoint, the JVM is a well-understood machine. Many more systems run in the JVM than run under Apache with Passenger. In the end, this is an adjustment in the server running the core Puppet Server and not a huge shift in paradigm.

Puppet Enterprise 3.7 is the first version to use this new Java-based Puppet Server.

More information on Puppet Server can be found at `http://puppetlabs.com/blog/puppet-server-bringing-soa-to-a-puppet-master-near-you`.

Finally, it should be mentioned that the core Puppet software is also improving. Version 4 is about to be released that will contain a new parser and a good amount of new functionalities. It's going to bring with it, the ability to solve a certain class of problems easier, with tools such as iteration, which are missing in Puppet today.

If you want to try some of these new features out today, you can use the future parser. This is the parser that is being worked on for Puppet 4. More information on the future parser can be found at `https://docs.puppetlabs.com/puppet/latest/reference/experiments_future.html`, and a presentation on Puppet 4 at `http://puppetlabs.com/presentations/future-goals-puppet-4-andrew-parker-puppet-labs-kylo-ginsberg`.

The Puppet community

No book would be complete without the mention of the excellent Puppet community. One of the reasons Puppet has been successful is because the community members are top notch and very helpful. We'll explore a few of the community resources available to you if you need assistance.

The first resource can be found at `http://ask.puppetlabs.com` site. This site is a place where users can go to post questions for the community to answer. It is in the style of various other question and answer sites. As your knowledge of Puppet increases, you can earn badges to help other users out, with questions they might have.

A second resource is the Puppet mailing lists. These lists are hosted at Google Groups. Lists exist for users and development efforts. A reasonable amount of discussion concerning future development and direction of Puppet takes place on the lists. This is a good place to read about development of new patterns and discussions on the future of Puppet. It is also a great place to go to ask questions if you get stuck with a problem. You can find the Puppet Users list at `https://groups.google.com/forum/#!forum/puppet-users`.

Finally, there is a page that discusses general community. There are many other community-based events available, including the Puppet Users groups in some cities, Puppet Camps that are smaller regional conferences, and the giant PuppetConf that draws thousands of Puppet users to one place. Additionally, there is an IRC channel available for use in asking questions in a more real-time fashion. Information on all of these resources can be found at `http://puppetlabs.com/community/get-help`.

Final thoughts

The journey to automation happiness is not one that happens overnight. Often times, the tasks ahead of you can seem daunting. However, there is a simple method that I use to approach such problems when they arise. Simply, start with your area of greatest pain. If you spend a lot of time reviewing logs on systems, then start using Puppet to implement centralized logging. If it's user and account creation, then start there.

The operations industry as a whole is beginning to embrace the concepts that were introduced in Japan after World War II. The description of the concepts often uses the word lean. There are several important concepts I will leave you with.

The first is Kata. Kata is the art of practicing something to obtain mastery. Growing up, you often did this in school, especially with math. As with those, you must practice your art to get better at it. As you engage in automating your environment with Puppet—either to make your life easier or to appease auditors, you will get better at it with practice. Do not be afraid to revisit the earlier code as you become better. Improving it, often times, can make new code development go faster.

The second and last concept I'd like to introduce is Kaizen. This is the concept of continuous improvement. You should consider your environments as never complete. You iterate on the work you've done to continuously improve. Perhaps as earlier, you started with centralized logging. As you iterate on it, you'll build improved grok patterns, dashboard, and other things that will make your environment better and easier to use and manage. Even in the simplest of environments, there is always room for improvement.

I hope that you learned a lot throughout the course of this book and it helps you move your environments forward. Go forth and automate!

Index

A

AppArmor
  URL 182
arildjensen module 125-129
attributes, audit
  content 30
  ctime 30
  ensure 30
  group 30
  mode 30
  mtime 30
  owner 30
  reference link 30
  selrange 31
  selrole 31
  seltype 31
  seluser 31
  type 31
audit
  about 39
  attributes 30, 31
  use cases 29
  using, on files 30
auditd
  about 182
  configuring, with community modules 197-200
  for audit logging 186
  references 187
auditd class, parameters
  config_override 197
  logagent 197
  package_name 197
  rules 197
auditing
  alternatives 40

audit meta-parameter 28, 29
audit system
  working 29
augeas 120
augeasproviders
  modules 121
  reference link 121, 125
  SSH, managing with 122-125
auth.conf file
  about 94
  reference link 95
autosigning certificates
  about 107
  basic autosign 108, 109
  naïve autosign 108
  policy-based autosign 110-113

B

bash scripting 83
basic autosign 108, 109
Bcfg2 3
Beaker
  reference link 95
best practice, for writing Puppet code
  reference link 32
built-in processors
  reference link 74

C

CentOS advisory
  reference link 91
Certificate Authority (CA) 102
Certificate Revocation List (CRL) 105
certificates
  revoking 104-106

[209]

signing 103, 104
Certificate Signing Request (CSR) 103
CFEngine
  about 2
  URL 2
Chef
  about 2
  URL 2
CIS benchmark
  URL 126
cis module 125-129
Cisco method, on-device management
  reference link 203
classes 5
client-server model, Puppet 5, 6
community modules
  about 62
  auditd, configuring with 197-200
  reference link 62
  SELinux, configuring with 192-196
community processors
  reference link 74
compliance, Puppet 17
components, Puppet
  about 6
  Hiera 7
  PuppetDB 6
configuration management tool 2
configuration options
  allow 94
  allow_ip 94
  auth 94
  environment 94
  method 94
  path 94
contexts 182
cron 6
custom facts
  using 56, 57

D

declarative systems
  properties 4
  versus imperative systems 3-5
default configuration settings, Puppet
  reference link 94
Domain-specific Language (DSL) 2

E

ebtables 140
Elasticsearch
  about 158
  installing 164-167
ELK stack
  installing 159-164
environment
  preparing, for examples 12

F

facts
  custom facts, using 56, 57
  Puppet roles pattern 55
  using, for compliance 55
files
  audits, using on 30
fileserver.conf file
  about 98, 99
  restricted file mount, adding 99-102
file system permissions
  URL, for wiki 160
file type parameters, SELinux
  selinux_ignore_defaults 191
  Selrange 191
  Selrole 191
  seltype 191
  seluser 191
firewallchain type 146, 147
firewall chain type, parameters
  ensure 147
  ignore 147
  name 147
  policy 147
  provider 147
  purge 147
firewall module 139, 140
firewall rules
  adding, to modules 151, 152
firewall type
  about 141-146
  reference link 142
firewall type, parameters
  action 141
  chain 141
  destination 141

dport 141
dst_range 141
ensure 141
jump 141
name 141
port 141
proto 142
reject 142
source 142
sport 142
src_range 142
state 142
tcp_flags 142
future parser
 reference link 206

G

git
 references 50, 53
 used, for tracking Puppet
  configuration 50-53

H

heartbleed
 reference link 88
heartbleed-vulnerable systems
 finding 88-91
herculesteam modules 120
Hiera
 about 7
 reference link 137
hiera-eyaml
 reference link 137
hiera-eyaml gem 132-136
hostmanager plugin
 reference link 95
 working with 96-98
hosts
 configuring, for reporting log data 176-180

I

imperative systems
 properties 4
 versus declarative systems 3-5

iptables
 about 140
 reference link 140

K

Kibana
 about 171
 installing 172-176

L

librarian-puppet
 URL 55
logging 158
Loggly 157
Logstash
 about 157, 158
 and Puppet 164
 installing 167-171

M

Mandatory Access Controls (MACs) 182
manifests
 about 5
 creating 31, 32
 history, tracking with version control 50
 used, for documenting system state 48, 49
modules
 firewall rules, adding to 151, 152
 modifying, for audit 36-39
 reference link 43
 tracking, separately 53, 54

N

Nagios 158
naïve autosign 108
National Security Agency (NSA) 182
Network Time Protocol (NTP)
 about 152
 drawbacks 153-155
noop
 about 28
 using 42-45

O

objects 182
open-source configuration management software
   URL, for comparison 3
open source Puppet 2
openssh configuration file 22
options, fileserver.conf file
   [mountpoint] 99
   allow 99
   deny 99
   path 99

P

package
   auditing 35
packages, ELK stack
   URL, for downloading 159
parameters, selboolean type
   name 188
   persistent 188
   provider 188
   value 188
parameters, selmodule type
   ensure 190
   name 190
   provider 190
   selmoduledir 190
   selmodulepath 190
   syncversion 190
params class
   about 62
   reference link 62
password file
   auditing 31
   modifying 33, 34
Payment Card Industry Data Security Standard (PCI DSS)
   about 47, 58
   authentication, to systems 71
   network-based PCI requirements 58
   secure systems, maintaining 71
   system protection, against malware 67-70
   URL 58
   vendor-supplied defaults 59-67

policy
   reference link 195
policy-based autosign 110-113
post rules
   creating 147-151
pre rules
   creating 147-151
presentation, Puppet 4
   reference link 206
providers 140
providers, augeasproviders modules
   kernel_parameter 121
   pam 121
   puppet_auth 121
   shellvar 121
   sshd_config 121
   sshd_config_subsystem 121
   sysctl 121
   syslog 121
Puppet
   about 1, 2
   and Logstash 164
   and SELinux 187
   and SSL 102
   client-server model 5, 6
   compliance feature 17
   components 6
   configuring 8-11
   declarative, versus imperative approaches 3-5
   installing 8
   reporting resources 204
   rerunning 33
   resources 205
   security feature 17
   URL, for configuration settings 10
   URL, for installation instructions 8
   used, for tracking changes 28
Puppet agent
   installing 10
Puppet Approved modules 118
Puppet authentication
   about 95
   second Vagrant host, adding 95
puppet-cis module
   reference link 129

Puppet community
  about 206
  references 206
PuppetDB
  about 6
  reporting 79-83
Puppet device management
  about 203
  references 203
Puppet Enterprise
  URL 205
Puppet Forge
  about 116-120
  URL 116
puppetlabs-firewall module 140
puppetlabs-stdlib module
  about 65
  URL 65
Puppet Labs ticket
  reference link 39
Puppet Labs Yum repository
  installing 8
  URL 8
Puppet Master
  installing 9
Puppet modules
  references 203
  testing 202
  writing 202
Puppet, on Junos
  reference link 203
Puppet report directory 75
Puppet reporting
  about 73
  last node runtime, displaying 77, 78
  references 74
  store processors 75, 76
Puppet roles pattern 55
Puppet scope
  reference link 41
Puppet security-related configuration
  about 93
  auth.conf file 94, 95
  fileserver.conf file 98, 99
Puppet Server
  URL 206
Puppet services 11

Puppet Supported modules 117
Puppet, used for securing openssh
  about 18
  code, running 23, 24
  module, building 20-22
  module, creating 20
  openssh configuration file, building 22
  site.pp file 23
  Vagrant virtual machine, starting 19
  virtual machine connection 20
Puppet versions
  reference link 75

R

r10k
  URL 55
reporting, for compliance
  about 88
  heartbleed-vulnerable systems,
    finding 88-91
reporting, on log data 171
reporting, PuppetDB
  about 79-83
  event counts, obtaining 85
  recent reports, obtaining 83, 84
  simple PuppetDB dashboard
    example 86, 87
report processors
  about 74
  HTTP 74
  PuppetDB 74
  Store 74
  Tagmail 74
Representational State Transfer (REST) 80
resource chaining 22
resource command
  reference link 35
resource ordering
  reference link 22
resources
  purging 42
resource types
  auditing 34, 35
  parameters 42
  references 35

rspec
  reference link 202
  URL 61
rspec-puppet
  reference link 202
rsynclocal module, parameters
  ensure 193
  ignore 193
  modules_dir 193
  source 193

S

Salt 3
saz module
  about 129-131
  reference link 132
scaling, Puppet
  reference link 12
security, Puppet 17
selboolean type
  about 187-190
  parameters 188
SELinux
  about 182
  and Puppet 187
  configuring, with community
       modules 192-196
  file type parameters 191
  references 185
SELinux Booleans
  references 190
SELinux framework 182-185
SELinux policy modules
  reference link 197
selmodule type
  about 187, 190
  parameters 190
services, Puppet 11
site.pp file 23
software repositories 68
spec tests, Puppet
  reference link 61
Splunk 157

SSH
  managing, with augeasproviders 122-125
SSL
  about 102
  and Puppet 102
  reference link 102
SSL extensions
  reference link 112
store processors 75, 76
subject 183
sudo module
  about 129-131
  reference link 132
system state
  documenting, with manifests 48, 49

T

types 182

V

Vagrant
  installing 13
  URL, for downloading 13
Vagrant Cloud
  URL 15
Vagrantfile
  creating 13-16
Version 4 report format, Puppet
  reference link 79
version control
  modules, tracking 53, 54
  Puppet configuration, tracking
       with git 50-53
  used, for tracking manifests history 50
VirtualBox
  installing 13
  URL, for downloading 13

Y

YAML Ain't Markup Language
  about 29
  reference link, for formatting 136

Thank you for buying
Learning Puppet Security

About Packt Publishing

Packt, pronounced 'packed', published its first book, *Mastering phpMyAdmin for Effective MySQL Management*, in April 2004, and subsequently continued to specialize in publishing highly focused books on specific technologies and solutions.

Our books and publications share the experiences of your fellow IT professionals in adapting and customizing today's systems, applications, and frameworks. Our solution-based books give you the knowledge and power to customize the software and technologies you're using to get the job done. Packt books are more specific and less general than the IT books you have seen in the past. Our unique business model allows us to bring you more focused information, giving you more of what you need to know, and less of what you don't.

Packt is a modern yet unique publishing company that focuses on producing quality, cutting-edge books for communities of developers, administrators, and newbies alike. For more information, please visit our website at www.packtpub.com.

About Packt Open Source

In 2010, Packt launched two new brands, Packt Open Source and Packt Enterprise, in order to continue its focus on specialization. This book is part of the Packt Open Source brand, home to books published on software built around open source licenses, and offering information to anybody from advanced developers to budding web designers. The Open Source brand also runs Packt's Open Source Royalty Scheme, by which Packt gives a royalty to each open source project about whose software a book is sold.

Writing for Packt

We welcome all inquiries from people who are interested in authoring. Book proposals should be sent to author@packtpub.com. If your book idea is still at an early stage and you would like to discuss it first before writing a formal book proposal, then please contact us; one of our commissioning editors will get in touch with you.

We're not just looking for published authors; if you have strong technical skills but no writing experience, our experienced editors can help you develop a writing career, or simply get some additional reward for your expertise.

[PACKT] open source
community experience distilled
PUBLISHING

Puppet Reporting and Monitoring
ISBN: 978-1-78398-142-7   Paperback: 186 pages

Create insightful reports for your server infrastructure using Puppet

1. Learn how to prepare and setup Puppet to report on a wealth of data.
2. Develop your own custom plugins and work with report processor systems.
3. Explore compelling ways to utilize and present Puppet data with easy-to-follow examples.

Mastering Puppet
ISBN: 978-1-78398-218-9   Paperback: 280 pages

Pull the strings of Puppet to configure enterprise-grade environments for performance optimization

1. Implement puppet in a medium to large installation.
2. Deal with issues found in larger deployments, such as scaling, and improving performance.
3. Step by step tutorial to utilize Puppet efficiently to have a fully functioning Puppet infrastructure in an enterprise- level environment.

Please check **www.PacktPub.com** for information on our titles

[PACKT] PUBLISHING open source
community experience distilled

Extending Puppet

ISBN: 978-1-78398-144-1   Paperback: 328 pages

Design, manage, and deploy your Puppet architecture with the help of real-world scenarios

1. Plan, test, and execute your Puppet deployments.
2. Write reusable and maintainable Puppet code.
3. Handle challenges that might arise in upcoming versions of Puppet.
4. Explore the Puppet ecosystem in-depth, through a hands-on, example driven approach.

Mobile Security: How to Secure, Privatize, and Recover Your Devices

ISBN: 978-1-84969-360-8   Paperback: 242 pages

Keep your data secure on the go

1. Learn how mobile devices are monitored and the impact of cloud computing
2. Understand the attacks hackers use and how to prevent them.
3. Keep yourself and your loved ones safe online.

Please check www.PacktPub.com for information on our titles

CPSIA information can be obtained
at www.ICGtesting.com
Printed in the USA
FFOW03n0251160116
20444FF

9 781784 397753